FROM THE MARGINS TO THE CENTRE

Popular Cultural Studies

Series editors: Justin O'Connor and Derek Wynne.
Series sub-editor: Maggy Taylor.

The editors are, respectively, Director and Research Director of the Manchester Institute for Popular Culture where this series is based. The Manchester Institute for Popular Culture, at The Manchester Metropolitan University, England, was set up in order to promote theoretical and empirical research in the area of contemporary popular culture, both within the academy and in conjunction with local, national and international agencies. The Institute is a postgraduate research centre engaged in comparative research projects around aspects of consumption and regulation of popular culture in the city. The Institute also runs a number of postgraduate research programmes, with a particular emphasis on ethnographic work. The series intends to reflect all aspects of the Institute's activities including its relationship with interested academics throughout the world. Current theoretical debates within the field of popular culture will be explored within an empirical context. Much of the research is undertaken by young researchers actively involved in their chosen fields of study, allowing an awareness of the issues and an attentiveness to actual developments often lacking in standard academic writings on the subject. The series will also reflect the working methods of the Institute, emphasising a collective research effort and the regular presentation of work-in-progress to the Institute's research seminars. The series hopes, therefore, both to push forward the debates around the regulation and consumption of popular culture, urban regeneration and postmodern social theory whilst introducing an ethnographic and contextual basis for such debates.

From the Margins to the Centre

Cultural production and consumption in the post-industrial city

edited by
Justin O'Connor
Derek Wynne

arena

Published by
Arena
Ashgate Publishing Limited
Gower House
Croft Road
Aldershot
Hants GU11 3HR
England

Ashgate Publishing Company
Old Post Road
Brookfield
Vermont 05036
USA

British Library Cataloguing in Publication Data

From the margins to the centre: cultural production
    and consumption in the post-industrial city –
    (Popular Cultural Studies)
    1. Popular culture 2. City and town life
    I. O'Connor, Justin II. Wynne, Derek
    306'.091732

Library of Congress Catalog Card Number: 96-83263

ISBN 1 85742 332 1 (Hardback)
ISBN 1 85742 333 X (Paperback)

Printed and bound by Athenaeum Press, Ltd., Gateshead, Tyne & Wear.

Contents

Acknowledgements

The papers included in this book represent the results of a collective investigation into the changing nature of the contemporary city and its associated 'city cultures'. The empirical investigations, rooted in a 'local' which is Manchester, while obviously peculiar to that city, do, nevertheless contain wider ranging implications for all 'industrial' and 'post-industrial' cities affected by an increasingly 'global' restructuring — a restructuring associated with not only economic change, but also cultural change. As such, while our investigations — and their results — are characterized by their embeddedness in a singular British, English, Northern, industrial (post-industrial?) city, we believe that many of the results of our investigations, and certainly the thrust of our arguments, will find an echo in other cities around the globe.

The editors would like to thank all of their friends and colleagues who have helped in countless ways to ensure that this project came to fruition. Certainly without the funding obtained from what was then known as the Polytechnics and Colleges Funding Council, the empirical work could not have been undertaken. For providing us with the necessary support we would like to thank Dr. Ian Roberts, Head of Research Development, and Dr Stephen Kirby, Dean of Faculty of Humanities and Social Studies at the Manchester Metropolitan University. For intellectual support we would also like to thank Pete Bramham, Sara Cohen, Eric Corijn, Mike Featherstone, Simon Frith, Larry Grossberg, Scott Lash, Celia Lury, Hans Mommaas, Jon Savage and Rob Shields amongst others. Finally to Maggy Taylor at MIPC — only she knows the enormity of our indebtedness to her.

Introduction

Justin O'Connor and Derek Wynne

The Institute for Popular Culture was set up at Manchester Metropolitan University in October 1991 as a way of bringing together a number of different research projects grouped around the Department of Sociology and the Unit for Law and Popular Culture created by Steve Redhead in 1991. The Institute was to be an interdisciplinary body within the faculty of Law and Humanities. It reflected our concern that the study of popular culture had reached an impasse; that it was taken seriously by the academic world only insofar as it was shunted off to that strange offshoot of English Literature and Sociology — Cultural Studies.

The Institute wanted to open up popular cultural studies to the debates raging in other disciplines; and to open these to the profound transformations taking place within popular culture. We began by looking at what was happening on our doorstep; trying to grasp the developments and to understand them in terms of those actually involved in their production and consumption. We did not want to confer a spurious respectability on the objects and desires of popular culture by a transposition of register and a display of intellectual pyrotechnics which could only confer a lucrative unrespectability on this 'transgresive' academic voice.

We started with rave, football and urban regeneration. The death of youth culture coinciding with a huge explosion of energy, imagination, irony, Peace, Love and drugs. Death on the terraces somehow prompting a re-invention of what it is to be in love with a game. The shiny happy buildings of a regenerated centre, announcing that the devastation of the city was just a bad dream — and then people taking them at their word and making the centre

1

their own.

We at the Institute felt that nobody was writing about this. As is often the case we have since found others who thought the same.

This book attempts to bring together and critically engage with two sets of debates. Firstly, that concerned with the construction and deconstruction of identities claimed by much of postmodern theorizing. Secondly, that concerned with urban regeneration, cultural policy and the changing role of the city.

A strong current of postmodern thought has placed the multiple uses of city spaces at the centre of its claims for the construction and deconstruction of identities. The proliferation and fragmentation of patterns of cultural production and consumption, it is claimed, makes the city a complex field of conflicting and overlapping activities whose juxtaposition undermines traditional cultural hierarchies. Across this field identity becomes fluid in a way that uncouples its close connection with fixed categories of class, gender and ethnicity. 'Nomads of the Present', 'Postmodern Tribes' have both been used to describe a condition of the contemporary city whose dynamics are governed by a symbolics of cultural consumption that opens onto a new 'postmodern sociology' (Melucci, 1989; Maffesoli, 1988; Chambers, 1986 and 1987).

We would argue that the positions outlined above have neglected any systematic empirical investigation in relation to the social practices of cultural production and consumption. While postmodern theories point to the dominant role of culture within contemporary societies, there is little discussion of the social practices and means whereby this is effected. It is often assumed that the alleged shift to a 'post-industrial' or 'service' economy is a sufficient explanation in itself (see Mole below). Such claims merely 'read off' consumption from production. Few empirical studies have been undertaken which attempt to assess the social and cultural changes that might be associated with the economic restructuring referred to in the work cited above.

If these above debates in social and cultural theory have attempted to place both the nature of 'culture' and of 'the social' in question, then the second major focus of this book links these with another debate — conducted for the most part in very different arenas — concerned with cultural policy. Writing on cultural policy has tended for the most part to remain separate from, or refer only obliquely to, these wider theoretical debates. One of the few grounds on which

2

these two meet is that of contemporary city cultures.

This meeting ground is more specifically that of culture-led urban regeneration. Here the concerns of urban theorists have been forced to confront very concrete questions of cultural policy and politics. However, we would suggest that whilst this has produced some excellent work — notably that of Mike Davies, David Harvey, Sharon Zukin — the meeting has tended to result in the concentration on urban form and social exclusion to the detriment of the question of urban culture. It has frequently led to over-generalized structural accounts of the dominance of capital and its elites within the city. We would argue that the debates in social science, referred to above, associated with 'post' or 'late' modernity — concerned with individuation, risk, ambivalence as well as globalization, displacement, space-time compression etc. — suggest that the 'cultural' aspect of this question cannot be reduced to that of the socioeconomic structure however complexly spatialized within urban theory.

Those coming to the city from cultural theory, on the other hand, have tended to ignore the concrete policy and political questions of urban form in favour of a textual approach to the city. Whilst this is valid to a degree, the impasse reached by Cultural Studies generally is repeated in this approach to the city. The city floats free, and the theorist floats with it. We would suggest a return to a situated analysis of urban cultures.

Those concerned directly — whether as academics, consultants, politicians or practitioners — with both cultural policy and urban regeneration have often been unwitting participants in a wide ranging review of the role of culture in contemporary society. Unwitting, because this debate only rarely refers to the theoretical debates in cultural theory. However, cultural theory rarely reflects this policy driven transformation of the 'culture' they are setting up for critique. This applies most especially to those writing about 'high culture', where the policy transformations are so often treated as secondary problems of 'delivery'. But it also applies to those writing on popular culture whose emphasis on current transformations can lack the specificity of the legal-political context within which policy can not just regulate (censorship, repression) but produce (see Lovatt below).

This book attempts to link social and cultural theory, cultural policy and urban regeneration in a way that addresses the theoretical and

3

political dilemmas these throw up. Furthermore, it attempts to situate the role of popular culture in a debate in which it has been frequently marginalized. The relationship between popular culture and cultural policy has been written mostly in terms of high and low; little attention has been paid to the way in which popular cultures are related to space and place, to local welfare regimes, to legal-political frameworks etc. When it comes to culture-led urban regeneration the silence is deafening, despite the fact that this popular culture has profoundly restructured the field within which cultural policy, especially in urban centres, has been conceived.

As such, a third major focus is implicit in the very intentions of this book; that contemporary popular culture is crucial to the understanding of the transformations to which all the authors refer; that the investigation of this popular culture needs to move beyond the parameters of cultural studies; and that this investigation places specific demands upon the researcher, the more so as this research moves towards the ethnographic.

Our title *From the Margins to the Centre* refers to three related themes that have run closely together in the debates around postmodernity and the city in the 1980s and 90s. Firstly, a process of restructuring in which many of those activities deemed peripheral to the activity of the 'productive' or 'Fordist' city have now moved centre stage and become a major concern for cities; that is, the concern with culture, consumption and image. Secondly, the notion of gentrification, whereby a reversal of the movement out of the city centre by the affluent classes results in a 're-centralization' of previously 'marginal' areas of the city centre. Thirdly, the process whereby previously 'marginal' groups and their activities have been made central to the city and/or have made the city centre central to themselves — not just residentially, but also by their uses of the centre, and by such usage being promoted, by themselves or others, as a primary sign of the 'centrality' of that centre.

The work presented in this volume emerged initially from a consultancy document produced by the authors for the regional arts board in conjunction with the local city economic regeneration agency, *The Economic Importance of the Arts Cultural Industries in Greater Manchester* (CER, 1989). This was later published as *The Culture Industry* (Wynne, 1992). This empirical research, running alongside our concern with the debates around 'postmodernism' and the changing role of the city, formed the basis of an ESRC funded

4

research project (R000233075) examining new forms of cultural consumption and the construction of lifestyle in the contemporary city. These new forms were associated with a range of development which included: i) the dramatic increase in the production and consumption of symbolic goods; ii) the shift of consumption from use value to sign value; iii) the destabilization of established symbolic hierarchies through the articulation of alternative tastes and styles; iv) the rise of popular and commercial cultures as alternative forms challenging established 'high culture'; v) the emergence of new urban spaces creating 'play spaces' for new forms of sociability, leading to; vi) new forms of display and social mixing representing a movement away from rational goal directed activity, permitting a more playful, carnivalesque exploration of emotions — a preoccupation with the aestheticization and 'stylization of life' as opposed to more fixed lifestyles.

This research was a systematic examination of these processes in the context of cultural consumption in the city centre and the lifestyles of selected inhabitants. We can pick out three significant results: i) the emergence of a 'mix and match' lifestyle amongst the 18-35 age group who are most prominent in the use of the cultural and leisure facilities of the city centre. The lifestyle emphasized 'anti-rationalist' values usually associated with artistic, bohemian or counter-cultural milieus — intuition, self-expression, creativity, the exploration of subjectivity and the body, pleasure and hedonism — but linked to a keen sense of the positional and distinction value of symbolic goods and services; ii) the extension of the notion of 'cultural intermediaries' from the new middle class to a much wider range of the population, through the increased involvement of popular culture in the creation of the new city centre sites of consumption; iii) these new and extended forms of cultural consumption, characterized by rapid turnover and complex distinctions, were feeding directly into involvement in cultural production to supply these new markets.

These findings formed the basis of a large scale investigation, funded by PCFC, into new forms of cultural production in the city. This study forms the bulk of the material presented in this book. The four areas of study were green or 'ethical' businesses; gay and lesbian leisure spaces in the city centre; micro-fashion designers; and the regulation of the night-time economy.

In all of these areas the research indicated that for those involved:

i) making money and making culture were activities difficult to disentangle; ii) there was a frequent inability and even antipathy to making a distinction between work time and leisure time; iii) there was a heavy reliance on informal networks for information and ideas; iv) there was an emphasis on intuition, emotional involvement, immersion in the field and an 'insider's' or 'enthusiast's' knowledge of the market; v) a realized ambition to 'work for themselves' and to 'break the 9-5'. This squared very well with the findings of the cultural consumption project.

The findings of both these studies pointed towards theoretical work in the social sciences which attempted to ground some of the claims of the 'postmodernity' debate in more empirical research. The research linked to the debates around 'reflexivity', 'de-traditionalization' and risk. It was argued that large scale social processes meant that the individual was decreasingly presented by objective social roles and had to construct her/his own identity in a situation of fluidity, anxiety and risk. The individuation of consumption thus brings an increased reflexivity, which tends to move away from a predominantly cognitive to an aesthetic reflexivity, increasingly mediated through aesthetic objects or symbolic goods.

These findings have led to the hypothesis, underpinning work in progress at the Institute, that if consumption is increasingly reflexive then so too is the production intended to satisfy that market. Predominantly located in the cultural industries, this sector uses different forms and circuits of knowledge, has a different conception and relationship to the consumer, and has a different approach to the very notion of 'running a business' — different, that is, from the conceptualization of this business practice in mainstream business education and training.

Contemporaneous with the research projects presented in this volume was a three year research project funded through a senior research fellowship post. This addressed two areas; I) the macro context of city economies; II) the role of culture in urban regeneration.

I) *The macro context of city economies involved three aspects:*

i) The shift from Fordism to post-Fordism involving the multiplication and fragmentation of markets, along with the acceleration of product turnover and volatility (or fickleness) of demand foregrounding the marketing and design functions of firms. Flexible specialization means margins of competitiveness depend on the generation and exploitation of new knowledge; successful firms are R&D and innovation intensive, constantly re-designing business organization to create the flexibility required to accommodate this. In terms of the marketing and design functions, this capacity can be defined as a cultural capacity — the ability to accumulate knowledge and manipulate symbols. This is clearest in those sectors which deal primarily with the production and distribution of symbolic goods — the cultural industries. This sector can be seen as cutting edge;

> ... ordinary manufacturing industry is becoming more and more like the production of culture. It is not that commodity manufacture provides the template, and culture follows, but that cultural industries themselves provided the template (Lash & Urry, 1994, p.123).

ii)   The informational economy refers to a new form of economic production and management characterized by the fact that productivity and competitiveness are increasingly based on the generation of new knowledge and on the access to, and processing of appropriate information (Castells and Hall, 1994). Thus the transformational aspects of this information society include a new and important association between the productive elements of the economy (knowledge generation and information processing) and the cultural capacity of society — that is, its ability to accumulate knowledge and manipulate symbols (Shearman, 1995; Castells, 1994).

iii) Cities can be seen as nodes within a global economy (Sassen, 1991) and the intersection of the global and the local becomes crucial in local economic development. Whilst the control and distribution functions may remain in centralized hands this can only be so on the basis of a sophisticated understanding of consumption patterns in specific and often very localized markets (Sassen, 1994). It is a knowledge of the local mediation of the global circuits of 'signs and space' that frequently defines the success of cultural industries in the local city context. This implies a knowledge of the local, but also a deep understanding for these specific forms of consumption. It is this knowledge that allows cultural industries to both innovate in the local sphere and extend their operations beyond that local.

7

All three points above underline the new centrality of knowledge, with an increased emphasis on the cultural and symbolic aspects of this knowledge. Local economic development increasingly depends on the mobilization of this knowledge, but the ability to do this depends on a range of historically specific social, economic, cultural and political factors.

II) The role of culture in urban regeneration

This aspect of the research derives from the ESRC project — the ethnographic study of the consumption of culture in the city centre. In line with the study as a whole it uncovered a tendency for a move from cultural consumption to cultural production. The increased centrality of culture in urban regeneration schemes since the late 70s is well documented (Bianchini and Parkinson,1993; Wynne, 1992). This research looked at the extent to which those public and private agencies involved in 'culture-led' urban regeneration could work with those actually involved in the production of culture — and especially popular culture. The research found that this collaboration was rare and fraught with difficulties.

The conclusion was that the languages of 'cultural' and 'economic' capital were very different (Bourdieu, 1984; 1993); that the latter found it very hard to come to terms with the former; that this had long historical roots in northern business and political culture; and that the inability at the level of culture-led urban regeneration suggested a more profound inability to respond to the demands of the global and informational economy.

Mole opens the empirical and theoretical terrain to be investigated, arguing that the changes experienced by Northern European and North American cities since the early 70s cannot be understood as simply inevitable, nor uniformly operative. Mole argues for the notion of post-Fordism as an explanatory framework, but insists on its attentiveness to the particularities of the local context. In this case the local is both the British State and Manchester. He argues, firstly, that Fordism was a belated and incomplete response to industrial decline and that it was introduced from the top (i.e. the State) at precisely the wrong time. He continues by contending, secondly, that whilst we can see a post-Fordist economy emerging (and that we should be wary of the more pessimistic commentators in this area) this is being pushed through in very distinct circumstances — that of

8

the free market Conservative party driven by political objectives. This, according to Mole, seriously hampers new economic growth and places the fluidity, flexibility and multiplicity claimed by postmodern theory under the sign of poverty, desperation and widening social division.

O'Connor and Wynne, in a specific examination of recent city centre housing projects and their residents, engage in an extended discussion with the related work of Sharon Zukin (1982 and 1992) and others. Here, they argue that the increasing commodification of cultural forms, the (re)emergence of play and pleasure and their associated spaces, together with an increasing 'individualization' of the social world, make the city a stage on/in which many of the most significant processes of socio-cultural change can be witnessed.

Through an investigation of changing work and leisure practices associated with the move from a manufacturing to a service economy, concentrating on the development of the cultural industries, particularly those associated with 'pop' music and fashion both Milestone and Purvis, through an examination of cultural production and consumption within 'youth cultural industries' illustrate the increasing centrality of such activities to the revitalization of certain quarters of the city. For Milestone debates about local identity, place and space frequently ignore the role of youth cultures, just as writing about the globalized pop music industry tends to pass over the local context of its production and consumption. Purvis' work on 'pop' fashion designers, their networks and their working practices, shows how production and consumption has become interlinked in new ways, and also points to a series of 'crossovers' between cultural forms, images and symbols (Lash, 1990; Wynne, 1992; Lash and Urry, 1994).

If Mole attempted to outline some of the problems of a uniform and unilinear approach to the shift from Fordist to post-Fordist economies, Lovatt attempts a more detailed critique of the regulationist approach to the city in the context of the changing mode of regulation of the night-time economy. This previously marginal zone of space and time is now being promoted as central to the image of a modern 'European' city. Lovatt investigates the difficulties with which a legal, political, and cultural local formation deals with shift, especially given the contradictory forces of Conservative moral ideology and the growing social divisions in urban space.

Ryan and Fitzpatrick, attending specifically to the gendered nature of urban space show how social spatialization and gender has traditionally been conceptualized in terms of the 'public' and the 'private'. Contemporary interest however in identity construction and reflexive modernization, provides a context for understanding how postmodern changes in work and leisure create a different spatiality within urban spaces, particularly for women. This new spatial experience of women — material, symbolic and 'political' — can be read as operating as part of a 'politics of difference' in everyday life alongside class, race/ethnicity and sexuality. In this context their ethnographic materials explore the relationship between lesbian and gay identities and the aestheticization of place in city centre cultures particularly those associated with the networks between popular music, fashion, and sexuality; the *flaneur*/stroller and gay spaces/ghettos; the 'bar/terrace' as opposed to 'pub'.

For Kennedy, insofar as postmodern society appears to revolve so much around materialism and the self expression of its citizens through symbolic consumption, the growth of green and ethical businesses poses both interesting contradictions and opportunities in the relationship between culture and the economy. On the one hand, there is flexibility amongst 'alternative' green businesses in terms of encouraging non-commercial functions such as democratic decision making and/or support for local political campaigns; on the other, the pursuit of these activities and their dislike of expansionist economics constantly threatens their very existence. Kennedy explores the contradictions, constraints and opportunities for green and ethical enterprises in the face of these apparent antagonisms. Purkis, writing from a not dissimilar position examines the city as a site of ethical consumption and a harbinger for the emergence of a new wave of radical environmental politics, which focuses its political campaigns on places of mass consumption. Informed by a variety of ethical sensibilities, and motivated to 'colonize' capitalist sites, the actions of certain 'green' organizations, lead us to re-examine how 'space' is conceptualized in the social sciences, and suggests that the consumer is less a victim and more a participant in contemporary life than some postmodern theorists would claim.

Finally, Lovatt and Purkis offer a view of the methodological difficulties that face the contemporary ethnographer and attempt to place this work within the theoretical context which has guided our investigations. In each of these studies, the authors have been concerned to relate their own empirical work to the theoretical issues initially outlined. As such, and in reflecting upon our own research practices, this book argues for a fundamental re-orientation of popular cultural studies which places such work both at the centre of current attempts to theorize contemporary socio-cultural change, and at the forefront of concerns regarding the cultural and economic regeneration of cities, together with their legal and social regulation. In addition it is argued that much of this work attempts to reflect a new sensibility in research methodologies. The changing role of the intellectual in contemporary society, means that research processes are complicated by the researcher's immersion in a number of contexts both central and peripheral to the area of study. As such, **the way** in which popular culture is studied becomes as important as the **subject** itself.

References

Beck, U. (1992), *Risk Society*, Sage, London.

Bianchini, F. & Parkinson, M. (eds.) (1993), *Cultural Policy and Urban Regeneration*, Manchester University Press.

Bourdieu, P. (1984), *Distinction*, Routledge, London.

Bourdieu, P. (1994), *The Field of Cultural Production*, Polity, Cambridge.

Chambers, I. (1986), *Popular Culture:The Metropolitan Experience*, Routledge, London.

Chambers, I. (1987), 'Maps For The Metropolis:A Possible Guide To The Postmodern', *Cultural Studies*, 1 (3).

Chambers, .I (1990), *Border Dialogues*, Routledge, London.

Cooke, P (1988), 'Modernity, Postmodernity and the City' in *Theory, Culture and Society*, 5(2-3).

Davies, M. (1990), *City of Quartz*, Verso, London.

Featherstone, M. (1991), *Consumer Culture and Postmodernism*, Sage, London.

Harvey, D. (1989), *The Condition of Postmodernity*, Blackwell, Oxford.

Lash, S. (1990), *The Sociology of Post-Modernism*, Routledge, London.

Lash, S. and Urry, J.(1987), *The End of Organised Capitalism*, Polity, Cambridge.

Lash, S. and Urry, J. (1994),*Economies of Signs and Spaces*, Sage, London.

Maffesoli, M. (1988), *Le Temps des Tribus*, Klincksiek, Paris.

Melucci, A. (1989) *Nomads of the Present*, Hutchinson/Radius, London.

Robbins, K. (1991), 'Prisoners of the City: Whatever could a Postmodern City be?' in *New Formations*, 15 (Winter).

Rose, D. (1984), 'Rethinking Gentrification: Beyond the Uneven Development of Marxist Urban Theory', in *Environment and Planning D: Society and Space,* 1: 47-74.

Sassen, S. (1991), *The Global City,* Princeton University Press.

Sassen, S. (1994), *Cities in a Global Economy*, Pine Forge Press, California.

Shields, R. (1992), 'A truant Proximity: Presence and Absence in the Space of Modernity', *Environment and Planning D: Society and Space*, 10.

Smith, N. (1987), 'Of Yuppies and Housing: Gentrification, Social Restructuring and the Urban Dream', in *Environment and Planning D: Society and Space,* 5.

Wynne, D. (ed.) (1992), *The Culture Industry,* Avebury, Swindon.

Thrift, N. (1993), 'An Urban Impasse?' *Theory, Culture and Society,* 10.

Zukin, S. (1987), 'Gentrification', *Annual Review of Sociology.*

Zukin, S. (1992), 'Postmodern Urban Landscapes: Mapping Culture and Power', in Lash & Friedman (eds.), *Modernity and Identity,* Blackwell, Oxford.

Zukin, S. (1988), 'The Postmodern Debate over Urban Form', *Theory, Culture and Society,* 5 (2-3).

Zukin, S. (1982), *Loft Living*, John Hopkins University Press, Baltimore.

Zukin, S. (1992), *Landscapes of Power: From Detroit to Disneyworld*, University of California Press, Berkeley.

1 Fordism, post-Fordism and the contemporary city

Phil Mole

Introduction

The purpose of this chapter is to examine the nature of urban economies in the early 1990s, in the light of the recent arguments in the social sciences about New Times (Hall and Jacques 1989) and postmodernity. While this is its central objective, it is also aims to provide a conceptual framework for analyzing the empirical findings of recent research into Manchester's 'cultural' industries, its clothing and fashion industries, and so-called 'green businesses', conducted by the Institute for Popular Culture at MMU and its PCFC research team (see other chapters in this volume). Manchester thus provides the empirical foundation for the discussion below, but the central theoretical question concerns the character and dynamic of the contemporary urban economy, especially but not exclusively in the UK.

It is important to emphasize the exploratory nature of the chapter, which acknowledges the complexity and scope of the issues involved, and the controversy surrounding the debates around postmodernity. The chapter does not accept some of the more ambitious claims of postmodern theorists, like Lash's assertion that the 'cultural' has become the most decisive moment in both economic and social life (Lash 1990). Its aim is much more modest: to examine some of the specific claims of postmodern theorists about the economy, and the light they throw on Manchester's current experience. To support this modest intention, I list below the tentative hypotheses which organize the chapter, so that the reader can assess how far it is fulfilled.

1. Of the various conceptual frameworks available for theorizing recent transformations in Manchester's economy — de-industrialization, post-industrialism, late capitalism, and Fordism/flexible specialization — the latter is the most useful;

2. that Manchester's economy, up until the late 1960s, was the centre of an industrial region which can usefully be described as Fordist, although this Fordism should be seen as an unsuccessful and short-lived response to industrial decline rather than a stable regime of accumulation and regulation;

3. that, unlike other cities and regions in Europe, and until recently, Manchester has failed to develop a sustainable post-Fordist economy, although certain elements of such an economy are now emerging;

4. that this failure was due to the particular patterns of 'embeddedness' of Manchester's economy, in an institutional matrix which perpetuated its crisis and prevented its resolution;

5. that the emergent elements of a post-Fordist, flexibly specialized, economy are not the result of some immanent postmodern logic, but the effect of a concerted neo-liberal attack on the City, and the stimulation of private consumption for electoral purposes;

6. and, finally, that Manchester will be unable to develop a sustainable post-Fordist economy without fundamental changes in policy and social institutions.

The political economy of postmodernity

It will not be the purpose of this chapter to examine the extensive literature which now exists in the social sciences on the political economy of contemporary western societies (see Piore and Sabel 1984; Urry and Lash 1987, and 1994; Harvey 1990). It will suffice merely to remind readers that there are a number of different, if partly overlapping, conceptual frameworks which have been put forward to characterize and explain the various developments in political economy over the last 20 years; among which the terms de-industrialization, post-industrialism, late capitalism, and Fordism/post-Fordism have been the most prominent.

The object of these conceptual frameworks is a set of apparently deep-seated and structural problems in western political economies which emerged in the early 1970s. After nearly three decades of economic growth, stable prices, rising living standards, increasing world trade, expanding welfare programmes, and full employment, the statistical indicators of economic well-being began to go into reverse. Of course, there were exceptions to these trends: the economic cycle still produced up-turns and down-turns, and some countries — notably Japan, West Germany (as it then was) and Italy — seemed to cope with the 'crisis' better than others. Looking back over this period in 1994, however, while some countries (notably the UK) seemed to continue to decline, and others changed their places in the capitalist pecking order, the overall picture looks decidedly grim.

Nowhere is this more apparent than in the traditional metropolitan centres of the advanced industrial countries, especially in the UK. Once the dynamic hub of manufacturing, commerce and administration, and the focus of population growth over many generations, cities have — since the 1970s — lost population, businesses and jobs, tax revenues and vibrant public services. No longer the privileged site linking local populations to national and international markets, many traditional cities appear to have been sidelined by some inexorable logic of multinational capital. Visible signs of economic collapse, physical decay, and social decomposition are everywhere evident: dilapidated buildings, derelict land, homeless people, begging, rising crime, racial tensions, riots, and much else besides.

De-industrialization

In the 1980s, many geographers like Champion (1989), Young and Mills (1983), Hall (1988) and Robson (1988), and social scientists like Blackaby, and Rowthorn (1986; 1986) attributed these problems to processes of 'de-industrialization':

> ... urban economic decline is no localised phenomenon, but part of a massive and continuing shift in the spatial structure of the economies of industrialized nations ... to place the local changes ... into a broader international and national context enables us to set aside the question of the impact of policies and programmes upon the urban economy, for ... that impact is unlikely to be significant and can hardly be expected to reverse the tide of urban de-

industrialization (Young and Mills, p.2).

Companies were quitting the city and relocating production and employment elsewhere, and urban population decline inevitably followed: 'urbanization has ceased in most of Western Europe and ... counter-urbanization is in the process of emerging as the dominant force' (Fielding, quoted in Young and Mills, p.35).

While this de-industrialization thesis may have appeared plausible in the 1980s, there are several grounds for questioning its validity as a conceptual framework for understanding the political economy of the contemporary city. Does it do anything more than describe what cities have self-evidently experienced in the last 20 years, the departure of companies and people? Does it offer a serious explanation of this phenomenon, except the truism that companies and people have sought to locate and live elsewhere? More importantly, perhaps, does it provide anything other than a purely negative conceptual model of the contemporary city, that it is no longer 'industrial' in the traditional sense? And finally, is it not simplistic in giving such priority to traditional industrial activities, while ignoring the wider institutional context within which economic activity is always embedded?

Post-industrialism

For many social scientists, urban de-industrialization has come to be seen as merely a staging-post on the way to the 'post-industrial' city. This term, first worked out by Daniel Bell in the 1960s (1974), looks at first sight a useful corrective to the purely negative model of the city implied by the term de-industrialization: in place of manufacturing activities come service activities, servicing people and companies takes the place of the production of products, information and cultural capital replaces physical capital. In his Presidential address to the Institute of British Geographers in January 1993, the UK government's leading advisor on urban policy, Professor Brian Robson, enthusiastically embraces the concept of the post-industrial city:

> Much of this, of course, is to spell out the elements of the post-industrial city for which I have argued for many years. At its

simplest this involves the creation of the city as a forum ... with specific new aims: for information; for face-to-face decision making; for producer services; for HEI-linked hi-tech activities; for entertainment and leisure (Robson, 1993).

Here again, however, the concept of the post-industrial city appears purely descriptive, of the dominant economic activities in the city. It tells us nothing about how these activities are organized, why they have become dominant, and how such a city is integrated into the world of 'goods-production', since it apparently does not produce material products itself. Indeed, the core concepts of 'post-industrialism' have been vigorously criticized ever since they were first formulated by Bell in the 1960s, notably by Gershuny and Miles (1983), by a variety of Marxists (Callinicos, 1989) and by neo-Keynesians (Reich 1978; Hutton 1994). The belief that UK cities in particular, and the UK in general, could flourish on the back of service industries, was a widespread prejudice among Government ministers — notably Chancellors Lawson and Howe — in the 1980s, leading to a devastating decline in the UK's manufacturing base, and an unsustainable trade deficit.

If the most obvious weakness of the post-industrial thesis is its (flawed) empiricism, its central theoretical deficiency is (as with the de-industrialization thesis which preceded it) the priority it gives to disembodied technical and economic phenomena, to which all else in the social is subordinated. Its overt evolutionism automatically discounts questions of individual and collective agency, social and political contradictions and struggles, and the different forms that social arrangements take across time and space. Characterizing contemporary Manchester as a post-industrial city, for example — either as reality, or 'in the making' — obscures the precise location of Manchester in its regional, national and international setting, and the arguably complicated processes which link its present to its past. There is no sense of the way Manchester's character and identity has been forged out of the interaction between a variety of constraints and possibilities, both external and internal to it.

Fordism and post-Fordism

At first sight, the concepts of Fordism and post-Fordism — or flexible specialization — might appear to suffer from the same kind of evolutionism criticized above. But since these concepts refer not just to production regimes, but also to consumption patterns, cultural forms, individual and collective identities, and patterns of social and political regulation (regimes of regulation and accumulation, as the French school describes them (Aglietta 1979); so the scope of analysis widens, and the worst dangers of evolutionism (determinism, formalism, functionalism) can hopefully be avoided. More specifically, since the concepts of Fordism and post-Fordism entail a recognition that economic activity is always 'embedded' in networks of social institutions and practices, and in 'space' and 'time', it would seem likely that their deployment should result in a greater understanding of Manchester's specificity.

Manchester as a Fordist city

Insofar as the concept of Fordism has a common-sense meaning, it lies with the notion of mass production — of standardized products, for homogeneous markets, on a global scale. In this particular sense of the term, Manchester has long been in the forefront of Fordist cities (perhaps the world's first), as the centre of the Lancashire cotton industry, which dominated world markets throughout the 19th century and into the 20th. The entire industrial archeology of the region — its mills, warehouses, canals, terraced houses, valleys, town halls, market places — still reflects this stupendous domination; and the economic history statistics document it in all the major indicators: output, exports, investment in buildings and machinery, employment etc.

If Fordist mass production characterized the output of the cotton industry, the typical enterprise producing the output also displayed some major Fordist features. Although most remained quite small in employment terms — in 1890 the average spinning firm employed only 155 workers — enterprises tended to specialize in only one stage of the production process (spinning, weaving, finishing, merchanting), and seldom integrated different stages: with expanding demand, they were preoccupied with economies of 'scale' not of 'scope'. Technological innovation and product design played a limited role in the industry's development, which was driven mainly by simply adding capacity (more mills, more looms, more spindles).

While there was no assembly line, speeding up and deskilling work and worker — that characteristic of Fordism associated with Henry Ford himself — the machinery was 'dedicated' and inflexible, and required great concentration but little skill of the textile operative. The pace of work dictated by the machine was intense, and the division of labour correspondingly strict, overladen with rigid gender divisions between skilled and supervisory males, and semi-skilled females.

Cottonopolis

If Cottonopolis — as Manchester has been called since the 19th century — displays many classically Fordist features (mass production, economies of scale, hierarchical and rigid divisions of labour, semi-skilled labour, inflexible machinery, impersonal global markets etc.), the cotton industry did not stand alone. Alongside it grew a vigorous textile machinery industry, a clothing industry, a warehousing and distribution network, and a banking system to match. A tradition of textile and textile machinery production provided the foundation for mechanical engineering, and later, electrical engineering: both producing on a mass scale for world markets.

By the 1920s however, the domination of world markets by the Lancashire cotton industry had come to an end, displaced in the high income markets of the USA and Europe by indigenous producers able to defeat the Lancashire competition by new technologies, new products, on price and on quality. Employment in spinning and weaving fell from nearly 800,000 in 1912 to under 500,000 in 1937 (Singleton 1991); unemployment among cotton operatives reached 43% in 1931. Forced out of the European and American high-income markets, Lancashire cotton became increasingly dependent on the protected markets of Empire; but even here Lancashire faced the rising, low-cost, textile industry of Japan, and new low-cost competition from India, Egypt and China. By the end of World War II, Manchester's textile Fordism had been in headlong retreat for nearly half a century.

To conclude from this summary account, however, that it is 19th and early 20th century Manchester that was Fordist, would involve a gross misuse of the term. Of course, the mass production and export

21

of homogeneous textile products (and textile and other machinery) to an impersonal world market, on an immense scale, impressed itself deeply on Manchester's social and cultural forms. But the concept of Fordism cannot simply be reduced to the existence of mass production industries, however dramatic or durable their dominance was. For Fordism involves (whether one takes the concept from the American institutionalists like Piore and Sabel, or from the Marxist French regulationists) a particular conception of mass production: one which is generated and sustained 'endogenously' by a whole network of social institutions and practices.

By contrast, the mass markets which generated and sustained the mass production of the Lancashire textile industry were largely overseas, secured in part by competitive efficiency but also by the predations of Empire. The textile industry was never a high wage industry, trading secure earnings and mass consumption for semi-skilled monotony at work. The heroic story of textile and clothing trade unionism in Lancashire is not one of incorporation and institutionalization: of mutual recognition and coordinated bargaining, of unified pay and conditions across the industry, of stable recruitment and apprenticeship training etc. And the industry was not sustained by interventionist government, at local or national level, maintaining full employment, universal welfare, and a supportive regulatory framework. This was, after all, the hey-day of laissez-faire, which was not jettisoned until the 1930s

In spite of appearances therefore, Cottonopolis cannot be described as Fordist on the strength of its traditional cotton industry, and the industries mentioned above which developed alongside, and often overlapped, with it. As recent research has shown, even the Ford Motor Company itself — set up in Manchester's Trafford Park in 1913 — was not strictly Fordist, employing as it did many skilled workers, in the production of many different products, with quite short production runs and 'flexible' production methods (MacIntosh 1993). And if the internal structure of Manchester's notable industries was not Fordist, the term also cannot be applied to Manchester's industrial structure as a whole, since it was not dominated by a few large, vertically integrated, firms. The vast majority of firms producing most of the output and providing the bulk of employment remained relatively small, often owned by individual families.

Again the cotton industry might be taken as fairly typical in this respect. Processes of amalgamation did not really get under way until the 1920s and 30s, and even here they were defensive in nature, protecting markets and prices, so as to avoid productive and corporate reorganization. This in spite of successive reports and ineffectual government recommendations, that the industry needed substantial contraction and reorganization. Even in 1959, there were 949 separate firms in the cotton industry, 855 of which had less than 500 employees, yet employed nearly 40% of total employment (Magatti, p.214).

This would seem to support the view that the economy of Manchester and its region must be described as essentially pre-Fordist until at least the middle of the 20th century. Indeed, it has many of the hall-marks of what Piore and Sabel (1984) describe as an 'industrial district', where a large number of small and medium firms, compete and cooperate in the production of a wide range of partly complementary goods, embedded in a supportive and regulative social and cultural framework (skilled labour market, cooperative shops, chapel, family and town hall). In sum, a complex industrial region which flourished in the 19th and early 20th century because of 'Free Trade Imperialism' (Semmel 1970), because its various advantages located it fortuitously in world markets. It began to decay after World War I precisely at the point when laissez-faire, in Britain and elsewhere, began to be challenged and displaced by Fordism.

Post-war Manchester

It is now generally agreed by economic historians that the British economy enjoyed a halcyon period after World War II, benefiting from post-war reconstruction and expanding world trade stimulated by national and international Keynesian policies (Skidelsky, 1979). It is also agreed however, that Britain's share in the post-war boom masked serious structural weaknesses in its economy, and delayed any serious attempt to resolve them until the 1960s. These weaknesses were nowhere more obvious than in the large industrial conurbations like Manchester, whose economic structure continued to resemble its 19th century past. Textiles and clothing, for example, still provided 15% of total manufacturing employment in Manchester itself as late as 1971, while in Rochdale they provided over 50%,

Oldham 35%, Bury 34% (Magatti, p.215). This concentration on declining industries, was exacerbated by a fragmented proliferation of small and medium firms unable to confront the new competition in home and export markets.

The explanation of these structural weaknesses of the UK economy in general, and Manchester's in particular, is usually attributed to the particular form that Keynesianism in Britain took. Concerned with maintaining full employment in the economy as a whole, through demand management, it lacked any serious engagement with regional and industrial structures. It left investment decisions to private capital; the global role of sterling and the Bank of England was left untouched; financial institutions and the stock market remained unregulated and committed to overseas and the short-term. Neither the state (unlike France) nor the banks (unlike Germany and Japan), nor employers or unions (unlike Germany or Scandinavia) concerned themselves with industrial reorganization (Anderson 1987). As with social welfare, this 'liberal collectivism' involved the minimum of collectivism and the maximum scope for individualism (Cutler et al 1986; Esping-Anderson 1990; Ginsburg 1992).

It was only in the 1960s that these structural weaknesses began to be addressed, and a belated 'Fordization' of Manchester's economy was initiated. It was in the 60s for example, that the then Labour Government encouraged the formation of large enterprises: in the textile and clothing industry this resulted in various amalgamations (Tootal, Courtaulds), substantial mill closures and the reorganization of production; in mechanical and electrical engineering, the merger of GEC with AEI; in motor vehicles, the merger of Leyland Vehicles with BMC to form British Leyland (see Lloyd and Shutt 1983, for other industries).

Alongside these developments, fostered by the Industrial Reorganization Commission (IRC) with its obsession with economies of size and scale, went attempts to reorganize industrial relations, fostering productivity bargaining, payment by results (Taylorism), a national redundancy scheme and centralized (corporatist) pay determination. In addition, the Donovan Report recommended the incorporation of informal and shop-floor industrial relations into a formal and national system, recommendations which were later embodied in the White Paper *In place of Strife* (but not enacted into law), and the Heath Government's Industrial Relations Act in 1971.

This belated, nationally orchestrated, attempt to restructure Manchester's — and Britain's — industrial structure along Fordist lines coincided with other developments stressed by the theorists of Fordism. If mass production is to be sustained, mass markets have to be assured, not only of individualized consumption but also collective consumption. So we see in the Manchester of the 1960s — as elsewhere — the bulldozing of part of the old city centre to make way for the Arndale centre on Market Street; and the wholesale clearance of terraced houses and the building of Hulme, Chorlton on Medlock, the Salford housing estates, and high-rise on Manchester's overspill estates in Hattersley and Hyde (Dunleavy 1981). These new housing estates were frequently graced by purpose-built primary and secondary schools, the latter replacing the traditional division between grammar and 'modern' with the 'comprehensive', which embodied many Fordist bureaucratic principles, especially those justified by the idea of 'economies of scale'. Birley High School (now closed), in the middle of Hulme, was a classic example.

The 1960s also saw the beginnings of the construction of motorways into the heart of the city, extending the travel to work (TTW) area, the spread of suburbia and 'out of town' residence and commuting. Meanwhile, the building of Salford University, and the formation of Manchester Polytechnic, added to UMIST and the Victoria University, made Higher Education one of the biggest industries in the city. Local government reorganization in 1968 tried to put an administrative seal on this 'Fordization', with the creation of Greater Manchester Metropolitan Council

The social and cultural effects of these processes, condensed into less than a decade, must have been dramatic. For example, Manchester had been known as the night-club capital of the North well before the 1960s; what was the effect of the new housing estates, new roads, new city centre, on this cultural vitality? The brutal modernism of the architecture of the new city sat uncomfortably cheek by jowell with the grand Victorian pretensions of the Town Hall and Royal Exchange, Albert Square and Piccadilly Gardens. The Halle Orchestra at the Free Trade Hall had long been internationally famed, but its fame became increasingly rivalled by the enormous national audiences for Coronation Street just next door, the flagship programme of the infant Granada Television. Mainstream and esoteric popular music, like the Hollies and Northern Soul, created a cultural dynamic in Manchester to rival that on Merseyside.

Finally, like the American cities which had pioneered and exemplified Fordism in the first two decades of the century — Detroit, Chicago, Philadelphia etc. — 1960s Manchester comprised a cosmopolitan population, of diverse origins, creeds and colours. Manchester had of course attracted and welcomed migrants from Scotland, Ireland and Europe for more than a century ; but the 60s saw an even more cosmopolitan population emerge with Chinese, Asian and African-Caribbean arrivals. Outside of London, no other British city has had such a diversity of cultures and communities, and no other city — perhaps even including London — has been quite as mutli-cultural as Manchester.

This also contributed greatly to the social and cultural transformations of Manchester in the late 1960s, which became an ethnic as well as a cultural melting pot, finally breaking many of its links with its 19th century (Lancashire) past. Even Manchester's football underwent this change: mass football audiences were not a monopoly of Manchester, nor unique to the 1960s; but the big monies of Edwards and Swales — the one made from mass meat sales to Manchester's schools, the other from electrical retail shops — pushed United and City into the forefront of the 'mass entertainment' industry, arguably leaving 'football' far behind (Dunphy 1991).

Belated Fordization

What is so strange about this 'Fordization' of Manchester was its lateness. This lateness has a double sense: first, it was belated in comparison with cities in other countries, notably the USA, where many of the familiar features of the Fordist city were being put together in the 1920s and 30s (see Aglietta, Piore and Sabel etc.). Even in Europe, war-time devastation of the physical and social environment meant the re-building of Europe's cities often from scratch: many German, Dutch and Belgium cities are unrecognizable from their prewar forebears. And the principles which animated their rebuilding were surely Fordist: architectural modernism, out-of-town industrial estates, mass housing, city centre shopping malls, mass urban transit systems, public spaces and straight lines.

The second, more important, sense of lateness about all this is that it was,arguably, too late. For Manchester's Fordism emerged at precisely that moment when the prerequisites and pillars of Fordism, both internationally and at home, were beginning to disintegrate. The devaluation of the dollar in 1971, and the 1973 OPEC oil price rises, undermined the system of fixed exchange rates and cheap energy which had sustained rising world trade; competition from old and new industrial competitors threatened Britain's mass markets, home and abroad; Keynesian policies of full employment and stable industrial relations were being challenged from the old left and the new right (Heath's Conservative Government of 1970 took office with a neo-liberal strategy which laid the foundations for Thatcherism in the 1980s). The old cultures of community, class and work which provided the social bases of post-war Fordism were being undermined by new popular cultures of leisure, gender, sexuality and age (Martin 1981; Bell 1974; Lasch 1991; and Lash and Urry 1987).

The consequences for Manchester of this belated adoption (or imposition from central government) of a Fordist strategy, in the face of the global crisis of Fordism, have been predictably disastrous; Manchester is still suffering these consequences. The few remaining large textile firms, for example, which had swept away hundreds of small and medium enterprises, continued to lose market share, to contract capacity and reduce employment. They became increasingly exploitative of a deskilled, low-waged, often female Asian workforce, surviving through the protection of the MultiFibre Agreement which limited textile imports from low-wage industries abroad, unable to compete and expand either in mass production or in the new fashion-conscious, niche markets. Other industries, companies and industrial locations — like mechanical and electrical engineering, GEC, and Trafford Park — have suffered likewise: closure, redundancy, declining investment and relocation elsewhere.

If we look at the other side of Fordism, that of mass consumption, the consequences of belated Fordism have been equally serious. Take Hulme for example: densely populated with people, small and medium industrial firms, shopping centres, corner shops, churches and chapels, terraced houses in the 1940s and 50s; swept away by the planners, architects and factory-builders in the 1960s, and replaced by the infamous Crescents and deck-access flats. Uniquely residential, it was designed for working class families whose male heads were assumed to enjoy high-wage, semi-skilled jobs in the city centre or neighbouring Trafford Park. However badly it was built, it was the surrounding industrial collapse which destroyed its integrity and vitality. As local labour markets contracted, Hulme had neither economic nor social resources to fall back on, and became fatally dependent on declining subsidies from the state, student occupancy, and a dangerous network of underground economic activity.

Manchester's Fordism in retrospect

I have argued that Manchester's Fordism was largely a product of the national strategy pursued by the 1964-70 Labour government, which found a willing accomplice in the local state. This strategy involved a number of interconnected policy areas: macro-economic policy (neo-Keynesianism), industrial policy (IRC), industrial relations policy (corporatism), social security (e.g. redundancy payments and pensions), transport policy (inner-city ring roads and motorways) and welfare policy (mass housing, comprehensive schools, wider access to Higher Education and the Open University) etc.

It was a strategy partly designed to extend the patchwork of post-war economic and social reforms instituted by the 1945 Labour Government, to which the subsequent Tory Governments reluctantly acquiesced between 1951 and 1964. But it was also an attempt to change the balance between liberalism and collectivism in favour of the latter, in the face of relative economic failure and renewed competitive pressure from Britain's trading partners.

My emphasis on the strategic and political dimensions of Manchester's Fordism is well illustrated by Magatti (*IJURR* 1993), which examines the radically different responses to industrial competition of Manchester's industrial region, on the one hand, and Ticino Olana — a similar textile industrial region in the North of Italy, between Milan and Varese — on the other.

> ... from being a most renowned traditional industrial district, Lancashire became the home of the largest Fordist textile industry in the world between the end of the 1950s and the end of the 1960s, while Ticino Olona switched from a paternalist to a post-Fordist style of industrial organisation, reinforcing its entrepreneurial features. In Lancashire, industrial transformation destroyed not

28

only the traditional specialization in cotton but also **any local industrial identity** (my emphasis), while in Ticino Olona adjustment took place by substituting old textile production processes and firms by modern ones, though control over economic forces remained largely within the locality (pp.216-7).

Magatti's general argument is that economic and industrial change — and by implication social change — is not:

... an ordered path of transformation determined by technological breakthrough ... (but) ... a much more scattered process of evolution ... basically related to the way in which societies are organized, actors act, and their strategies fit together (p.217).

More specifically, if Ticino Olona managed to develop a post-Fordist, or 'flexibly specialized', textile industry in the 1970s — while Lancashire was going in the opposite direction — it did so because of a complex of institutional features and social processes rooted in the locality of Northern Italy. The so-called Third Italy, of course, figures prominently as an exemplar of flexible specialization in post-Fordist texts, like Piore and Sabel, Murray, Harvey, and Urry and Lash.

Precisely what social and institutional processes does Magatti identify to explain the trajectory of Ticino Olona's textile industry? They include the following: 'the weakness of the national state and of traditional business elites' (p.230); the strength of the family, as '... the focal point for mobilizing resources within the market, while the household was the physical location in which new economic activities took place' (p.223); 'the financial system, with its strong local identity ... generating and supporting local entrepreneurship'; 'the local employers' organization legitimized and supported the role of small firms in the development of the local district'; 'and the local authorities contributed to maintaining conditions suitable for rapid growth' (p.222).

As Mingione (1991) and Weiss (BJS, 1987) have shown, much of this activity takes place — or at least originates — in the informal economy, and is actively fostered by the central and local state — by tax privileges for small businesses, for example — extended family networks, and the availability of a largely female workforce excluded from formal employment. The absence, or weakness, of universal welfare provision, labour market fragmentation and weak national

29

trade unionism, and a strong Catholic culture of mutual reciprocity and self-provisioning, are also factors adduced by Magatti to explain Ticino Olona's industrial success.

In Lancashire, by contrast,

> ... workers had learnt for generations to protect themselves through collective agreements and arrangements aiming to regulate the market rather than through individualistic or family mobilization (p.224).

Highly unionized, workers looked to the nation state to secure stable employment conditions and to provide collective services, and the 1964 Labour Government's Fordist strategy sought to satisfy these aspirations. Employers too sought to regulate the market by price fixing and market sharing, and happily acquiesced in Labour's restructuring strategy as prices fell and markets shrank. Creative entrepreneurial adaptation to the changing market was as lacking among employers as among workers:

> ... any economic adjustment was blocked by an 'alliance of losers' between employers and employees, both interested — for different reasons — in maintaining the status quo (p.225).

When change did come in the 1960s, '... the advent of large companies was largely legitimized by the political project within which it was framed' and:

> ... the Lancashire textile district became entirely controlled from the outside, while the economic and social climate in the locality grew increasingly unfavourable to the emergence of new small firms (p.227).
>
> The result was an almost unrestrained company-led development which implied the loss of control by social forces over economic organization and the progressive decline of the British textile industry.
>
> Employment collapsed, skilled workers left, leaving a residual workforce of women, immigrants and low-skilled or older white men (p.227).

From the 60s to the 90s

I have argued so far that Fordism is best understood as a national political strategy which was initiated in unfavourable circumstances in the 1960s, which unravelled in the 1970s and finally collapsed in the early 1980s (Overbeek). Greater Manchester's economy, its labour market and industrial structure, is still suffering the consequences of that failed national and political strategy, as is well documented in Peck and Emmerich's paper: *Recession, Restructuring and the Greater Manchester Labour Market — an empirical overview* (1992).

Their conclusions can easily be summarized: continuous and massive loss of manufacturing employment; service industry employment increases, but insufficient to compensate for the decline in manufacturing employment, and itself suffering job loss in the recent recession (1989 to date); the proliferation of poorly-paid and part-time work, especially suffered by women; high aggregate levels of unemployment nearing 15% on pre-1982 definitions, and appallingly high levels approaching 50% in some wards of the city, for some age groups and ethnic minorities. 'Almost one in seven of the labour force are out of work, while more than one third of the city's population live in poverty' (p.20).

In the kind of empirical evidence presented and analyzed by Peck and Emmerich, there is almost no indication that any post-Fordist economy might be emerging in Greater Manchester, more than two decades after the failure of the Fordist strategy. In fact they explicitly warn against any extravagant claims made on the strength of Metrolink, the Olympic (and now Commonwealth) Bid, Granada and Castlefields, the cultural industries etc. 'It is important that a positive approach does not descend into unfounded "local boosterism"':

> ... the celebrated cultural industries employ less than 1% of the workforce, while the financial sector has been shown to consist of branch-office operations, themselves now shedding workers (p.19).

While Peck and Emmerich's warning is a salutary one, there are grounds for questioning the empirical basis on which the warning rests. Generally, these grounds involve the contention that official

31

statistics — of unemployment levels, employment by industrial sector, full-time and part-time jobs etc. — might well mask the extent and significance of an emergent post-Fordist economy, having been developed to record conventional or traditional Fordist economic processes. While the PCFC research on the cultural industries, fashion, and 'green' businesses is principally qualitative and ethnographic in nature, and does not attempt to be quantitative, it would be useful to survey the possible deficiencies in conventional quantitative indices.

The literature on post-Fordism, for example, suggests that labour markets become fragmented, in place of the organized and unionized labour markets typical of Fordism. In fragmented labour markets, distinctions between full-time and part-time work, and between work and non-work, become blurred: people may 'slide' from full-time into part-time work, or into self-employment, or into unemployment, and back again (see Mingione 1991). This may occur over time, or within a working day or week, as people pass from day-time activity to night-time, or working in a different location — or in 'different social relations' — on weekends rather than on weekdays. Conventional employment statistics tell us nothing of these possibilities. Again, the aggregate number of part-time jobs, and the percentage of part-time to full-time, does not tell us who does these jobs: separate individuals, or individuals who combine a number of part-time jobs, or part-time with full-time jobs.

And of course the official figures on Manchester's employment tell us nothing about the extent of employment outside the formal economy, concealed either because it is deemed trivial (e.g. too few hours worked), to avoid taxation and safeguard benefits, or because it is criminal (Hakim, Mingione etc.). They tell us nothing about people who are primarily or partly dependent on benefits, a major omission given the levels of benefit dependency in Manchester. And they tell us nothing about the arguably huge economic and cultural significance of Higher Education in the city. If the official statistics show that the formal economy sustains fewer and fewer people through wages and salaries, it is surely vital to investigate the alternative ways Manchester's population sustains and reproduces itself.

If there are legitimate theoretical doubts about the employment and unemployment statistics, so too are there about industrial classifications. Manufacturing employment statistics may include many service activities e.g. marketing, or design, or personnel; service industry statistics may include productive activities, e.g. theatres producing food, advertisers published material, nightclubs or music groups producing videos and tape recordings. The important work by Gershuny and Miles (1983) showed over 20 years ago how precarious the manufacturing/service distinction is, and how interrelated productive and service activities are. This is especially true for the activities researched by the PCFC team: it is by no means clear where cultural industries, fashion, or 'green businesses' should be located or discovered in the conventional industrial classifications.

Finally, post-Fordism is associated with organizational structures different from Fordist ones: non-hierarchical, flat or 'soft'; cooperating as well as competing with others; involving 'networking' among employees, suppliers and customers; flexibly moving from one product or service to another; transcending the boundaries between work and non-work, production and consumption. Evidence of these varied and interconnected changes must require, at least initially, qualitative and ethnographic investigation, and it is to these that we now turn.

The PCFC research

The culture industry

A number of recent studies by Derek Wynne et al, and Wynne and O'Connor, (1989, 1992, 1993) have documented the nature, extent and significance of the 'cultural' industries in the Manchester region. Their 1989 report, *The Culture Industry*, estimated that the annual product of the arts and cultural industries as a whole was around £350 million, and that they employed around 10,000 people. Even in narrow and quantitative economic terms, therefore, the significance of 'culture' in the city's economy is clearly substantial.

For our purposes, however, this research has generated empirical findings which are more interesting. For example, the majority of organizations operating in the arts and cultural industries are small, employing less than 10 people (Wynne and O'Connor 1992 p.114 passim). In addition, while these organizations produce and sell for a market, they are not wholly dependent on 'box office' revenue for their survival: they depend considerably on a variety of other sources of funding (like the Arts Council, urban aid projects, sponsors and advertisers, enterprise allowances, and financial and other practical council support). While 40% of these organizations are nominally 'private' (limited companies, partnerships, co-ops, sole traders), 37% are in the voluntary sector and 23% are classed as 'public' organizations (op cit Tables 3 and 4, pp.116-119). In other words, simple distinctions between private and public, market and non-market, do not begin to encapsulate the diversity either of organizational forms or sources of income which one finds in this sector.

This diversity is parallelled by the employment patterns found here: while the majority of employment and self-employment is categorized as full-time, 4 out of every 10 employees are either part-time, casual, voluntary or on a training scheme. This 'informalization' of the employment patterns in the arts and cultural industries is complemented by an elaborate informal network of relationships between individuals, organizations and institutions: 'personal and informal contacts are the principal modus operandi of artists and cultural producers (op cit, Table 5, p.117).

These organizations cooperate as well as compete, sharing information, cultural initiatives, sponsorship bodies, and often offices, equipment and workspaces. They are, in other words, embedded in an institutional and cultural setting which they mutually sustain and reinforce, not only as 'producers' but also as 'consumers'.

These studies also show, finally, how these arts and cultural organizations transgress the boundaries between one art/cultural form and another (music, dance, film, photography, drama etc.); and between arts and culture together and everyday life. 'The vast majority of those questioned were unable to identify themselves as working in any one single art form' (op cit Table 7 p.119).

> The sheer volume of cultural products, the sheer extensiveness of the circulation of images and sounds ... has led to the contention that there has been a de-differentiation between art and everyday life (op cit, p.121).

Manchester's pop fashion designers

In the last decade, the changing face of fashion has frequently been used to validate the general claims of certain theorists about flexible specialization, niche marketing and post-Fordism (Murray, *In New Times* 1989, Urry and Lash 1994). This has purported to show how the once elitist, expensive and luxury end of the the clothing industry — associated with high culture as in the term haute couture — has been invaded by a 'democratization' of fashions. This, they claim, has transformed both the 'fashion' and mass produced clothing industries simultaneously.

Sarah Purvis' research on Manchester's pop fashion designers (this volume) confirms and amplifies this thesis. She documents a close, symbiotic, relationship between Manchester's pop culture scene — its music, dance, clubs, bars etc. — on the one hand, and the fashions of its producers and consumers and its designers and producers, on the other. This has produced a series of niche markets, innovative designs, and flexibly specialized units more fragmented, diverse and rapidly changing than those apparent in mainstream clothing markets served by Benetton, or Next. Here the product is sold (or otherwise exchanged) in Affleck's Palace, on street stalls, or in the clubs themselves; the designs change overnight, and yesterday's fashion is tomorrow's collector's item. These fashions often mirror the playful and syncretic styles of popular music and dance, combining traditional and contemporary motifs in a variety of ways (colours, pictures, words) on a variety of themes. Various paraphernalia celebrating Coronation Street character Reg Holdsworth (jewellery, key rings, T-shirts) jostle with garments documenting the fates of Manchester's football teams, and others advertising the merits of particular bands, clubs or 'scenes'.

Like the majority of 'organizations' in the arts and cultural industries, Manchester's pop fashion designers are small businesses, often self-employed 'one-man bands'. Sales of their designs and/or their products are only one source of income: equally important are enterprise allowance grants, welfare benefits, informal support from family and friends, and various 'benefits in kind', like sharing telephones, back-rooms, or equipment.

In conventional economic terms, these 'businesses' look both ephemeral and peripheral, unlikely to expand or consolidate, and equally unlikely to survive the ups and downs of the business cycle, recessions, and local and foreign competition. One might assume that they are merely an alternative to 'proper' full-time jobs, which the fashion and clothing industry has been unable to provide in recent years; that they are an apprenticeship for the full-time jobs which the industry will eventually want filling. One might claim that they are 'no choice' businesses (see Nicholson 1986) for those temporarily — or permanently — marginalized in the urban labour market: in the case of some of the pop fashion designers, the unemployed graduates of local Art and Design departments.

Purvis' research challenges this kind of prejudiced critique in showing the dense networks of friends and business associates which sustain both the lifestyles as well as the productive capacities of these fashion designers. The smallness and informality of these enterprises is a choice, not a fate, which permits them to anticipate or react to changes on the streets or in the clubs, sensitively and quickly.

They successfully create and occupy their market niches precisely because they are small and informal, and they (and their networks) consume as well as produce. They do not need Benetton's point of sale computers to tell them what is, and what is not, selling. They are durable because they are embedded in a cultural scene in which transgressing the boundaries of the conventional is positively encouraged.

Manchester's green businesses

Paul Kennedy's investigation of 75 'green' businesses in Manchester and the North and North West (this volume), covers a range of activities from health food shops to ethical financial services, recycling manufacturing operations, to the production and retailing of non-toxic paints and biodegradable plastics. They thus include businesses involved in the production, wholesaling and retailing of 'green' products, either as an exclusive activity or one among others. His special focus is on those businesses for whom 'greenness' is central and exclusive, of which there are around 30 in the study. These he labels 'radical' or 'alternative' green businesses.

The fundamental paradox confronting such businesses, he argues, is the need to generate a financial surplus sufficient to pay rents, wages and suppliers, by selling products — either direct to the consumer, or to other green businesses — defined essentially by their 'greenness' rather than their price or utility. These consumers, it has to be said, are deeply sceptical of the profit-making, commercialized materialism of contemporary life. This 'commodification of ethicality', as Kennedy describes it — or the moralization of consumption — 'locks entrepreneurs and consumers into a mutually validating cultural embrace' (Kennedy, 1994, p.5).

> Selling goods that embody certain ethical claims ... invites scrutiny and calls for proof. An inability to substantiate such demands would involve severe risks (p.4).

The radical green businesses respond to this paradox in very specific ways. First, by the adoption of strict criteria of ethical purity, validated by the specialized green media (like the *Green Consumer* magazine). Second, by a refusal to compromise on the ethical quality and range of products bought and sold. Third, by a reluctance to expand, especially if such expansion would threaten the ethical purity of the business (this 'self-limitation' is common to the organizations in the arts and cultural industry, and the pop-fashion designers). Fourth, by a commitment to a wider ethos of greenness in business practice e.g. participation in recycling schemes, home deliveries by bicycle, acting as a focus of environmental campaigns etc. Fifth, by an adherence to alternative work patterns, like rotating jobs, eschewing skill differences and hierarchies, democratic work meetings, putting new employees and volunteers on probation etc. Sixth, by a commitment to an alternative, ethical 'lifeworld', such as vegetarianism or veganism, and a non-materialistic life-style.

Finally, by a more or less explicit commitment to non-profit-making activity, such as community, cultural and political activity, for which the business acts as a focal point. In addition, many of these businesses deliberately avoid conventional legal status, setting themselves up as cooperatives, companies limited by guarantee, and community businesses.

Kennedy's study of green businesses has run alongside complementary investigations by the PCFC research team into radical environmental groups (see Purkis, this volume), and into local trading systems (LETS). One of Manchester's Local Economic Trading Systems uses a currency called Bobbins, a Mancunian term meaning 'rubbish'! We cannot go into these researches here, but they support Kennedy's claim that his green businesses are embedded in a complex network of agencies, organizations and practices which are mutually supportive:

> ... in seeking to operate within a specialized market niche of

highly responsive consumers, they also tended to nestle within an interlocking set of support groups, sometimes national as well as regional and local in orientation (op cit, p.14).

The diversity and vibrancy of this set of networks bears some resemblance to the kind of industrial districts which, according to Piore and Sabel (op cit 1982), preceded the era of Fordism and mass production. We would argue, however, that these environmental (or green) networks represent not so much a return to some pre-modern Arcadia (as even some of its protagonists might aspire to); but the cutting edge of an incipient post- (or late) modern economy, whose structure and functioning is best understood in terms of reflexivity, informalization, and de-differentiation.

It is to these more general theoretical considerations that we now turn.

Postmodern Manchester: immanence or contingency?

The research reviewed above suggests that, among activities that have flourished in Manchester in the last decade — even as recently as the last 5 years — elements of a novel type of economy are emerging. Here, entrepreneurship is not solely concerned with the bottom line, profit-maximization, and absolute authority; businesses cooperate and 'network', as well as compete; workers seek fulfilment, not just money, from their work; consumers are willing to trade price for style or ethical commitment. Indeed commitment — cognitive, aesthetic, moral or political — and 'reflexivity' (see Giddens 1991; Beck 1992; Lash and Urry 1994) are values apparently integral to all these activities. They also indicate processes of 'de-differentiation', as the boundaries between work and non-work, production and consumption, economy and culture etc., become blurred; processes of cultural 'commodification'; and what Urry and Lash call the economy of 'signs and spaces'.

While much of this has been widely anticipated in much of the literature on New Times, post-Fordism, and indeed postmodernism, we need to acknowledge that that literature has often been speculative and generalized, and occasionally devoid of empirical content. Many of the critics — like Williams et al, 1989; Callinicos, 1989; Rustin, 1989; Sivinandan, 1989 — have expressed a justified

38

scepticism about the 'novelty' of these activities, their extent and significance, and their durability. Do they represent a different 'logic", or modus operandi, of the city's economy, or are they marginal and superficial? Is their potential scope and significance greater than is indicated in the kind of statistics marshalled by Peck and Emmerich? Are they anything more than the 'lifestyle choice' of an unrepresentative, urban middle class, for whom post-Fordism and postmodernism have become a self-serving ideology with universalistic pretensions? (Pfiel, 1990; Featherstone, 1991).

I would argue that they are indeed significant, but that we need to understand their nature, emergence, and extent in terms of "politics" and 'strategy', rather than in terms of some immanent, evolutionary logic rooted in economy, society or culture. For all the supposed concern with 'time' and 'space' in the post-Fordist (postmodern) literature, fashionable notions about the global village, the informational city, the niche producer, the discretionary consumer etc. threaten to eclipse any concern with particular places (e.g. Manchester), at particular times (the 1990s). The emergent, or nascent, post-Fordist economy in Manchester — if such is what it is — needs to be put into its social context, the most important parameters of which are, in my view, political and strategic.

The assault on the city

Two articles by Mike Davies in recent editions of the *New Left Review* (1993) set the scene for what follows. Analyzing the events leading up to the 1992 Los Angeles riots, Davies shows how the city has been the victim of a systematic and relentless attack, orchestrated by Reagan and Bush from Washington, and actively prosecuted by local policy-makers, interest groups and power-brokers. Animated by neo-liberal ideology, and articulated by rhetorical crusades against public expenditure, local taxation, public services, welfare 'scroungers', illegal immigrants, ethnic minorities, single parents etc. — often lumped together as an 'underclass' — the attack has devastated the economic livelihood of the city's population: their access to jobs, welfare support, public services, housing and physical security. As his earlier monumental history of Los Angeles — *City of Quartz* — shows, the local social roots of this political attack lie in the successive waves of segregated suburbanization of Los Angeles

39

residents, which has created a plethora of (normally white) middle class interest groups remote from, and hostile to, the city.

Direct comparison between US politics, and indeed US cities, and their British counterparts, is not what I intend by this brief reference to Davies. Indeed, while I would argue that there is some convergence between British and American cities, the real 'fault-line' seems to me to run between European cities on the one hand, and American cities on the other; and that British cities share more features with the former than the latter (e.g. a civic tradition, restricted suburbanization, inclusive public services, open spaces for leisure and public life, and a strong local identity).

If British cities have become more and more detached from this European model, and more 'Americanized', the key factor has arguably been the virulence of free-market politics in both the US and the UK in the 1980s.

For the attack on Britain's cities in the 1980s — which still continues today — has been no less systematic and relentless than that on Los Angeles. The attack has ranged widely and deeply: on city finances, its services, its employees, their managers, and their elected representatives; through financial and legal measures, it has forced cities to cut and privatize services, and divest them of power and discretion; and it has created new institutions to by-pass elected city authorities and undermine them. Insofar as right-wing ideology has a vision of the city at all — which is debatable — it is a wholly impoverished one in which a regulatory shell, with limited democratic accountability, presides over a network of services whose providers, employees and consumers relate to each other in purely contractual ways. Voters and citizens become consumers and tax payers; the ballot box is replaced by consumer charters, competition, and market choice; the city becomes a void underpinned only by the cash nexus.

The social roots of this attack in Britain are indeed different from those in the USA, where local elites and interest groups are probably much more significant. The USA has a federal system, which confers wide powers on federal and local government. Britain, by contrast, has a highly centralized, 'unitary', constitution, where the laws and powers of local government are wholly at the mercy of Westminster. Britain's unitary constitution, and its electoral system of 'first-past-the-post', has permitted successive Tory governments wholly unrepresentative of Northern and urban populations, to inflict almost terminal damage on Britain's older, once industrial, cities. Just on the financial front alone, it has been estimated that Manchester lost more than £500m in government grant between 1980 and 1990, and local taxation — which accounted for over 30% of local revenue in 1980 — now raises only 10%.

The fact that almost all British cities, like Manchester, have Labour councils, adds a special animus to the bitter conflict between central and local government. However, the fact that the Labour Party has, until recently, subscribed both to the unitary constitution and to the winner-takes-all electoral system, has fatally compromised its ability to withstand and resist the attacks of central government. For if the 1980s Tory governments were unrepresentative, and especially so of the Northern and urban electorate, so too are Labour-controlled councils, elected as they are on an even smaller percentage of local electorates.

If the neo-liberal attack on Manchester constitutes the main parameter within which the elements of an emergent post-Fordist economy has emerged, it is important to recognize that this attack has involved not just an interconnected set of policies, but a systematic electoral strategy. This has involved targeting and undermining the social bases of Labour's electoral support (sometimes illegally, as in Westminster) — e.g. public sector trade unionism, council tenants, public transport users etc. — while simultaneously subsidizing and privileging private consumption among the employed, the comfortable and the wealthy. The overt discrimination in favour of private over public/collective consumption — in the fields of housing, health, pensions, transport etc. — has been breathtaking; the consequent widening inequalities in income, wealth and life chances, has been massive. This bias in favour of private as against collective consumption was reflected in popular idiom: the 'Yuppie' became the mildly satiric label for the extravagantly wealthy, while the poor were (de)moralized as an 'underclass'.

It is no exaggeration, therefore, to claim that Manchester — and other similar British cities to a greater or lesser extent — has been the site of a tremendous struggle over the last 15 years, and that what we have tentatively labelled 'Manchester's emergent post-Fordist economy' has to be seen against that background. If the people involved in the cultural industries, fashion, and 'green' businesses have a 'semi-detached' relationship to the formal labour market, this is as much to do with the absence of full-time, secure jobs, as it is to do with any attitude (or cultural) change on their part. If Manchester's labour market has been fragmented by a declining full-time workforce and a massive increase in work which is part-time, subcontract, short-term, self-employed, or 'underground', this is principally to do with government, which has systematically privileged the latter over the former.

It has often done this, moreover, in direct defiance of European legislation, and is continuously breaching decisions of the European Court of Human Rights (see Hutton 1994).

Declining student grants, for example, and the abolition of housing benefit and social security for students, have forced many students into the part-time and informal end of the labour market; students have become part of a post-Fordist workforce. Compulsory Competitive Tendering has forced many once full-time workers to accept part-time, and/or short-term, work. The Enterprise Allowance Schemes have encouraged many to accept redundancy, or come off unemployment benefit, and enter self-employment. The 'demand' for labour by employers has also been skewed towards part-time workers, whose employment rights have been heavily restricted by government.

Similarly, if a cafe society is developing in Manchester, a night-time economy, a gay village, cultural tourism etc., is this not in large part a consequence of the stimulation of private consumption in the 1980s, by a combination of tax cuts, credit sprees, housing and stock market booms, and privatizations? The fact that many of the activities which the PCFC researchers have been examining have shown some resilience in the face of the recent recession, merely suggests that the kinds of consumers they cater for have been relatively immune from that recession. Consumption of 'culture', of fashion, or green products is not just a matter of wants, desires, attitudes, culture etc.; but of money.

Governments, especially those since 1979, have been very important in putting money into (certain) people's pockets — by taxation changes, privatizations, welfare benefits, direct employment etc. — and thus influencing directly, as well as indirectly, the extent and pattern of consumption. Increasing FE and HE student numbers means increased aggregate student grants and expenditure, for example, on housing, food, transport and leisure. It also means increased fee income for the FE and HE institutions, and increased construction of new buildings to house and teach them. Deregulating financial institutions has eased the availability of subsidized credit for house purchase, thus contributing directly to the 'gentrification' of parts of inner city Manchester. Various tax breaks for private savings (Tessas and Peps), life and health insurance, pensions etc. have fuelled the growth of the financial services industry.

Finally, much of Manchester's inner-city activity in the last decade has been fuelled by the urban development corporations, public-private sector partnerships, Task Forces and City Challenges. Manchester's night-time economy, the club-cafe-music scene, and the promotion of cultural tourism has direct parallels elsewhere (London, Liverpool, Tyneside docklands and waterfronts), and they owe a great deal to the various government initiatives to by-pass local councils, and to 'hoist the free market flag' in 'those inner cities' (cf. Robson, 1988). Cynics might compare the postmodern spectacle of Manchester's canal, Whitworth Street and Piccadilly Village with the Potemkin villages along the river Niva, built to impress the Tsar and obscure the squalor and deprivation behind them.

Conclusion

... [C]entral state policies involve accruing increasing powers to Whitehall, then generalizing a model of local economic development which is largely private sector and consumption based. The spectacular housing, leisure and entertainments schemes now being mapped out for depressed inner cities everywhere reflect the strength of property and finance capital and the relative weakness of industrial capital in the country. It is, of course, partly a cultural question. Whereas in the European examples quoted there seems to be some cultural attachment to the idea of self-sustained, often collectively organized enterprise, that tradition may, especially in manufacturing industry, be impossible to revive in areas that were swamped long ago by capital concentration and Fordism.

... [F]or too long, Britain's economy has been run from a centre that is clearly inadequate to meet local needs, other than by generalizing a consumers' paradise of urban spectacle. Localities can, if they wish, develop along a different trajectory (Cooke, in

Campbell, 1990, pp.39-40).

I have tried to argue in this chapter that, just as Manchester's Fordism has to be understood as the product of politics and strategy, at local and national level, so too are the fragments of an emergent post-Fordism which the PCFC research has uncovered. While they may be the consequence of irreversible and deep seated transformations in culture and social structure, they have also been decisively marked (if not stunted) by right-wing ideology and practice, to which the values and traditions of public service, collective provision, civic pride — even the very idea of the social — is anathema. To deduce from this, however, that this right-wing strategy is itself a comprehensive post-Fordist strategy, and one which in time will produce a durable post-Fordist Manchester, is surely mistaken. For it is a strategy rooted in the exigencies of Britain's antique constitution and electoral competition, and its success is entirely limited to its repeated delivery of Tory election victories.

What Manchester's fledgling post-Fordist economy needs, above all else, is the breaking of this political stalemate. Without this, the forging of an institutional and cultural setting conducive to a durable and expanding post-Fordist economy looks well-nigh impossible. For such an economy needs a dynamic, innovative, and democratic local government, with substantial financial and legal powers. It needs a labour market which is flexible not simply for the convenience of employers, but employees and the self-employed as well. It needs a welfare system which does not stigmatize claimants, discourage informal work, and condemn the jobless to actively search for non-existent work. It needs a taxation system which encourages the formation of networking small businesses, investment in training and new technology by established business, and a banking system sensitive to local needs.

Above all, it needs a shift from private consumption to collective consumption and investment, and from markets to new forms of social regulation, because cities are so much more than networks of monetary transactions. The ruling idea that these two principles — private/public, market/regulation etc. — are incompatible and antagonistic, is no more than a political prejudice; but one whose continuation condemns Manchester's post-Fordism to fragility and marginality.

References

Aglietta M. (1979), *Theory of Capitalist Regulation*, NLB.

Anderson P. (1987), 'Figures of Descent', *New Left Review,*

Beck U. (1992), *Risk Society,* Sage.

Bell D. (1974), *The Coming of Post-Industrial Society,* Heinemann.

Blackaby F. (1986), *De-industrialization,* Gower, Aldershot.

Callinicos A. (1989), *Against Postmodernism,* Polity.

Champion A. G. (1989),*Counterurbanization,* Edward Arnold.

Cooke P. (1990), in Campbell M. *Local Economic Policy,* Cassell.

Cutler A. J. et al (1986), *Keynes, Beveridge, and Beyond*, RKP.

Davies M. (1992), *City of Quartz,* Vintage.

Davies M. (1993) 'Who Killed Los Angeles?", and "Los Angeles on Trial" in *New Left Review.*

Dunleavy P. (1981), *The Politics of Mass Housing*, Clarendon.

Dunphy E. (1991), *A Strange Kind of Glory; Sir Matt Busby and Manchester United*, Heinemann.

Esping-Anderson G. (1990), *3 Worlds of Welfare Capitalism,* Polity.

Featherstone M. (1991), *Consumer Culture and Postmodernism,* Sage.

Gershuny J. and Miles (1983), *The New Service Economy*, Frances Pinter.

Giddens A. (1991), *Modernity and Self-Idenity,* Polity.

Ginsburg H. (1992), *Divisions of Welfare*, Sage.

Hall P. (1988), *Cities of Tomorrow*, Blackwell.

Hall S. and Jacques M. (1989), *New Times*, Lawrence and Wishart.

Harvey D. (1990), *Condition of Postmodernity*, Blackwell.

Hutton W. 'Britain fulfils de Gaulle's prophecy' in *The Guardian*, 27.6.94.

Kennedy P. (1994), 'Consumerism and Green Businesses in Manchester', unpublished paper for PCFC research group.

Lasch C. (1991), *The Culture of Narcissism*, Norton.

Lash S. (1990), *Sociology of Postmodernism*, Routledge.

Lash S. and Urry J. (1987), *The End of Organised Capitalism*, Polity.

Lash S. and Urry J. (1994), *Economies of Signs and Spaces*, Sage, London.

Lloyd P. and Shutt J. (1983), *Recession and Restructuring in the North West Region*, North West Industry Research Unit, Working Paper 13.

MacIntosh I. (1993), *Ford in the UK*, Unpublished PhD thesis. Manchester.

Magatti M. (1993), 'The Market and Social Forces' *International Journal of Urban and Regional Research*.

Martin B. (1981), *Sociology of Contemporary Cultural Change*, Blackwell.

Mingione E. (1991), *Fragmented Societies*, Blackwell.

Murray R. (1989), 'Benetton Britain' in Hall and Jacques, *New Times*.

Overbeek H., Peck J. and Emmerich (1992), *Recession, Restructuring, and the Greater Manchester labour market — an empirical overview*. Unpublished working paper from Geography Department, Manchester Victoria University, Manchester

Pfeil F. (1990), *Another tale to Tell,* Verso.

Piore M and Sabel C. (1984), *The Second Industrial Divide,* Basic Books.

Reich R. et al (1978), *The Capitalist System,* Prentice-Hall.

Robson B. (1988), *Those Inner Cities,* Clarendon.

Robson B. (1993), 'No City, No Civilisation', *Regenerating Cities,* Issues 3 & 4.

Rowthorn B. and Martin R. (1986), *The Geography of De-industrialization,* Macmillan.

Rustin M. (1989), 'The Shape of New Times', *New Left Review.*

Semmel B. (1970), *The Rise of Free Trade Imperialism,* Cambridge.

Singleton J. (1991), *Lancashire on the Scrap heap,*

Sivanandan (1989), 'The Hokum of New Times', *Race and Class.*

Skidelsky R. (1979), 'The End of World Keynesianism' in Crouch C. (ed.) *The State and Economy in Contemporary Capitalism.*

Williams K. et al (1987), 'The End of Mass Production?' in *Economy and Society.*

Wynne D. et al (1989), *The Culture Industry,* Centre for Employment Research, Manchester Polytechnic.

Wynne D. and O'Connor J. (1992), 'Tourists, hamburgers and Street Musicians' in Reichardt R. and Muskens G. (eds.) *Post-Communism, the Market and the Arts.*

Wynne, D. and O'Connor, J. (1993,) *From the Margins to the Centre*, Working Papers Series I, No.7, Manchester Institute for Popular Culture.

Young K. and Mills C. (1983), *Managing the Post-Industrial City*, Heinemann.

2 Left loafing: City cultures and postmodern lifestyles

Justin O'Connor and Derek Wynne

In this chapter we will examine the claims that any transformation towards the 'postmodern city' can be tied to the operations of a designate class or class fraction who, more than any other social group, are concerned with the promotion of a 'postmodern lifestyle'. We will draw on our empirical research(1) in order to do two things. Firstly, to argue that some of the claims made about 'gentrification' and the social groups involved are mostly over generalized, and that any characterization of this process must acknowledge the local context in these 'global transformations'. Secondly, to suggest that the attempt to tie the emergence of postmodern lifestyles to the distinction strategies of a particular class fraction may need to be seriously modified.

Landscapes and the counter-culture

Gentrification, which was increasingly commentated on in the 1970s, carries the sense of a 'return' to the centre by the middle classes, but by a new fraction within this 'middle class' who are seen to be 'on the rise' and hence often 'new'; it also involves a sense of displacement of lower social groups. We describe gentrification as the 're-centralization' of areas that had lapsed into marginality. This implies a shift in power based on the economic, but also cultural power.

The economic explanation usually revolves around a notion of 'rent gap'. The gradual move out of the city by industry, followed by residents and offices, causes an undervaluing of the centre. The potential value remains, because of its centrality and the historic/aesthetic buildings in which capital was still tied. As rent and prices fall below this potential value capital moves back in. It has been argued that the withdrawal from industrial production in the late 1970s coupled with the undervaluation of the city centre meant that development capital began to pour into the centre, producing new buildings and a general rise in rents.

Gentrification was seen to be part of this cycle. The return was an economic move by an 'enterprising' middle class ready to defend their self-refurbished new homesteads in the midst of hostile social groups, ultimately to recoup their investments when social and economic 'health' returned to the centre.

However this direct economic argument cannot stand alone. Why should centrality be important, why did its value suddenly emerge as undervalued? Arguments centre on the revived symbolic importance of centrality for an increasingly globalized financial capital, now severed from a connection to specific locations of production and the importance of networking opportunities for higher management and associated business services. Be that as it may, central business districts underwent a rapid expansion in many cities in the 1980s at a level that went beyond any advantages related to undervaluation.

The growth in professional-managerial employment associated with the expansion of the central business district (CBD) does not necessarily mean that all these employees will live in the centre. An alternate or associated explanation is to be found in the sphere of 'reproduction and consumption':

> The consumption style of this urban, professional-managerial group is partly one of conspicuous consumption, the acquisition of commodities for public display. It is facilitated by the postponement of familial responsibilities, and the accumulation of savings ... In addition, more and more consumption takes place outside of the household in 'public' realms ... The postponement of marriage facilitates this consumption, but it also makes it necessary if people are to meet others and develop friendships (Beauregard, 1986, pp.43-44).

Thus for Beauregard whilst these new consumption habits are 'not dissimilar from those of other professional, middle-class individuals not in the city' (p.44) they crucially intersect with the postponement of marriage.

Conspicuous consumption is thus part of clustering. Centrality facilitates this clustering, hence the desirability of living in the city. Those social opportunities, moreover, though possibly no more numerous in cities than in suburbs, are decidedly more spatially concentrated and, because of suburban zoning, tend to be more spatially integrated with residences (p.44).

The economic rationality is ever-present, as it is clear that to buy into a soon to be gentrified area is an investment, especially for young people at an early stage of their careers — it is also a statement of 'affluence and taste'.

But this sort of functionalist explanation is severely limited. The conspicuous nature of consumption is reduced to its ability to facilitate sexual and other social encounters. Many questions about why this group have no other rituals of encounter go unanswered, but it is the explanation of the importance of 'conspicuous consumption' and the centre as a site of such that is most lacking. It seems clear that there is more than the necessity of sexual encounter in operation in the following account.

Clustering occurs as these individuals move proximate to 'consumption item' and as entrepreneurs identify this fraction of labour as comprising conspicuous and major consumers ... these tendencies are also obviously important for the gentrification of commercial districts. The potential gentry represent an 'up-scale' class of consumers who frequent restaurants and bars, and generally treat shopping as a social event. The objective for the entrepreneur is to capture the discretionary income of the consumer by offering an experience that is more than a functional exchange (p.44).

Sharon Zukin's work (1982; 1992) represents an extremely useful examination of the dynamics of gentrification. Put baldly, her contention is that the gentrification of the centre is about the shift from production to consumption, that this shift is, importantly, about the imposition of a cultural power, and the crucial role in this shift is played not by developers, nor even some general professional-managerial class, but by precisely those 'entrepreneurs' referred to above. We shall focus, firstly, on her account of the transformation of the landscape of the city centre, and, secondly, her account of the

51

activities of these cultural entrepreneurs.

For Zukin the transformation of the city centre or downtown is located within a series of global economic shifts. These include the increasing abstraction of the market, the internationalization of capital and the centrality of consumption to the structuration of the economic system. The new city centre has been reorganized around consumption, but a consumption dominated by abstraction and internationalization. The restructuration of the centre is one not of the 'creative-destruction' (Harvey, 1986) of the built environment but one of the imposition of a new perspective on the city, a perspective based on cultural power. This cultural power emerges in a context of mass cultural consumption, giving rise to new mechanisms of inclusion and exclusion, and in a context of globalization, where the market of cultural consumption is increasingly abstracted from place based production and consumption, and driven by globalized flows of information, capital and cultural goods.

This cultural power acts upon the downtown area in a way that brings the fragmented vernacular of the old productive communities into an aesthetic landscape based on cultural consumption. Disputing the simple equation of centrality and power, Zukin argues that city centres have included both symbols of centrality — political and economic — but, as centres of industrial production, also contained a large working class population. The landscape was one structured by an opposition of the CBD, with its 'assertion of power at the centre', and the vernacular of the working communities. Both densely built and historically layered, downtown is the 'urban jungle' that pits the cultural hegemony of economic power against its alternative image of social diversity. It is also a fragmented landscape, where each section was organized around the social and cultural worlds of small scale production centres. As industry and wealthy residents began to move out capital in the centre declines, leading to 'its temporary abandonment as a landscape of power'.

Until the mid-70s ... downtown remained a patchwork of social and economic values. It included sedimentary concentrations of capital investment from the past, empty lots that formed a holding pattern — often under the aegis of publicly sponsored urban renewal — against the loss of economic value, and low rent quarters for local, declasse and traditional ethnic uses. These were all excluded from the landscape of power (Zukin, 1992,

52

p.196).

It is this situation that allows for the economic and cultural project of gentrification. If it was undervalued in economic terms this value could not be realized as undervalue until the vernacular was reabsorbed into a landscape, made to reflect the economic, social and cultural priorities of power. These priorities were now written in terms of consumption, and the reformation of the fragmented vernacular into a single landscape achieved by a cultural labour.

> Deindustrialisation, corporate decentralisation and real estate development are responsible for downtown's recent creative destruction. Unlike in Westchester County, however, they interact not to build a new landscape that looks different from what went before, but to impose a new perspective on it. They incorporate downtowns' segmented vernacular into a coherent landscape on the basis of cultural power (p.198).

This imposition is an aestheticization of both the buildings and of the vernacular associations of downtown. It is an imposition based on the cultural labour of a certain social group, though these may not be the main beneficiaries of this labour. This group Zukin calls the 'critical infrastructure', the cultural specialists who both promote and have expertize in the production and consumption of cultural goods. Sometimes this group are dupes of a game they thought they were in control of, sometimes they tend towards the role of 'necessary' (and thus functionally produced) agents of capital.

Relative autonomy

The transformation of the urban downtown vernacular is the focus of *Loft Living*. The argument is well known, though its complexities are not often spelled out. SoHo, as a downtown vernacular was next to the financial district intent on expansion in alliance with political forces that saw no future for manufacturing on Manhattan. The future lay with finance. The attempt at a classic 1960s style development was successfully resisted by the artist and ancillary community that had moved into the old 19th century lofts, attracted by the cheapness and space in a New York now at the centre of the world art market. The victory, through an alliance of a growing communitarian and anti-development movement of the 1970s led to the designation of SoHo as an artists' zone. But the end result was that manufacturing and 'down market' retail was pushed out by this zoning, and the old vernacular became prime real estate as 'loft living' became a desirable commodity. Ultimately, many artists found it impossible to buy or rent, and any indigenous bohemian artist quality now became totally packaged, landscaped, for wealthy residents.

Global and local

The narrative in *Loft Living* is complex. Zukin wants to show how those dealing in cultural knowledge were responsible for the transformation of SoHo, creating a new value that could be recouped by development capital. Two forces are prominent. Firstly, the historic buildings' groups began to see the cast iron frontages as aesthetic objects that should be protected rather than torn down. This, along with a more general appreciation of Victorian and early 20th century industrial artifacts, represented an aestheticization of past use which immediately devalued current industrial usage (Smith & Williams, 1986). The current legitimate usage of these buildings was increasingly restricted to those who could appreciate this historical aesthetic. Secondly, often ignoring those other groups and users in the area, the artists' community claimed the central role in the revitalization of a 'derelict' district. The economic importance of the artists to New York was stressed, but it was their cultural impact on the area that was primary. The Loft was a metonym for an artistic lifestyle which, drawing on the bohemian and countercultural elements of the 1960s, would bring back a new vibrancy, to the downtown. However, although this vibrancy drew on the qualities of the downtown vernacular, it was now based on a 'lifestyle' no longer linked to a productive community. It was a lifestyle that could be consumed, whether in the form of the newly fashionable lofts, or the bohemian ambiance of the restaurants, bars, galleries and shops.

Thus the aestheticization of the vernacular achieved by cultural specialists mediated its emergence as an object of consumption. Once this cultural work had been done and the vernacular reabsorbed into the cultural landscape the cultural specialists lost ground to those *pioneers!*

wielding economic power. In *Loft Living* the outcome is paradoxical, where the victors ended up the losers. That developers quickly appreciated the importance of cultural consumption is the revalorization of undervalued downtown areas. After SoHo they became proactive. We will argue that the attempt to transpose this model has its problems. But it is clear in that work (and more so in the postscript) that this mediating role of the cultural specialists was a more widespread phenomenon. As we move to the later book the dupes tend to become unwitting 'agents' of capitalist restructuring around consumption.

The growing popularization of the artistic-bohemian lifestyle was part of a much more widespread shift in cultural hierarchies and an increasingly reflexive construction of lifestyle. Consequent on the expansion of Higher Education and the cultural radicalisms of the 1960s, knowledge of cultural goods expanded enormously. At the same time the transgressions of the artist, the experimentation with new experiences, the desire to create the self as a work of art became absorbed into a wider culture. These changes fed into the growing incorporation of art and culture into the design of consumer goods, and into the techniques of advertising and marketing. In *Landscape* Zukin is much more explicit in linking the operations of the new groups of cultural specialists in both the promotion of consumption and the gentrification of the city.

> Production units function best in clusters of customers and suppliers. Historically these clusters gave downtown its specialised aura of variety and innovation. But consumption units are increasingly spread out, diffused, standardised and reproduced. Decentralization reduces the power of consumption spaces: it requires conscious action to restore their specific meaning. Under these circumstances, mediating the dialectic of power and centrality depends on a critical infrastructure for cultural production and consumption. Here I am thinking of men and women who produce and consume, and also evaluate, new market-based cultural products. Like artists, they both comment critically on, and constitute, a new kind of market culture. Their 'inside' view opens up new spaces for consumption. They enhance market values even when they desperately want to conserve values of place (pp.201-2).

55

This is the tragic function of the counterculture. Ultimately, their concern with culture merely opened a new field of consumption, which, exposed to the forces of abstraction and internationalization, destroys the object of their desire.

> The organisation of consumption thus has a paradoxical effect on downtown space. Initially treated as unique, the cultural value of place is finally abstracted into market culture (p.195).

For Zukin, the role of these cultural specialists is functional to social distinction in an age of 'mass produced and mass distributed culture' (p.203). In the absence of 'hierarchies based on personal networks and social position' (p.203) cultural specialists, 'the critical infrastructure', emerge to promote and to guide us through the new landscape of consumption.

> Today cultural consumption follows the lead of several mediators: the artist, the primary consumer, and the designer, who interpret desire and direct the consumer to equate awareness of consuming with awareness of life, and the line producer in new service industries, catering to a jaded consumer 'who yearns for homespun to ease the chintz' (p.204).

Zukin's work represents a severe indictment of the project of culturally based urban renewal, and of the role of cultural specialists as both mediators of the new consumption and as destructive of the values of place. This is crucial because it is precisely along these lines — the promotion of cultural production and consumption — of, and in, the city — and the attraction of cultural specialists, the creation of a critical infrastructure — that cities in Britain and Western Europe have attempted to engage with the problems of the 'post-Fordist' city. We would argue that these global shifts must be understood in terms of a specific spatialization, involving a complex mediation of the local/global nexus, and that the 'renewal' of the city centre around cultural production and consumption is open to a range of different outcomes and meanings.

We have seen above that the importance of cultural consumption in revalorization was quickly recognized by developers. The logic of standardization and repetition meant the rapid elaboration of regeneration models that could be sold to different city governments.

By the late 1970s a number of large cities in North America, especially those in the north with historic centres, began to invest in these regeneration models (Wynne, 1992). It was clear that whilst the 'artists community' was often brought in to these local growth coalitions, it was the developer who held the upper hand. The transformation of historical and/or waterfront areas into retail/leisure and residential developments was based around 'up-market' consumption coupled with a high cultural input. This could include cultural animation programmes, artists residences, subsidized workshops and a public art that fitted well with a new 'postmodern' aesthetic. Such cultural input was encouraged by city governments employing 'percentage for art' programmes, and 'planning gain' initiatives. These areas thus had an 'up-market' ambiance of speciality shopping and 'designer' restaurants and bars. They also aimed at establishing the sense of vibrancy that once attached to downtown areas, but a vibrancy now mediated by a bohemian image represented by the presence of artists and 'artisans'. The vibrancy was one of an aestheticized 19th century, where the image of the downtown was reappropriated via the image of the artist-bohemian in the guise of *flaneur*. The new-old spaces of urbanity were not the ones of the productive communities but the middle class stroller who had the time and the cultural knowledge with which to stroll through the landscape and absorb the vernacular as aesthetic.

It is this ersatz urban realm which was initially characterized as 'postmodern', in a way that confused the debate. Both admirers and critics seemed to see this as an incarnation of the postmodern *zietgeist*, without inquiring as to how people used these places and to what extent, and on what basis, they were successful. It will be our argument that the transposition of the model of regeneration by developers is fraught with problems. If the imposition of a landscape of cultural power is to have any chance of success, even defined in narrowly economic terms, a critical infrastructure is necessary. Despite Zukin's occasional functionalisms this critical infrastructure cannot just be created as required. As specialists and insiders they have a relative autonomy and a close knowledge/relationship to place and it is in this context that a specific localization involves a series of negotiations around the new emergent landscape which can be laden with meanings very different to the standardized 'postmodernity' of the development models.

This model of urban regeneration, development around historical-cultural urban centres, was directly imported into Britain in the early 1980s. In this transposition the specificities of the local context were crucial. Firstly, the Thatcher Government, having won a resounding second term in 1983, made 'inner cities' its target, especially after the riots in 1981 had underlined these inner cities as symbols of the 'British disease'. Secondly, these cities were mainly held by the opposition Labour party. Central government was loath to give these credit for any possible success in these programmes, but also, they blamed these councils for the socialist-bureaucratic failures of the 1960s and 1970s. Urban regeneration was to be a symbol of Thatcherite Britain's escape from the cycle of post-war failure. Thirdly, the Government wanted to use a free enterprise approach which demanded deregulation and a more flexible planning system. To this end a whole series of legislative changes were enacted restricting local government, freeing private capital's access to public land and development contracts and creating new semi-autonomous bodies outside the control of local government. Fourthly, this was done at a time of massive and catastrophic de-industrialization. Apart from its social and economic consequences it was also a process of great cultural disruption, especially in the Northern industrial towns where identity, much more than in the south, was centred on work, on manual and industrial labour. Urban regeneration was based on a conscious and explicit shift of the economic base from manufacturing to service industries, symbolized by the redrawing of the old historical industrial areas in terms of leisure and consumption. Thus, fifthly, this work of urban regeneration was seen by many on the Left as a symbol of Thatcherism, and despised as such. The debate around the yuppie, gentrification and 'postmodernity' in 1980s Britain cannot be divorced from this political context.

Manchester is England's third largest city, although in terms of its historical role as ideological centre of the industrial revolution, it could be considered the second city, capital of the North (Sheilds, 1991). In 1988 a large swath of land just south of the CBD and civic centre was given to Britain's first city-centre Urban Development Corporation. The Central Manchester Development Corporation (CMDC) a semi-autonomous body (responsible to London), was given a brief to cut through the socialist red-tape and bring private money into city centre regeneration by using public funds as leverage.

Its initial task was to draw up a plan for the area, and to then present the image of the new city to developers, private entrepreneurs and the people of Manchester.

The CMDC's physical area can be seen as a crescent weighted towards one end. At either end is a canal basin linked to a wide canal network. A canal runs the length of the area between the basins. The eastern basin was to be a retail/office and residential development. The western basin, which was much larger, was a site of historic importance in terms of industrial archeology. It was here that the industrial revolution moved from the countryside into the town; Manchester was the world's first industrial city. The area already had a major industrial and science museum near the site of the world's first passenger railway station, and the whole area, Castlefield, was to become Britain's first urban industrial heritage park. Along with the museums went the promotion of waterway events on the canals and other animation programmes. The area also had a private residential development.

Between Castlefield and the centre a large area of disused land and parking lots was ear-marked for Manchester's 'cultural quarter', and nearby, some of the old 19th century warehouses would be converted for residential use, forming 'Whitworth Village' a 'village in the heart of the city'. It is this area that was seen to be a prime site for the 'arts and culture' led model of urban regeneration.

The Cultural Quarter was to be — in the words of one planning officer — 'Manchester's Montmartre'. It was clearly developer driven. Manchester's local authorities had already transformed a centrally located disused railway station into an exhibition hall and occasional concert venue. Next to this on CMDC ground was a huge, elaborately decorated late Victorian goods warehouse. This was to be developed into a 'Festival Shopping Centre' by the same development company responsible for others in North America. This has still to materialize. On the other side of the exhibition hall a concert hall on the site of a car-park was to be built, uncovering the old canal arm around which offices and apartments would be constructed, along with the inevitable restaurants, bars and retail outlets. The apartments, in a refurbished warehouse, together with some of the office buildings have been finished for two years. The remaining projects began just after Christmas, 1993.

'Whitworth Village' is now completed. Whitworth Street runs more or less the whole length of the crescent, following the canal. The

* city centre living as regeneration after 1988 creation of UDC.

residential area includes five large building complexes, though two of these existed before CMDC was created. If we include the other residential developments in the CMDC area, and two others which were built in the early 1980s, we calculate that there are currently around 7000 people living in the city centre. Before 1978, there were almost none.

The CMDC attempted to use private developers to transform the landscape of the city centre. It is clear that this was to be around the consumption of the historical and cultural values of this landscape. The cultural quarter and the residential areas were directly linked to the promotion of Manchester as a cultural landscape, as a sight and a site of cultural consumption. The image of the city as a whole was tied up in this; it was crucial for the success of the landscape, but it also formed a justification for the project of transformation — Mancheste's new image would have direct economic advantages.

That the CMDC recognized the crucial role of image, of perspective, can be seen in the promotional literature that was concerned not just to outline the plans of the Corporation, but to present the centre as an aesthetic object. The historical qualities of the Victorian city were brought out in terms of aesthetic qualities; detail and cropped shot photography de-contextualized the buildings to present them to the gaze. This is by no means new in terms of marketing strategies, what was new was that this was applied to the city. Warehouses, long time symbols of northern industrial gloom re-emerged as Renaissance Palaces, Greco-Roman Temples, brooding Gothic Piles. Images of night-time in the city, early morning, and aerial shots, all worked on the perception of a city built on anti-aesthetics.

The CMDC took the prime role in the above, and it is clear that it was the argument as to the economic value of cultural consumption that was uppermost in both its political orientation and in its approach to the developers. The old landscape of industrial production was to be offered up for aesthetic consumption, but also as 'investment opportunities'. Thus the Cultural Quarter with its 'flagship' concert hall would attract those with disposable incomes into the city after 6 pm to encourage spending on leisure and retail. Similarly the area's cultural profile would attract 'prestige' offices occupied by those business services and creative professions that both developers and sociologists believed to be intimately connected.

In order to enhance the Cultural Quarter, Manchester's artist community, was to be brought into consultation. The CMDC were to work closely with these in terms of public art, recognising the role of art in the image of cities, their brochure using Barcelona and the Pompidou centre as examples. There was talk of subsidised artists workshops as a way of promoting the creative ambiance which would both attract the 'culture crowd' and the creative professions. As such it represents an attempt by the CMDC to bring in and direct the critical infrastructure (cultural intermediaries), which in Zukin's terms, was crucial for the creation of a cultural landscape in SoHo.

Discussion of the relationship between cultural intermediaries and capital is, as Zukin makes clear, also about the process whereby this capital learns about the value of culture. This is part of the story of post-Fordism, flexible specialization and the emergence of creative, designer-led industries from the mid-1970s onwards. It would also need to include the ways in which public agencies learned about this, and in what context. The CMDC as an organization and in terms of its personnel began to learn this model of cultural regeneration through seminars, fact-finding missions and consultancy reports all within the context of a Thatcher government explicitly hostile to 'intellectuals' — the 'chattering classes' as they were being dubbed. Both the counter-culture and the 'permissive society', symbols and causes of Britain's social and moral decline were laid at the door of the liberal cultural establishment. The CMDC, like this cultural establishment themselves, became a cultural intermediary cast in the role of justifying cultural value via its direct relationship to economic value. This also appealed to property developers, the local business elite, and the city council. Both culture and consumption had been marginal concerns. In this context, as the urban renewal programmes began to take hold, a wide range of cultural agencies were pushed to the fore, albeit through an economic justification of their activities.

For Zukin (1992) the two are run together:

> Significantly, cultural value is now related to economic value. From demand for living lofts and gentrification, large property-owners, developers, and elected local officials realised they could enhance the economic value of the centre by supplying cultural consumption (p.194).

While the context in which it emerged in Manchester's urban

61

regeneration was closely tied to economic arguments, this tends to undermine the cultural in two important areas. Firstly, as Bourdieu (1984) makes clear, cultural capital, whilst related to economic capital, must also stress its distinction from it. Too close a connection undermines the claim of culture to be disinterested, to be more than economics. Whilst we must ask the question as to what extent this is true in the context of any postmodern cultural field, and indeed whether Bourdieu's fields themselves are not tied to an older notion of aesthetic distinction(2), it is certainly true that cultural value can suffer from too close a connection to the economic. Secondly, cultural intermediaries are precisely that: intermediaries. They are able to interpret, package, transmit and manipulate symbols and knowledge in a way that produces new value. As both producers and consumers they are able to claim an expertise, a close knowledge of the inner dynamics of the cultural field.(3)

The initiation of culture based urban renewal by a quasi-political body dominated by a 'free enterprise' ethos with an anti-cultural bias, and one that worked primarily with a development capital using tried and trusted models for the formation of a cultural landscape, was damaging. It meant that the resultant development, whilst based on images of leisure and consumption and aestheticization taken up by urban boosterists and sociologists alike (but with opposite intentions), had limited cultural resonance, and especially amongst those whose labour would be crucial to the transformation of the centre into a cultural landscape — the cultural intermediaries.

This can be illustrated by looking at some of our findings regarding the residential developments that we have studied. Three facts need to be stressed. One, there was no displacement of an existing population. Two, there was no tradition in Manchester, as in other non-metropolitan English cities, of living in the centre. Three, the majority of the residents moved in within a six year period, after urban renewal had begun. Thus, within a short period of time a large number of people moved into the centre precisely because it was the centre. The lack of a tradition of living in the centre meant that such a tradition had to be invented.

One current, but rejected image, was that of 'yuppie' gentrification. In the two areas where new build houses were located on old disused industrial land next to 'deprived' inner city estates — and both were modelled on the London docklands, already a symbol of the Thatcher dream — they took on an air of gentrification which many of the residents resented. The term 'yuppie' was always resisted by them because for a great number it disturbed the self image of what they were doing:

> *Accusation of gentrification I think is not really valid. Gentrification to me means the sort of thing that you see sometimes in London, where you've got housing which hitherto had been relatively cheap and there's a history of people living there in purpose built houses relatively cheaply and then suddenly you get the Volvos and the labradors and people start tarting it up, and whatever, and the prices rocket. That I would see as gentrification, and I can see the arguments both ways. But here, in all the ones I've seen, it's new developments and where it's not new it's doing up what was previously commercial buildings. Now I can see the point that some people would argue that if you're going to do that it ought to be done to provide lower cost housing for people, and the answer is, yes, I can see that that could be done, but then again, you presumably have to accept the commercial argument that if a development company, speculative company, is going to do it they've got to get a return, and in order to get a return you need to be dealing in prices that are fairly high. If you want to do it for people who can't afford higher prices then it ought to be done through local government, and I think that's a separate question about whether the central government should be providing local government with additional funds to be able to do this. I mean, I think they should. I think it's a slightly separate question. Gentrification, if I was living in a converted artisans cottage in Islington or something, sometimes I would feel that perhaps I had taken away from somebody else by being part of an artificially increased market. That I'd perhaps deprived somebody else an opportunity. I don't feel that so much really* (case 6 page 8 of transcript source material).

The 'village in the city' contained private and rented apartments, ranging from £38,000 to £140,000. There were five sites in this area (our study covered 11 in all), with a sixth, subsidised housing development, for people in housing need. The five were 'design and build', the developer using the in-house architect. 'Village in the city' indicates the ambivalence felt towards city living. The promotional images stress its protected, village scale. The convenience of central amenities were to be a part of this village atmosphere. The exteriors of the warehouses were protected by 'listed' status, but any leeway in the regulation was exploited to stress the developers' notion of prestige exclusivity for up-market consumers. Georgian style door furniture, plastic awnings and other 'individualized' features now become standardized in a manner that David Harvey (1990) has pointed to with regard to postmodern gentrification. The interiors were 'Laura Ashley', country-cottage style, mixed with a vague 'Victoriana'. Pictures of antique cars in brass frames lined the lobbies. All the communal areas were aimed at a similar 'suburban' style, which was the developers only image of what a prestige buyer could be.

The residents almost universally disliked the way that the apartments had been refurbished and decorated. Many scoffed at the mock-georgian elegance, others were angry at the missed opportunity to respect the historical integrity of the buildings, some redecorating against the original, 'new' interiors. One or two apologised for the areas that they could not redesign, such as the kitchen and bathroom fittings in 'glorious floral'. In some buildings pictures in the communal areas have been taken down and replaced. The 'yuppie' image picked up by the developers was seen to be completely misplaced. We would contend that people were attracted despite the presented image and with a mission to impose their own. This indicates how far the imposed models of the developers stood outside the cultural field in which they were attempting to intervene. This could be illustrated in countless areas.

Zukin (1992) argues:

> Gentrification received its greatest boost not from a specific subsidy, but from the state's substantive and symbolic legitimation of the cultural claim to urban space. This recognition marked cultural producers as a symbol of urban growth (p.194).

We have argued that this legitimation on the part of the CMDC and the developers was in exclusively economic terms, where cultural production has direct economic consequences. We have suggested that the imposition of a model in these terms denies the autonomy of the cultural field, excluding cultural specialists to the detriment of cultural value. We must go beyond this and suggest that the unavailability of an image of city living — of centrality, meant that it had to be created by cultural producers — and that this was done in a complex field in which the 'state's substantive and symbolic legitimation of the cultural claim to urban space' was far from fixed, and was indeed a product of negotiation and conflict.

City centres are periodically abandoned as landscapes of power. Manchester's landscape is paradigmatic of the way this occurred in the industrial cities of Britain. Industrial capital abandoned the centre after the second world war (residents had left before) leaving large swaths of the central area to decay. These abandoned areas, if reclaimed for the vernacular, were reclaimed in ambivalent fashion. In Manchester they became representations of northernness; industrial wasteland and old canals — old rails sunk into grassy cobbles. As sources of identity they were also an unwanted past, an unusable past — it is easy to forget this mix of attachment and redundancy. The vernacular of northern wasteland became a symbol of economic decline, which is why it became so central to Thatcher's economic miracle. Regeneration, however, worked on a vernacular that few were willing to defend. It coincided with a local cultural renegotiation of both northernness and the world of industrial work crucial to this identity. Very often presented as a devastating disorientation it was also taken as a possibility of change.

CAPITAL SCHEME FOR INVESTMENT IN CULTURE REALISES ITS HIGH POTENTIAL

Since the Cottonopolis boom in the 19th century Manchester has been seen as the cultural capital of the North-west region ... At last the cultural assets of the city are coming to be seen as a form of economic and social capital ... Until recently, local authority investment in the arts was justified as simply being good for the soul ... Then it became fashionable to advance economic arguments ... Now as manufacturing declines the arts and culture industries are beginning to justify themselves in their own right, in hard cash terms ... The city is beginning to take its cultural assets seriously and learn to use them ... the city's bid to be the Arts Council's City of Drama in 1994 has brought together a range of arts organisations who previously hardly spoke to each other, and the city council has initiated a study of Manchester's cultural scene with the appointment of Consultants Urban

Cultures Limited (Robin Thornber, *The Guardian*, 24 January, 1992).

If part of this change can be understood in terms of the emergence of a cultural landscape it is crucial to locate the precise meanings, functions and beneficiaries of this transformation in a specific spatialization of the global, national and local. There are a number of factors involved here. As we have seen, this cultural landscape was to be promoted in the context of a re-imaging of the city. This was part of a general recognition by councils throughout the country that their 'smoke stack' image would work against them in the attraction of inward investment, especially those centres around business services and 'high tech' industries. By the time CMDC was created, marketing consultancies were a common feature in Manchester's local councils. This re-imaging was initially centred on the offering of facilities that would attract professional-managerial 'executives' — golf-courses, waterfront leisure developments, 'high' cultural venues and museums. This was a simple and direct version of the equation of cultural production with urban growth. Like the CMDC, Manchester City Council entered a learning curve of how to operate within the field of symbolic knowledge. It began to establish links with cultural intermediaries. As this linkage of networks between council (and to a lesser extent the CMDC) and cultural intermediaries proliferated, operations within this symbolic field became more sophisticated. Though not stated in such terms, it was recognized that the obvious association of cultural strategy with the attraction of 'executives' was limited, precisely by this close link to economic rationale. Similarly, the consumption desires of these 'executives' had become standardized to such a degree that most cities could claim to offer them in abundance. Competing at a European and global level the city had to promote its cultural value in 'disinterested' fashion. Its cultural authenticity, and thus desirability, derived from its intrinsic and autonomous cultural production. The city as 'city of culture' had to present itself as a vernacular. The close association of Manchester's image with a distinctive historical and cultural tradition would, it was felt, be crucial to the future success of the city. Thus the entry of relatively autonomous cultural intermediaries into the political and economic fields of local government saw a convergence of interests within the cultural field. Whilst the abstraction and internationalization of global finance undermines place in the elaboration of markets, local government has an interest in attenuating this. Developers, imposing a formula, find it relatively easy to disinvest as profitability declines. Local governments, stuck in place, must look to the longer term. It is not in the interest of the local state to allow the abstracted global market to act too disruptively on local cultural capital. This is of course a matter of politics, education and often brute financial power, and is a project by no means guaranteed, in terms of either conception or execution, as the landscape of many British cities can illustrate. Local government needs a local cultural infrastructure with a specific expertise which gives it a relative autonomy from the circuits of abstracted global finance. Its expertise involves a knowledge and feeling for place, which is, despite Zukin's pessimism, crucial for the successful localization of capital in the form of cultural landscaping. Cultural intermediaries will be affected by the new networks and changing working practices; but if the dictates of this new cultural field presented new problems with regard to their negotiation of autonomy and creativity, it also gave them a new and expanded scope of operations. Previously distant from local politics and economics (in the larger 'strategic' sense) they are increasingly proactive in lobbying public agencies for the importance of cultural investment — a fairly obvious stance from their point of view — but also for the need to defend their autonomy from short term economic fluctuations, and to assert the particular *modus operandi* of this sector and its close relationship to the local sphere, as opposed to the larger and more abstract models transposed by globally financed cultural regeneration.

The relationship between market and place is, as Zukin (1992) rightly points out, a crucial component of the landscaping of cities. As we have seen, cultural intermediaries are crucial to this process.

> Their 'inside' view opens up new spaces for consumption. They enhance market values even when they desperately want to conserve values of place (pp.201-2) ... Initially treated as unique, the cultural value of place is finally abstracted into market culture (p.195).

We have argued that this in itself can lead to a decline in value, especially if taken over directly by global finance. But the relationship between place and consumption in this context is much more complex. A sense of place can be negotiated precisely through the opening up of new spaces of cultural production and consumption.

Let us return to the residential developments. If they were not attracted by the images of 'prestigious exclusivity' presented by the developers, what did attract these residents? It was clear that, given the price of the apartments in relation to houses that could be bought not too far from the centre, and not necessarily in 'boring' suburbia, that those who moved in were attracted by the central location. This was borne out by our questionnaires and in-depth interviews. Of what does this centrality consist?

If the English city lacked an image of centrality as a place to live then the model would be provided not by North America but by Europe. The new centrality that would replace the old vernacular was elaborated around the 'European city', a space of socialization, cultural and cultured consumption on a non-exclusionary basis. The reality of this image may be another question. It was also given different twists by different users, but was enough itself to give a unity to an image of cafes, restaurants, spaces for strolling and sitting, of diverse social interaction, of galleries and concerts. While cafes and croissants came to be the quintessential attribute of 'yuppie' consumption in the mid-1980s these sorts of images also provided ways in which various identities were being negotiated.

TOP OF THE TABLE!
CAFE SOCIETY IS URGED TO BACK OUTDOOR STYLE

Cafe society in Manchester is being urged to try a taste of the great outdoors ... all in the cause of being good Europeans of course ... Councillor Spencer Manchester's Planning Chairman — is urging more cafe and bar owners to set up open-air tables. Several have already set up street cafes with permission from the city council. But the town hall is keen to promote the European influence in Manchester with even more pavement tables (*Manchester Evening News*, June 1992).

The promotion of the 'European city' can be seen as part of a new globalized competition, and as an imposition of a specific habitus in the interest of cultural status for cultural intermediaries and the expansion of the cultural sector to which it is tied. Each of these are correct to an extent. But this idea of the 'European city' is also about identity. In a political context of economic and political domination from the centre, 'Europeanness' was a means of redefining the relationship of Northernness to Englishness in a way that by-passed London's cultural dominance. Thus Glasgow and Edinburgh stressed that they were European and not English cities. It was a negotiation of identity through a reworking of its location in the matrix of cultural space. 'Provincial' culture could now become semi-autonomous as it opened out into the 'Europe of the regions' and looked (enviously) to the great city-states of Europe. The 'European city' was about the possibility of new images of self, of the possibilities of transformation as Manchester attempted to map itself onto a transnational 'cosmopolitan' space. The Europeanization of centrality located this cosmopolitan space at the level of the local.

> *... in a city that's really international, in that it welcomes lots of groups, you can feel that what you're part of reflects the wider picture. The world, what's reflected in the world. So I like the idea of being something that's embracing wider issues rather than being somewhere where you could be getting a blinkered view but not realise you were. So it's more challenging in a way to live in a place that has many different cultures all interacting together and, you know, you can go to an Italian restaurant and it will be like a real Italian family; you go to a Jewish restaurant, you've got Jewish culture; you've got Chinese, you've got real Chinese; Indian, you have real Indian in Rusholme or somewhere. You wouldn't be having Deal's* (Deal is a small town, previous residence of subject) *version of an Indian, and then the shops and the same in the museums and stuff. Just you're getting, by mixing together like that, you get creative new things come out of it* (case 1 page 11 of transcript source material).

This local was also one of northern culture. This was the industrial city with a strong sense of working class identity, in which even the local establishment portrayed itself as 'down to earth', 'straight speaking', concerned with work as opposed to the *rentier* elite of the South. Manchester's recreation as a cultural city was, as we have seen, deeply involved with de-industrialization and the re-imaging process associated with competition for inward investment. But it involved real cultural shifts, a real renegotiation of identity. While the specific dynamics of this are not yet clear to our research, Manchester, along with other northern cities, asserted its concern with culture and cultural production in terms of an authenticity derived from place, as opposed to what was seen as London's concern with money and hype. This was a traditional opposition to the 'unearned' incomes of the capital, but now mediated not through 'hard graft' but through culture. The community spirit deeply embedded in northern mythology transmuted into the vibrant public realm so desired by cosmopolitan Manchester, a European city of culture.

> S. *Yeah, I think it..that's obviously what they're trying to ... Manchester City Council or whatever are putting all their money into improving the city are probably trying to do that. They're trying to..Obviously if they got the Olympic bid that would be really good, and then they're building all these outdoor ... these cafes where you can sit outside. Very sort of Europeanised. So it does seem to be going that way.*
> D.M. *Do you feel you've got a personal commitment towards that, in as a belonging to the city?*
> S. Yeah. *I feel I do. I've lived in the city centre now for nearly two years and it's nice to see that they're trying to improve things here. I feel sort of quite closely involved in that, and I'm glad that they're doing that* (case 11 page 2 of transcript source material).

The nature of this 'cosmopolitan' could be considered in terms of the distinction strategies of a specific group, but again, whilst this is in part true it also ignores the political component of this image of centrality. The 1980s saw a general revaluation of the qualities of the urban across a wide range of cultural fields. Not just a site of decay and abandonment it was increasingly celebrated as a vibrant realm in which a wide variety of people rubbed shoulders. The complex sources of this re-evaluation cannot be explored here. However, the attempt to characterize this urban realm as that of the *flaneur*, floating signifiers, disembodied eddies of desire, etc. by sociologists either friendly or critical of some 'postmodern urban experience' tended to miss another crucial component of this re-evaluation. In an age of privatism, of the disappearance of the social (whether by Baudrillard or Thatcher) the urban realm was one of the few images of sociality remaining. The 'cosmopolitan city', the 'European city' were cities that would promote urbanity, a mixing and meeting of classes and groups and races in a way that would provide for an active citizenship.

To live in the suburbs of Manchester where there isn't anything..in Wythenshawe, (a council estate — subsidised housing on outskirts of city) *which is where I come from, there's no, you know, it's very... Perhaps I don't really mind, but what I thought..I've found actually a little..they're not open-minded people — the people actually living in Wythenshawe and staying in Wythenshawe and spend their lives in Wythenshawe have almost tribalistic tendencies, and if you don't sort of..if you reject their values then they don't really accept you. You know, I find Wythenshawe, like I say I find Wythenshawe, I find it quite a hard place to live. It's not cosmopolitan enough for me... whereas I think if you live in say like Wythenshawe, or something, you tend to find that most people agree..I don't know whether that's fair or not. You know, they just seem to get entrenched in their own lifestyles, and don't sort of see outside that. Their own lifestyle is because of the poverty there, that's there as well. There's a lot of poverty, a lot of unemployment and if people are just faced with..I think they get 'Oh no' in those environments ... I mean I still like music, I still like clubs and most of the people my age in Wythenshawe don't..they don't go to clubs anymore, they tend to go to the pub, and then when they go to the Vaults and then play darts and that can be about the end of it, and it hadn't changed in twenty years. It's still the same as like when I left it twenty years ago.*
D.M. Right. So the benefits of the city are that there's more diverse people, easy access to different cultural pursuits?
K. Yeah. There's less constrictions about like personal behaviour. I mean, you could get quite lot of people in Wythenshawe, for example, quite a lot of them tend to be homophobic, whereas if you come to the city centre then there's just a general acceptance of gay people. I mean, that's just an example, but it's like the way it is, yeah. There's no, er, I would think gay people in Wythenshawe probably have a very hard time whereas gay people who live in the city centre, it's more easygoing about them, you know. Except for the odd exception..you still see it

around but it doesn't..they're not bigotted people. Whereas in Wythenshawe, by accident they become bigoted through ignorance really.

It was in this way that urban and cultural policy began to realign within the Left in the mid-1980s. This connection was less the work of the Labour party than that of the Greater London Council (GLC). At a time when the Thatcher Government looked to the United States, the GLC, across the water from Parliament, controlled by Labour, operating with an enormous budget and responsible for 6 million people, looked to Europe — especially the Italian cities (Bianchini, 1989). Again, the roots of this cannot be explored here but can be related to the growing recognition of the importance of cultural politics. Here the Gramscian politics of the Italian communist cities was taken as a model by the GLC, with the need to promote a sense of democratic citizenship around a post-proletarian, multi-cultural London. The use of culture here was taken at its widest, and 'popular culture' given a new priority. The shift from pedagogy to entertainment in subsidized culture is not just down to commodification, but a democratizing impulse towards popular participation.

Such an approach had its problems as 'the popular' fragmented into client groups. It also stressed cultural consumption rather than production, with a cultural industries strategy left to be developed by other local councils (Wynne, 1992). But the fact that it promoted popular cultural events, and that it opened up the spaces of the city to these events, transformed the relationship of large sections of cultural producers and consumers to these spaces, and to the possibilities of a locally funded cultural sphere. In terms of local cultural policies it was the single most influential statement of the first half of the decade.

Centrality then operates in a complex set of fields and at a number of levels of meanings. We cannot here examine the theories of spatialization that Zukin draws upon in the final section of her book. However, she argues that space is both structured and structuring. It is structured in that it reflects macro-level economic forces, but it is structuring in that it:

... structures people's perceptions, interactions, and sense of well being or despair, belonging or alienation ... Space also structures metaphorically. Because they are easily visualised, spatial changes can represent and structure orientations to society. Space stimulates both memory and desire; it indicates categories and relations between them (p.268).

This is fine, but the problems emerge when Zukin reduces this to the fundamental opposition of landscape and vernacular. Shifts between these two are the result of **both structural changes in the economy and cultural strategies for social and spatial differentiation** (p.269).

But both are operating under the same logic and mesh ever closer together — the movement towards consumption and the incorporation of place into the market. She uses the word liminality to describe 'the cultural mediation of these socio-spatial shifts':

> Liminality in our sense depicts a 'no-man's-land' open to everyone'' experience yet not easily understood without a guide. Defining the symbolic geography of a city or region, liminal spaces cross and combine the influence of major institutions: public and private, culture and economy, market and place. As the social meaning of such spaces is renegotiated by structural change and individual action, liminal space becomes a metaphor for the extensive reordering by which markets, in our time, encroach upon place (p.269).

This is surely a singular logic in which macro and micro combine to insert the local landscape into the global organization of consumption. It seems to ignore the **structuring** qualities of local space and the ways in which local action can intervene in such spatialization. It also ignores the fluidity by which landscape and vernacular — if we can separate the two out — interpenetrate in the city centre. The liminality of the centre need not be conceived as a one-directional move from vernacular to landscape. Thus areas of Manchester's abandoned landscape have become vernacular based around cultural production and consumption. This is certainly the case with at least two areas of the city that we have examined.

Manchester's 'rave' and 'house' scene emerged in certain clubs located throughout the city centre and beyond. However the Oldham Street area of the city centre has become an important meeting place for the style connoisseurs of this scene. A previously thriving working class area of the city both for work and residence, the area was neglected in the 1960s and 1970s as many workplaces closed and residents left. Today Manchester's 'youth cultural' scene has developed the area with shops, bars and clubs dedicated to promoting that 'scene'. Afflecks Palace, a previously disused three story building, has been converted into low rental units where producers and consumers of this 'pop' culture can be found. The building was due to be demolished to make way for the city's new tram and light rail system but this decision was reversed when it was realised just how important Afflecks Palace had become to the developing image of the city as a place for consumption and play. Other instances which illustrate the degree to which 'pop' culture has been 'taken up' by the city can be seen in the development aid given to the creation of workspace units for the city's 'pop' cultural entrepreneurs, and in the support given to the *In The City* conference and convention held for the pop music recording industry in 1992 (Milestone, 1992).

Is one of the products of the cultural industries a cultural landscape, or does it give rise to production communities with an associated vernacular, in Zukin's sense? It could be argued that the new landscapes created by urban renewal, **precisely because** they attempted to invoke centrality, have invited new uses of the spaces that return them to the vernacular. This has already been argued in the case of shopping malls (Sheilds, 1992), those 'totally programmed spaces' which Zukin seems to concentrate on (Thrift, 1993). In Manchester, the cultural quarter and the residential 'village', presented as landscape, were taken up into spaces of pleasure, spaces of cultural production and consumption not foreseen by the planners and property developers. One of Manchester's most animated areas is around the 'Gay village' which was not a part of CMDC's cultural landscape, just as the colonization of one of the residential sites by gays was not foreseen by the in-house architect whose refurbishment included the 'Georgian door-knockers'.

What has now become known as the Gay Village is a small area of the city centre located around the Whitworth Street corridor and the adjoining canal. Previously neglected, apart from policing activities associated with club and bookstore 'raids', the area has become a vital site for the celebration of alternative sexualities. The refurbishment of old warehouses into studios and one or two bedroom apartments in the area has proved popular with many who choose to live there. Far from creating a 'power soaked' landscape the area now presents an open and unashamedly 'gay vernacular' to the city. Policing activities have changed from ones of confrontation to cooperation with the recent appointment of a 'gay liaison' police officer to the area (Whittle, 1994).

We must pose the question as to what is vernacular and what is landscape? How are we to define these, and do we not risk a nostalgia for a 'free' vernacular versus a 'power soaked' landscape. We could see them as different levels of intensity, different proximities to different flows of information and capital, different weavings of memory and desire. We must look at the liminality whereby the vernacular of gay or pop culture is taken up into the promotional image of the city, where once marginal activities now come to symbolize creativity and vitality. In Manchester the impact of the rave scene of the late 1980s completely redrew the cultural landscape of the city and the relationship of the local agencies to it.(4) Whilst looking to the cultural flows of Olympics and symphony orchestras Manchester was briefly locked into the very centre of the global flow in the guise of 'Madchester'. The dialectic of vernacular and landscape runs close. Cultural power may depend on landscapes presenting themselves as vernacular, just as vernacular resent being taken up by landscape. Thus the 'gay village' is very ambivalent about gaining a respectability it has so long loved to shun (Whittle, 1994).

Cities are liminal places, ones structured by macro-forces, but macro-forces in complex interaction with local spatialities. These spatialities themselves must be seen to be liminal, not in the move from production to consumption, not in the united logic of macro and micro, but in a complex interaction of fields and meanings within which local (and non-local) actors intervene. The cultural landscape is heavy with contested meanings, with the eddies of memory and desire, well-being and despair; it forms a place within which global flows are localized, and in this lies the possibility of meaning and sense (sens) (Hodge, 1993).

Put more strongly, we would argue that the initiation of the process whereby Manchester was to be culturally landscaped actually created new spaces within which cultural contestation and exploration could emerge. Whether we call these landscape or vernacular or not, they represent complex conjunctions of cultural production and consumption, local and global, market and place. These spaces can be about hedonism and urbanity, civility and the frisson of anonymity; they can be the image of the social and the anti-social, the nomad and the villager. They are to be negotiated best by Berman's 'low modernism', the shout in the street (Berman, 1991).

Finally, centrality may produce new spaces not just in terms of power and exclusivity, but also as exposure, as stage, as theatre. In this one of the attractions of centrality may be its liminality, not in the sense of a transition between production and consumption, but in terms of the weakening of fixed roles. The recreation of the landscape of the centre, the very promotion of its status as centre, allows this centre to act as marginal, as *liminoid* in Turner's sense (Turner, 1969). The questions we must then ask are about the relations between marginality and habitus, and how they structure this centre.

Here it is worthwhile to examine some of the links which might be suggested between Zukin's conceptualization of the 'critical infrastructure' and our colleague Mike Featherstone (1991) in his use of Bourdieu's 'cultural intermediaries' and his examination of the relationship between these and postmodern culture.

In bare outline, he argues that rather than seeing the features associated with postmodernism as a general implosion of social structures and hierarchies, they may be seen to be a result of shifting power relations between social groups. His programme with respect to the 'aestheticization of everyday life' undertaken by these cultural intermediaries appears close to Zukin's in spirit.

> It is ... necessary to raise the stark sociological questions of the specific locations and degree of generality. Here we investigate the socio-genetic historical origins of particular cognitive styles and modes of perception which arise in the changing interdependences and struggles between figurations of people (Featherstone, p.71).

With reference to gentrified inner city areas and what he regards as some of the key sites of 'postmodernization' he argues:

> ... we also need to inquire into the process of the articulation, transmission and dissemination of the experience of these new spaces by intellectuals and new cultural intermediaries to various audiences and publics and examine the way in which pedagogies
> xx

of these 'new' sensibilities are incorporated into everyday practises (p.70).

Side-stepping the new class debate he concentrates on these cultural intermediaries as the new petty-bourgeoisie — producers and distributors of a vastly expanded range of symbolic goods. They also promote the consumption of these with an emphasis on stylization, on the artistic life, on an openness to new experiences.

> These are engaged in providing symbolic goods and service ... the marketing, advertising, public relations, radio and television producers, presenters, magazines journalists, fashion writers, and the helping professions (social workers, marriage counsellors, sex therapists, dietitians, play leaders etc.) ... They are fascinated by identity, presentation, appearance, lifestyle, and the endless quest for new experiences. Indeed, their awareness of the range of experiences open to them, the frequent lack of anchoring in terms of a specific locale or community, coupled with the self-consciousness of the auto-didact, who always wishes to become more than he/she is, leads to a refusal to be classified, with the injunction to resist fixed codes as life is conceived as open-ended (p.44).

Clearly this stylization of everyday life can be linked to the aestheticization of the vernacular in gentrification.

> The process of gentrification is of interest because it not only points to the redevelopment of the cultural fabric of the inner city areas, it also provides a higher profile for groups within the new middle class who are in many guises the producers, carriers, consumers of lifestyles which entail the culturally sensitive 'stylisation of life' and have developed dispositions which make them receptive to postmodern cultural goods and experiences. They therefore have direct and indirect interests in the accumulation of cultural capital both on a personal basis, and in terms of that of their neighbourhood and the wider city (p.108).

Zukin (1992) is clear on this. She quotes an Italian designer:

> I knew that a new culture of consumerism was not the answer.

Rather, I wanted to make the consumer aware that he is consuming. This shift in perspective is the principle product of the critical infrastructure ... [Thus] they play a critical role in a new organisation of consumption (p.204).

We have already seen the function of this role, it is to guide us through 'mass produced and mass consumed culture'. In the classic game of distinction to be guide is also to be gatekeeper; in acting as cultural intermediaries they establish their taste as the guide to taste. After destabilizing existing cultural hierarchies their taste, in the classic game of distinction, is presented as the taste of the social. Featherstone, following Turner, uses liminality in terms of a suspension of social roles at a point of transition to other social roles:

The liminal points to the emphasis within these essentially delimited transitional or threshold phases upon anti-structure or communitas (Featherstone p.22).

Following Turner's restriction of liminality in its full sense to 'traditional society' and using it in the sense of liminoid, Featherstone sees this concern growing in importamce within the artistic and bohemian counter-cultures of the 19th and early 20th century, with their emphasis on the dissolution between art and life, and the heroic life as the artistic life. He sees the move to the postmodern as emerging from the vastly expanded volume and appeal of the goods and lifestyles associated with this transgressive liminality — a process associated with the distinction strategies of those groups who have most expertise in this field and stand to benefit most from its expansion.

This can be clearly related to Zukin's account of the emergence of the critical infrastructure from the counter-culture, and its central role in the shift to consumption. However there are a number of problems associated with this. One is the tension between difference and imitation central to fashion. As a style becomes more popular, it loses its distinctive power. Distinction, here, is a zero-sum game. This is clearly the tension felt in Zukin's critical infrastructure, driven from one fad to the next in order to keep ahead in the game of tasteful consumption. But at the same time, if this new social group is concerned to destabilize fixed cultural hierarchies and promote a new attitude to lifestyle as such, it is difficult to see how they are to

No - habits.
'fakes' are
easily spotted.

78

'keep the lid' on the process. Featherstone sees this in terms of the prospects for re-monopolization. Can this new petty bourgeoisie, after 'blowing open' the hierarchies and introducing liminality into the heart of the system, then manage to remain as gatekeepers and guides in any meaningful sense? Featherstone becomes more doubtful as his book proceeds.

He argues that these techniques of destabilization have effects on groups above and below this new petty bourgeoisie. There is thus a general tendency to fluidity of lifestyle, to liminality. This we take to be the thrust of Bernice Martin's work (1981; 1991) who concurs with the above to the extent of seeing the crucial role played by the counterculture in destabilizing the cultural hierarchy and changing attitudes to lifestyle, but who sees this as a much more general and widespread process than the distinction strategies of a particular group. Essentially Martin argues that the post war generation of the 1960s engaged in an 'expressive revolution' which she sees:

> ... as an important catalyst of full grown consumer culture in Britain ... it was an enormous dramatisation of the protean possibilities of Desire. The counter-culture served to popularise, initially through shock and outrage, the apprehension that the narrow, ritual limits within which desires had been contained in the inter-war period of scarcity and unemployment, were seriously out of date by the affluent sixties (Martin, 1991, p.16).

The process whereby economic and emotional 'rationality' begin to penetrate across a wide range of professions, and not just 'the cultural' points for her, to a breaking down of the puritan subject. This goes beyond the distinction strategies of one particular class — it is seen to have a deepening social momentum of its own. Those areas in which this interpenetration of economic and emotional rationality is highest attract a wide range of people in a way that militates against the notion that one can call them a class which can 'rise' or 'pursue strategies'.

Moreover, this integration of the emotional into the field of reflexivity is in constant tension. Whimster's account of the 'yuppie' (Whimster, 1992) argues that their social operations, obviously deeply embedded in a 'capitalist rationality', are not part of some 'off-the-peg' postmodernist game but are often confusing and disturbing questions of identity. In many studies it has been found that this integration of the emotional is unstable, whether manifested as guilt or transmuted into cultural compensation — '68 as an ur-world of dreams.

Featherstone attaches liminality to the spaces of the city by an identification of certain spaces as priveleged sites of liminality. It is clear that gentrification and the new petty bourgeoisie can be linked in this way, as they can through aestheticization. The informalization and relaxation of these experiences can be seen as part of a 'controlled de-control of the emotions' in which rules, surveillance and mechanisms of exclusion operate for those without the cultural competence to exercise this control. The mixture of 'security' and 'liminality' in shopping malls is taken as an example.

> As cities de-industrialise and become centres of consumption one of the tendencies in the 1970s and 1980s has been the redesigning and expansion of shopping centres which incorporate many of the features of postmodernism in their architectural design of interior space and simulated environments: use of dream-like illusions and spectacles, eclecticism and mixed codes, which induce the public to flow past a multiplicity of cultural vocabularies which provide no opportunity for distanciation (de-distanciation) and encourage a sense of immediacy, instanciation, emotional de-control and childlike wonder (Featherstone, 1991, p.103).

However, the establishment of new social spaces may provoke new uses which can be described as liminal and which go beyond the rules of controlled de-control of a specific habitus. The creation of the centre as a theatre of liminality may affect other groups and other forces in ways that go beyond this exclusionary habitus. As Featherstone suggests later, to what extent may these changes:

> ... mean that the conditions for dominant elites to exercise global hegemony over taste and culture are destroyed with the unlikelihood of foreseeable re-monopolization, thus pointing us towards a historical development in which some of the impulses detected and labelled postmodern may become more widespread? (p.111).

It is here we would argue that 'popular culture' becomes operative in ways that we have suggested earlier with regard to the emergence of the 'Gay Village' and 'Madchester'. In discussing what we take to be the importance of popular culture to Manchester it is necessary to consider the effects of an increasing commodification of culture, both high and popular. We would argue that it is this commodification, together with a pervasive liminality which is primarily responsible for the destabilization of cultural hierarchies and taste distinctions such that, not only is the game of distinction itself threatened, but also that such a collapse invites the emergence of an 'articulation of alternatives'. As a result, social identities may no longer be 'read' from an individual's class or occupational position, but rather exist as a combination of choices, articulated from a series of possible alternatives made available by this collapse. Such alternatives may not only be discovered in the *bricolage* of consumer goods, but also in:

> ... all the underpinning patterns of taste, modes of feeling, styles of understanding — including self-understanding — and presentation of identity which are involved in 'lifestyle construction' (Martin, 1991, p.22).

As Beck (1992) has argued, albeit in a somewhat different context:

> The Individual himself or herself becomes the reproduction unit for the the social in the life world ... Biographies too, are becoming reflexive. People with the same income level, or put in an old-fashioned way, within the same 'class', can or even must choose between different lifestyles, subcultures, social ties and identities ... Individualisation of life situations and processes thus means that biographies become self-reflexive ... Under those conditions of a reflexive biography, 'society' must be individually manipulated as a 'variable' (Beck, 1992, pp.130-1).

The aestheticization of everyday life may then be understood in terms of this 'articulation of alternatives' produced, in part, through self-reflexive biographies. Two of these 'alternative articulations', Madchester and the Gay Village, could be seen as cultural spaces which have become prominent in the city's new image.

In conclusion we have suggested that the position taken by Zukin, initially in *Loft Living*, and latterly in *Landscapes of Power* fails to grasp some of the complexities that our own research has uncovered, and to which Featherstone, Martin and others have pointed. Such an observation does not necessarily involve any questioning of the findings reported by Zukin, but does question the one-dimensional logic which ties cultural to economic capital in her account which allows for the transformation of a vital, culturally located 'vernacular' into a power soaked, economically located 'landscape'. Rather, as we have attempted to argue above, the work of Featherstone, Martin and others, together with our own research, suggests that any analysis of 'new cultural intermediaries' needs to consider important cultural shifts operative throughout contemporary societies which may not be contained solely within the distinction strategies of one particular class fraction, but instead signify a more complex process of contemporary cultural change.

Notes

1. We are grateful to the ESRC for the funding which allowed this project to be undertaken. The research was conducted by the authors, Mike Featherstone and Dianne Phillips. The work involved the collection of both quantitative and qualitative data and the transcripts and other materials presented here form part of that project. Further details are available from the authors, or the Economic Research Council of Great Britain quoting grant ref no. R00023-3075.

2. Here our suggestion is that Bourdieu's analysis may be less applicable today precisely because of the increased commodification of the cultural and the associated destabilization of cultural hierarchies. While it is always possible for distinction strategies to differentiate cultural practices, monopolization of the 'judgement of taste' may no longer allow for the kinds of 'capital conversion' available in the recent past. As Martin (1991) has observed: 'Bourdieu is notably reluctant to admit to any serious disturbance of basic class patterns' and:

   > One indubitable member of the old gentlemanly class (higher ecclesiatical branch) recently remarked to us that in order not to be mistaken for a Yuppie today it has become neccessary to live among considerable decay, sagging 1920s sofas and the kind of ugly heirlooms that no self-respecting Yuppie would be caught dead **buying**.

3. Thus we can see the ad-hoc way in which these professions grew up often in the interstices of larger concerns in order to offer services that these often did not know they needed or could not understand why they consistently failed. There is a history of how these larger concerns both learned to recognise how much they needed this new expertise, the specific modus operandi of this new sector (flexibility, creativity, 'counter-cultural values' etc.) and how (to a degree) these could be reproduced within their own organizations. There is also a history of how large concerns could fail to recognise this, with damaging consequences. That is a history familiar in Britain.

4.   In 1992 Manchester's local authorities launched the Greater Manchester Visitor and Convention Bureau. The launch was held, not in a hotel, exhibition or conference centre but in The Haçienda, which had become Manchester's premier club and discotheque for the rave and house scenes. The club, partly owned by one of Manchester's most prominent 'pop' cultural entrepreneurs played a major role in articulating a 'pop' cultural bohemia centring on music, dance and fashion. In spite of a history of problems with regard to its relationship with authority; licensing, policing and the use of dance drugs such as Ecstasy, the club was chosen because it epitomized the changing image of the city from work to play. At this launch invited guests were treated to an entertainment collage which began with a 'Northern working class' tableau of 'cloth caps' and 'pigeon fancying' and ended with lycra clad dancers moving to the latest 'house' sounds.

References

Beck, U. (1992), *Risk Society:Towards a New Modernity*, Sage, London.

Berman, M. (1986), 'Take it to the Streets: Conflict and Community in Public Space', *Dissent* (Summer 1986).

Berman, M. (1992), 'Why Modernism Still Matters' in Lash, S. & Friedman, J. (eds.) *Modernity and Identity* Blackwell, Oxford.

Beauregard, S. (1986), 'The Chaos and Complexity of Gentrification', in Smith, N. & Williams, P. (eds.)*The Gentrification of the City* Allen & Unwin, London.

Bianchini, F. (1987), 'GLC R.I.P. Cultural Policies in London', *New Formations*, 1.

Bianchini, F. (1989), 'Cultural Policy and Urban Social Movements: the Response of the 'New Left' in Rome (1976-85) and London (1981-86)', in Bramham et al (eds.), *Leisure and Urban Processes*, Routledge, London.

Bianchini, F. & Schwengel, H. (1991),'Re-imagining the City', in Corner, J. & Harvey, S. (eds.), *Enterprise and Heritage* Routledge, London.

Bianchini, F. (1991), 'Urban Renaissance? The Arts and the Urban Regeneration Process' in Pimlott, B. & MacGregor, S. (eds.) *Tackling the Inner Cities?* Open University Press, Milton Keynes.

Bianchini, F. & Parkinson, M. (eds.), (1994), *Cultural Policy and Urban Regeneration* Manchester University Press.

Bourdieu, P. (1984), *Distinction* Macmillan, London.

Chambers, I. (1990), *Border Dialogues* Routledge, London.

Cooke, P. (1988), 'Modernity, Postmodernity and the City' in *Theory Culture and Society* 5(2-3).

Crane, D. (1992),*The Production of Culture,*Sage, London.

Ehrenreich, B. (1990), 'The Yuppie Strategy', in Ehrenreich, B. *Fear of Falling: The Inner Life of the Middle Class.*

Elias, N. (1939), *The Civilising Process,* (reprinted 1994 Blackwell).

Fainstein, S. et al (eds.) (1986), *Divided Cities,* Blackwell, New York and London).

Featherstone, M. (1991), *Consumer Culture and Postmodernism,* Sage,London.

Fisher, M. & Owen, C. (eds.) (1991), *Whose Cities,* Penguin, London.

Frith, S. & Savage, J. (1993), 'Pearls and Swine', *New Left Review,* 198.

Haider, D. (1989), 'Marketing Places; the State of the Art', in *Commentary,* (Spring).

Haider, D. (1989), 'Making Marketing Choices', in *Commentary,* (Summer).

Hammond, J. & Williams, P. (1988), 'Yuppies', in *Public Opinion, Quarterly* 50.

Harvey, D. (1986), *The Urbanisation of Capital,* Blackwell, Oxford.

Harvey, D. (1988), 'Voodoo Cities', in *New Statesman and Society,* 30 September.

Harvey, D. (1989), *The Condition of Postmodernity,* Blackwell, Oxford.

Hodge, J. (1993), *Rethinking Temporality: Heidegger, Sociology and the Postmodern Critique,* Working Paper No 5, Manchester Institute for Popular Culture, The Manchester Metropolitan University.

Jager, M. (1986), 'Victoriana in Melbourne' in Smith, N. and Williams,

P. (eds.), *The Gentrification of the City*, Allen & Unwin, London.

Kellner, H. & Heuberger, F. (eds.) (1991), *Hidden Technocrats: the New Class and the New Capitalism* Transaction Press, New York.

Law, C. (1988), 'Urban Revitalisation, Public Policy & Redevelopment: Lessons from Baltimore and Manchester' in Hoyle, B. et al, *Revitalising the Waterfront,* Belhaven Press.

Lewis, J. (1990), *Art, Culture and Enterprise,* Routledge, London.

Martin, B. (1981), *A Sociology of Contemporary Cultural Change,* Blackwell, Oxford.

Martin, B. (1991), 'Qualitative Market Research In Britain: A Profession on the Frontiers of Postmodernity', in Kellner, H. & Heuberger, F. (eds.) (1991), *Hidden Technocrats: the New Class and the New Capitalism,* Transaction Press, New York.

Myerscough, J. (1988), *The Economic Importance of the Arts in Britain,* Policy Studies Institute, London.

Milestone, K. (1992), *Pop Music, Place and Travel,* Paper presented at Leisure Studies Conference, Department of Leisure Studies, Tilburg University, The Netherlands. Alternatively, the author is a former researcher at The Manchester Institute for Popular Culture, Manchester Metropolitan University.

Mulgan, G. & Worpole, K. (1986), *Saturday Night or Sunday Morning?* Commedia, London.

Robbins, K. (1991), 'Prisoners of the City: Whatever could a Postmodern City be?' in *New Formations* 15 (Winter).

Robson, B. (1986), *Those Inner Cities* Manchester University Press.

Rose, D. (1984), 'Rethinking Gentrification: Beyond the Uneven Development of Marxist Urban Theory' in *Environment and Planning D:* Society and Space 1 pp.47-74.

Sassen, S. (1991), *The Global City Princeton,* University Press.

Sassen, S. (1994), *Cities in a World Economy,* Pineforge.

Savage, J. (1992),'Structures of Feeling', *New Statesman & Society,* 18 September.

Shields, R. (1991), *Places on the Margin,* Routledge, London.

Shields, R. (ed.) (1992), *Lifestyle Shopping,* Routledge, London.

Shields, R. (1992), 'A truant Proximity: Presence and Absence in the Space of Modernity', *Environment and Planning D*: Society and Space 10.

Schulze, G. (1993), *Die Erlebnisgesellleschaft: Kultursoziologie der Gegenwart,* Campus Verlag, Frankfurt.

Simpson, C. (1981), *SoHo: The Artist in the City,* University of Chicago Press.

Smith, N. (1987), 'Of Yuppies and Housing: Gentrification, Social Restructuring and the Urban Dream' in *Environment and Planning D*, Society and Space 5.

Smith, N. & Williams, P. (eds.) (1986), *The Gentrification of the City,* Allen & Unwin, London.

Thornley, A. (1990), *Urban Planning Under Thatcherism,* Routledge, London.

Thrift, N. (1993),'An Urban Impasse?' *Theory, Culture and Society* 10

Turner, V. (1969), *The Ritual Process: Structure and Anti-Structure,* Allen Lane, London.

Walzer, M. (1984), 'The Pleasures and Costs of Urbanity', in *Dissent,* (Summer).

Whimster, S. (1992), 'Yuppies: A Keyword of the 1980s', in Budd, L.

and Whimster, S. (eds.) *Global Finance and Urban Living*, Sage, London.

Whittle, S. (ed.) (1994), *Gay Culture and The City*, Arena, Swindon.

Worpole, K. (1992), *Towns for People: Transforming Urban Life*, Open University Press, Milton Keynes.

Wynne, D. (ed.) (1992), *The Culture Industry*, Avebury, Swindon.

Zukin, S. (1987), 'Gentrification', *Annual Review of Sociology*.

Zukin, S. (1982), *Loft Living* Johns Hopkins University.

Zukin, S. (1992), *Landscapes of Power: From Detroit to Disneylworld*, University of Clifornia Press, Berkeley.

Zukin, S. (1992), 'Postmodern Urban Landscapes: Mapping Culture and Power', in Lash, S. and Freidman, J. (eds.), *Modernity and Identity*, Blackwell, Oxford.

Zukin, S. (1988), 'The Postmodern Debate over Urban Form', *Theory, Culture and Society*, 5 (2-3).

3 Regional variations: Northernness and new urban economies of hedonism

Katie Milestone

Is the immense texturology spread out before one's eyes anything more than a representation, an optical artifact? It is the analogue of the facsimile produced, through a projection that is a way of keeping aloof, by the space planner urbanist, city planner or cartographer. The panorama-city is a 'theoretical' (that is, visual) simulacrum, in short a picture, whose condition of possibility is an oblivion and a misunderstanding of practices.

The ordinary practitioners of the city live 'down below', below the thresholds at which visibility begins (Michel de Certeau, 1984).

... radio signals commercial mainstream pop pap; TV shows marginal — not networked — rock slot hosted by longhair Catholic on a stool. All is quiet in the dusty village (Richard Boon, 1992).

During the past few years there have been extensive debates and theories in circulation centred around issues of locality, identity and place(1). The frameworks and boundaries for these debates are vast and have been situated amongst a cluster of local/global, centre/periphery and national/regional paradigms. Amongst these issues about place, locality and identity are a set of concerns about ways in which these entities are represented and 'sold' — especially within postmodern economies of consumption.

In this chapter I want to focus on pop culture with respect to some of the themes outlined above. In particular I want to look at ways in which the cultural status and identity of the 'North' and the regions has been altered because of the emergence of 'regional' music, club

91

and other pop cultural industry infrastructures.

We will examine 'local' pop cultural scenes, which include bands and clubs, fashion and graphic designers, promoters and people working in the technical sphere of live and recorded music, and look at how these cultural infrastructures have contributed to altering the identities of certain regional cities. In this respect I argue that it is through popular culture, and in particular pop culture, rather than high culture, that cities such as Leeds, Liverpool and Manchester have become established as credible sites for the production and consumption of culture.

Within this framework I want to look at two main areas; firstly I want to focus on the people who were responsible for catalysing these changes — groups of working class bohemians, working predominantly in association with the pop industry, who played crucial roles in redefining the cultural position of provincial urban areas. Drawing on the work of Featherstone (1991) and Bourdieu (1984) I want to argue how their definitions of the new middle class and new cultural intermediaries need to be expanded to include groups such as these 'working class bohemians'. For example Featherstone describes 'new cultural intermediaries' as being:

> ... engaged in providing symbolic goods and services ... the marketing, advertising, public relations, radio and television producers, presenters, magazine journalists, fashion writers, and the helping professions ... If we look at the habitus, the classificatory schemes, and dispositions of the group we should note that Bourdieu (1984:370) has referred to them as 'new intellectuals' who adopt a learning mode toward life. They are fascinated by identity, presentation, appearance, lifestyle, and the endless quest for new experiences. Indeed their awareness of the range of experiences open to them, the frequent lack of anchoring in terms of a specific locale or community ... leads to a refusal to be classified (1991 p.44).

The cases that I refer to in this chapter differ from the descriptions offered by Featherstone above. Firstly notions of community and a focus on a specific locale are central concerns of the urban working class pop bohemians. Secondly the symbolic goods and services of the pop bohemians tend to be produced on a small scale , and are often 'one off', DIY in nature and can usually be described as being alternative/subcultural products and spaces. They are not in themselves explicitly part of mass or global culture — although at certain times their existence is picked up on and circulated within global flows of information(2). Most often people working in regional post-punk pop cultural industries are self employed or part of small businesses rather than being part of large national and multi national companies.

Secondly, I want to look at the way in which there was an aestheticization of 'Northernness' which was again important in terms of establishing regional pop scenes in redefining urban identities. How did certain Northern cities use their existing (mainly negative) images, manipulate them, commodify them and make what was once unfashionable, fashionable? These types of shifts began to occur in the late 1970s. Using Manchester, Sheffield and Coventry as examples I will elaborate on these arguments. Although strictly speaking Coventry is part of the Midlands rather than 'the North' we use the term 'Northernness' as a synonym for industrial, hard, regional and other terms which could describe a city such as Coventry just as easily as they could Sheffield or Leeds. Furthermore Coventry is 'well north of Watford', London and the affluent South East.

Ghost towns

The late 1970s was a bleak period in the history of Britain's city centres. It was a period of political and economic transition in which the city was losing its identity as a place of production, and commercial and social exchange, growing increasingly less animated through people working, interacting and participating in civic culture. Poor employment prospects, racism, conflicts with the police, the weakening of the Welfare State, industrial decline and desolation of the environment became increasingly more prominent aspects of urban life. The physical effects of this decline were witnessed in many British cities which were becoming characterized by wastelands, disused and derelict buildings, despondent graffiti and cracked paving stones.

I want now to focus on Manchester to look at an example of a city which has forged a new identity centred around pop culture. Although Manchester had a fairly prominent role in the sixties beat boom, with a large number of coffee clubs and night clubs and a number of mainstream groups such as the Hollies, Hermans Hermits and Wayne Fontana, it was not able to fully establish its pop cultural infrastructure at this time primarily because of an exceptionally ironhanded Chief Constable, J. A. McKay who was hell bent on trying to ensure that Manchester had no pop cultural spaces at all. As C. P. Lee points out:

> So concerned was the Chief Constable that by August 1965 he had almost single-handedly generated a moral panic sufficiently large enough to warrant the passing of a special Act of Parliament allowing the Police sweeping, some would say draconian, powers to deal with the problem created by the so-called 'coffee clubs' (1995 p.7).

Because so many clubs were either closed down by the police or knocked down to make way for the city's new Arndale Centre, Manchester, like the majority of provincial cities, was overshadowed by London which held the nucleus of the country's emerging pop cultural infrastructure in terms of both production and consumption spaces. Gradually over time this situation has altered and certain cities have managed to displace some of the power of London.

With the case of Manchester there have been four distinct players (although probably several more less easily definable ones) in the formation of the city's new identity — the Labour-controlled local authority, the private sector, the Urban Development Corporation and the new cultural intermediaries or entrepreneurs of which the pop bohemians were central figures. It was not until the mid to late 1980s that the first three groups (listed above) began to incorporate culture into their regeneration and image-making strategies. However, as the work in this chapter seeks to demonstrate, groups of young, frequently working class Mancunians, who participated in the formation a new punk-generated cultural infrastructure, were highly instrumental in laying the foundations of Manchester's cultural transformation almost a decade before more politically and economically powerful groups began to acknowledge the potential of pop culture.

All is quiet in the dusty village ...

It is important to convey a sense of what Manchester was like in the
mid 1970s, not least to put into context the changes that have
occurred in recent years. Like many other provincial cities at this
time Manchester was overshadowed culturally by London. The
clubs, shops, scenes, record companies and the media were firmly
rooted there. At this time there was an apathetic acceptance that
that was just the way things were — after all it was the capital city.
Certainly in the North West region there was a strong Northern Soul
scene(3) but for many this scene merely epitomized the North's quirky,
inward looking working class values. The majority of beat clubs that
had thrived in the city during the sixties had either closed down or
been razed to the ground. Pop culture, even when it was highly
successful was not valued by the mainstream — the seventies for
instance was the decade in which Liverpool City Council sanctioned   X
the knocking down of the Cavern only to spend much of the eighties
trying to reinstate its 'Merseybeat' identity.
   The once dynamic and spirited (although poor) inner city
communities of Hulme and Ancoats had been broken up and their
populations were moved to peripheral estates.   The smoking
chimneys and factory sirens that had been present in sixties films such
as *A Taste of Honey, Hell is a City,* episodes of *Coronation Street* and
Lowry paintings began to fall silent. Manchester was no longer
characterized as a working class, work a day city heaving under the
weight of furnaces and turbines. Whilst Coronation Street continued
to depict to the nation a caricature of a close knit working class
community in reality such 'communities' were being broken up and
the working classes' opportunities to work were being diminished.
The city was not only being stripped of its economic and industrial
purpose but also of its role as a place of culture, sociability and civic
participation.   The physical effects of de-industrialization were
witnessed in many parts of the city — not least with the majority of
architectural reminders of the city's previous commercial power
laying empty. The belated attempts of the city to modernize itself
were contingent on destroying previous sites of popular culture.
This, coupled with an especially authoritarian and puritanical police
force further suppressed spaces of leisure and popular culture. The
cultural facilities that did exist became increasingly parochial and
pedestrian. Andy Spinoza (1992), a journalist who began his career in

Manchester during this period, describes the city at this time as follows:

> Manchester, 1976. The 'scene' that we now take for granted — Situationist nightclubs, designed bars, independent record labels, hometown pop stars living in their hometown, art galleries and art cinemas — did not exist ... Mainstream discos ruled the city centre , soccer bootboys ran wild on the estates. Pop culture like national politics , was filled with complacency. The time was ripe for change.

Although the city, from the late sixties had a fairly vibrant underground press scene(4) there were very few 'alternative' physical spaces in the city for the majority of the 1970s. From the late sixties onwards the city was subjected to planning and zoning which left large patches of the centre in a marginal position. These were the spaces that were no longer considered valuable — the old working class shopping districts, warehouses and factories. Although the exclusion from development and investment in some of these spaces left them to deteriorate considerably they were, in some cases, to provide the alternative spaces that the city had previously been lacking. Left mostly unnoticed by the council and corporate investors Manchester's pop bohemians were able to claim and use these areas to create, over a period of time, their own cultural environments in places such as the Oldham Street case area (now known as 'the Northern Quarter'), Hulme and what is now Manchester's nationally recognized site of gay and lesbian culture — the Gay Village.

'You measly berks from the North'

It was punk that was to begin an enormous change in the Manchester pop cultural scene — it had an effect on both the cultural production of the city and on the lifestyles and working practices of its inhabitants. Although London's control of the pop production machinery and other media forms continued well into the seventies the DIY ethos that emerged with punk totally revolutionized the structure of the national and international music industry and music making itself. The now legendary relationship between the Sex

96

Pistols and EMI called the power and control of the majors (and by implication the domination of the metropolis) into question for ever. **'This is a cord, this is another, this is a third. Now form a band'** urged a 1976 fanzine (cited in Jon Savage's book *England's Dreaming*, 1991) and people did. Punk created a mechanism for release of the frustration, anger and boredom experienced by Britain's youth. More than any youth subculture that preceded it, punk renegotiated the power structures of pop culture.

In June of 1976 the Sex Pistols played at the Lesser Free Trade Hall in Manchester, a month and a half later they played in the city again but this time they were supported by two local bands — The Buzzcocks and Slaughter and the Dogs. People who were later to be key players in the Manchester pop scene repeatedly refer to the huge impact that the Sex Pistols concerts had in terms of influencing people to reject the sleepy boredom and unimaginative provincial youth culture scene. As Richard Boon recalls:

> These two Pistols gigs were fundamental in bringing our previous cast of disparate isolates out of the wings, out of hiding, out of the woodwork. Heavy networking. At least you could do nothing and go nowhere with new found friends and acquaintances. The virtual stage was set, waiting only to be invaded. The '70s incarnation of the mythical Manchester scene developed from there (1992, p.10).

The Manchester punk scene acted as an important focus point for bringing previously disenfranchized groups of people into contact with one another so that they could begin to take greater control over their cultural environment. Punk also unleashed ambitions to change things as this description from Greil Marcus's *Lipstick Traces* also reveals:

> At a certain time beginning in late 1975, in a certain place — London, then across the U.K., then spots and towns all over the world — a negation of all social facts was made, which produced the affirmation that anything was possible. 'I saw the Sex Pistols' said Bernard Sumner of Joy Division (later, after the band's singer killed himself, of New Order). 'They were terrible. I thought they were great. I wanted to get up and be terrible too' (1989 p.7).

Will Straw, in his article 'Systems of Articulation, Logics of Change: Communities and Scenes in Popular Music', makes reference to the importance of punk in generating local alternative scenes. He writes:

> As local punk scenes stabilized, they developed the infrastructures (record labels, performance venues, lines of communication etc.) within which a variety of other musical activities unfolded (1991 p.375).

Straw's observations are highly applicable to what happened in Manchester and other regional cities, and, as this chapter seeks to point out, punk has been highly influential on the development of urban pop cultural scenes.

During the rest of 1976 Manchester's punk scene exploded not least because of the opening of a punk venue — the Electric Circus. Situated in a run-down peripheral part of the city and housed in a former working man's club the Electric Circus soon gained a national reputation. Most importantly though it provided a distinct site where the previously divergent Mancunian youth could meet like minded people, network and organize. When the December hosting of the Manchester leg of the 'Anarchy Tour' again saw the Sex Pistols returning to Manchester supported by the Clash and other punk bands, the audience at this event included future members of bands such as Joy Division and the Smiths as well as people who were to work closely allied to the subsequent Manchester pop scene. As Jon Savage notes:

> In early 1977, Manchester started to develop as England's second Punk city after London and, as the capital quickly became Punk saturated, its most creative site (1991, p.298).

The speed at which the Manchester scene developed must in part be attributed to the attitude of the London punk scene that had wanted little to do with the provinces. Rather than become part of a national punk scene, a more self-contained, regional one emerged instead. To give an example of this I describe an occurrence which Jon Savage cites in *England's Dreaming* that happened at the McLaren organized Midnight Special at London's 100 Club. Manchester's Buzzcocks, the only non London members of the line-up recall feeling ostracized. Howard Devoto said that; **'There was a feeling that we**

were outsiders. The Clash and the Sex Pistols were from London and we weren't' (1991, p.208). Speaking of the same event and confirming all that Devoto had felt the Clash's Joe Strummer remembers:

> We were mean to the Buzzcocks because we were the London crews, and we looked at them sitting in a row thinking 'You measly berks from the North'. Now I really like those Buzzcocks records; they were also very good that night. It shows how mean we were: we didn't think of them as part of our scene. There was no solidarity (1991, p.208).

This of course is just a one-off event and cannot claim to 'prove' anything concrete. Yet it fits with the North/South divide debate that has come to hold so much currency in recent years. Rob Shields in his book *Places on the Margin. Alternative Geographies of Modernity,* (1991), dedicates a whole chapter to exploring the ways in which from 19th century novels to late 20th century media products the 'North' has been represented as being distinctly 'different' to the sophisticated South. The 'North' then was held as being backward, unsophisticated, artless. It was widely accepted that not only did you have to go to London to be part of the most current and hip pop cultural scene but that you would want to. As Iain Chambers notes:

> It was to London that the Animals (Newcastle upon Tyne), the Spencer Davis group (Birmingham), Them (Belfast), and countless other groups, migrated during the period 1963-5. London's record companies' headquarters, now alerted to new developments in the wake of the Northern invasion, were clearly crucial (1985, p.75).

Until very recently the North was represented as a place 'behind the times' in almost every respect. However, in terms of the music industry at least, the cultural status of London began to be increasingly challenged by the provinces. Because of the changing structure of the record industry brought about by punk, the regions were no longer entirely dependent on London. Manchester and other provincial cities increasingly began to reject the authority of London as the sole British site of pacesetting cultural innovation. There was a rebellion against mainstream culture as well as a negotiation of the spatialization of this resistance.

In February of 1977 The Buzzcocks released their first record *Spiral Scratch*, on their own label; New Hormones. Jon Savage notes the tremendous ramifications produced by The Buzzcocks putting a record out on their own label — as he points out:

> ... it struck a permanent blow for regionalism. In the Liverpool Beat Boom of the early 1960s, groups had to go to London just to record, let alone become successful. By 1977, both Liverpool and Manchester had small but active musical communities that were proud of their autonomy, and 'Spiral Scratch' cemented this: here was a record, produced and manufactured by a local group, which had as big an impact as any that came out of London (1991 p.298).

The Buzzcocks were also one of the first bands to experiment with innovative design-conscious record covers and began a tradition for Manchester bands to use Manchester based designers for the generation of their visual images. Richard Boon (the bands manager) relied on graphic designer Malcolm Garrett to introduce a ground breaking graphic style to the Buzzcocks record covers. Garrett persuaded the band to break away from the accepted seventies record cover format of either using photographs of the band or air brushed fantasy landscapes. Through his use of mixing influences from Dada, Pop Art and Typography, Garrett was able to set new standards in which design was of tantamount importance. Tim Chambers acknowledges the legacy of Garrett's work:

> His importance in setting the agenda for many graphic designers who followed him at Manchester and beyond, with his unique form of 'pop Constructivism' ... cannot be underestimated (1992, p.5).

In the aftermath of punk, cities such as Sheffield, Coventry, Liverpool and Manchester began to retain their pop talent and create their own pop infrastructures, But more importantly their own sounds and looks. Bands and performers began to be self-conscious about their local identities and infused this into their lyrics, record covers and overall image. Although the tremendous implications of this renegotiation of Britain's cultural geography remained for several years predominantly only valued and disseminated within

100

subcultural space, these shifts were later to became frequently used as currency for mid to late eighties city image makers as a means of demonstrating that provincial cities were innovative, sophisticated and hip. This was often in spite of the fact that the agencies engaged in these cultural promotion campaigns were often working on behalf of organizations who for years had been at best heedless and at worst obstructive to the development of clubs and bands.

Rather than trying to fit in with the London dominated scene and suppressing their regional identity, cultural entrepreneurs in regional cities began to play with and exploit their local culture and their 'Northernness'. The hard-edged grimness of a declining industrial landscape was in many ways inspirational in generating the angry post-punk sounds. The destructive aspects of punk and post punk echoed the destruction of the landscape, the disused warehouses and factories provided ideal sites for bands to rehearse in and as backdrops for promo videos and other visual images. Often these spaces were daunting, sinister and sometimes brutally beautiful — seeping a sense of understated power and melancholy . The widely held public opinion that the North was dour and depressing was manipulated by bands such as Joy Division — they sounded miserable and looked miserable — but this was highly germane to the mood and spirit that they sought to convey. The suicide of Ian Curtis, the band's lead singer, permanently sealed the bands melancholic aura. This composed miserablism — or call it what you will — was an important facet in the creation of a distinct Manchester sound and image. Likewise bands such as Coventry's Specials sang about the *Concrete Jungle* and *Ghost Town*.

People involved in the Manchester pop scene took select aspects of what it was supposed to mean to be Northern, provincial, Mancunian and renegotiated these elements to construct something that was cool, frightening, imposing and urbane. Furthermore the bringing together of academics, artists and Manchester's indigenous youth in the clubs led to this 'Northernness' being refracted and negotiated with references to *avant garde* literature and art. This had an impact not least because it was unexpected. Working class lads from depressed Manchester housing estates were not supposed to truck with this type of culture. They were supposed to be hard, crass and deliberately philistine. In the early eighties, Wythenshawe bred Morrisey (of the Smiths) continued to break the rules of what it meant to be a non-university educated, male, working class

101

Mancunian in writing poetic and playful lyrics inspired by the sites and experiences of his hometown, brandishing flowers and being excruciatingly public about his shyness, androgyny and celibacy. He aestheticized the idiosyncratic (dis)ordinariness of the provincial city and made mythical tiny corners of the suburbs and estates. In terms of Smiths record covers he also drew upon visual elements of 60s kitchen sink iconography juxtaposing media images of traditional working class Northernness with a new type of working class Northernness which he embodied.

The mixture of people involved with Manchester's initial post-punk scene included working class Mancunians, the art school contingent and university educated, Situationist influenced Tony Wilson. This produced a period of pop creativity which frequently alluded to avant garde art and intellectual movements. Although, as authors such as Frith and Horne (1987) have pointed out, increased working class access to higher education and in particular, art schools, has had a great impact on a number of post war British subcultures this had more typically involved art students forming bands. In Manchester however the relationships between art and pop were sometimes different to the scenario drawn out by Frith and Horne — many of the musicians and designers had not themselves been educated within Higher Education or Art Schools but associated socially with people who had. It was frequently through this mode of exchange that Manchester's working class pop bohemians were introduced to *avant garde* ideas. This is not to suggest however that the Art School/pop cross-over described by Frith and Horne did not also take place in the Manchester of the late seventies and early eighties — there are numerous examples of these relationships too.

Salford born Tony Wilson, who was to have an enormous impact on this creativity, was involved during his period as an Oxford undergraduate with the translation of Raoul Vaneigem's Situationist text *The Revolution of Everyday Life*. Texts such as this were passed on to people such as Joy Division and Factory manager, Rob Gretton, a non-university educated working class Mancunian. When the Haçienda opened in 1982, it took its name from Ivan Chtcheglov's Situationist treatise *Formulary for a New Urbanism* at the suggestion of Gretton. Especially in its early years Factory records were frequently self-conscious in their referencing of Situationism and as Dave Laing has acknowledged in his book *One Chord Wonders* Situationist ideology was noticeably strong amongst members of the Manchester scene:

> In Britain, the pro-Situationists were a small circle of drop-outs, art students and intellectuals who included Malcolm McLaren, Tony Wilson and Richard Boon. Their activities were intended to conform to true Situationist practice, which aimed imaginatively to disrupt the everyday life of capitalism in order to expose its oppressive nature (1985, p.126).

The art/pop crossover experienced a particular intensity in the Manchester of the late seventies and early eighties as bands increasingly turned to their graphic designer peers to design their logos, record covers and flyers. In October 1977 The Buzzcocks released their first single for United Artists, a major record company. The cover was designed by Malcolm Garrett, a student at Manchester Polytechnic and also incorporated a photomontage by Linder who had also been at the Polytechnic and fronted seminal band, Linder and the Ludus. Linder was a key participant in the Manchester punk scene and was also to design for New Hormones (the label to which she was signed) as well as designing Magazine's first record cover. Likewise when Factory was formed in January of 1978 there was an intense use of locally based artists in the production of flyers and record covers. One of the most prolific Factory designers at this time was Peter Saville who incorporated a sense of northern industrialism with his interest in Functionalist design. Saville gained knowledge of avant garde design via books leant to him by Malcolm Garret. Saville subsequently became fascinated by the history of graphic design and art movements, such as Futurism, Modernism and Pop Art. Design became almost as important as the music in Manchester's pop scene and as Tim Chambers has pointed out, a whole network and Manchester design aesthetic emerged:

> Punk marked a point of crisis within pop culture, which allowed the intervention of design articulate entrepreneurs to give patronage to a new generation of graphic artists and theoreticians. Many of these were located, or associated with Manchester, whether educationally, professionally or socially. The resultant audio visual graphic was an attempt to reject the perceived cultural standardisation and social regimentation of

> that time. Subsequently, their practices and products have produced some reverberation beyond the confines of the pop culture industry (1985, p.2).

Gradually from 1976 onwards alternative or resistant spaces emerged in Manchester in which punk and post punk were to play a crucial role. The habitus of Manchester's pop bohemians became imposed on spaces of the city centre and abandoned sites became captured and reinterpreted. The Manchester pop scene had a physical and symbolic impact on the environment yet, at the same time, it was inspired and impressed upon by the landscape, architecture and mood of Manchester and the North.

During the eighties Factory Communications was to have an enormous amount of influence on the changing cultural landscape of Manchester. Apart from helping to retain bands of global significance such as New Order and The Happy Mondays within the cultural economy of Manchester, the company was also responsible for opening the world's first Situationist inspired nightclub, the Haçienda which opened on Friday, 21 May 1982. Situated in a vast yachting warehouse, the club's interior was designed by Ben Kelly who had been introduced to Factory by Peter Saville. Factory gave Kelly a great deal of freedom. It was an incredibly adventurous project in the context of a time when, even in London, clubs were not consciously conceptualized or innovatively designed. Despite being thirteen years old the club's interior is still remarkably striking and contemporary with its design style still being imitated in the development of more recent clubs and bars.

On the club's opening night Bernard Manning was hired for the opening ceremony — a blatant example of stereotypical working class Northernness being sardonically decontextualized.

At first the club did well when specific bands and events were put on, but not so well when it attempted to operate solely as a discotheque. However as the eighties progressed and the clubs DJs introduced more and more underground black American dance and soul music people began to come to the club to dance. There was a change in attitude towards black music in the underground as the decade progressed — where once there had been a big split between what was seen as frivolous, commercial and tacky disco music and more serious and esoteric rock, punk and new wave people began to realize that there was an experimental and innovative edge to dance

disconnection bet
culture (club) +
economic capital) Haçienda
punk etc

music. Many of the Haçienda's early DJs had been participants in the Northern soul scene — Rob Gretton, Mike Pickering and Graeme Park — who retained a commitment to searching out rare Black styles. The Haçienda became one of the first clubs in the country to discover and play new dance musics such as Go Go in 1983, Electro and Rap in 1984-1986. It wasn't until August of 1986 however that the Haçienda was ever full for a club night — this was for Dave Haslam's 'Nude' nights. In the following year club nights such as 'Zumbar' and 'Hot' in 1988, which changed the Haçienda into a beach party environment with palm trees and a swimming pool, were enormously successful. With the emergence in 1988 of Acid House, House and Baleric Beat the Haçienda was widely acknowledged as being at the forefront of this dance orientated culture — constantly packed out and constantly in the gaze of the media. This period also coincided with an era in which 'Madchester' happened. Again regional/local identity was a crucial element to the latest phase in Manchester's pop cultural history when a distinctly Northern (some said scally) working class hedonism was played out in the lyrics, attitude, lingo and style of dancing of bands such as the Happy Mondays, Northside and the Inspiral Carpets.

Within Manchester the opportunities to aestheticize everyday life (Featherstone) became opened up in the sphere of pop culture. As the 1980s progressed and the pop infrastructure became more developed, if you were not in a band yourself it became possible anyway to work closely allied to the sphere of the Manchester music scene. People began to see it as increasingly more viable to work in the production of their leisure time as managers, promoters, visual designers, fashion designers, DJs, sound technicians, lifestyle journalists, bar and club architects and designers. Although Bourdieu (1984, p.371) argues that the new cultural intermediaries engage in the cultivation of a stylized lifestyle in which almost anyone can have access to spheres previously guarded by intellectuals he identifies people in such groups as emerging from the 'new middle class'. It is more accurate in the Manchester example to refer to a working class bohemianism. Bourdieu also refers to the careers engaged upon by the 'new middle class' as typically being those such as marketing, advertising, public relations, radio and TV production and the caring professions, but there is an implied suggestion that these professions, whilst often in the realm of popular culture, are part of mainstream, national and global networks and organizations. Using the examples of the types of jobs and personnel in the Mancunian pop infrastructure, we can see that these definitions given by Bourdieu (and to some extent Featherstone) are too general and do not refer to locationally specific differences or to diverse and resistant cultural practices . The suggestion is that popular culture became legitimized and accepted into the mainstream. Whilst this is in many respects true it is also the case that it is possible to become a cultural intermediary in a more grass roots, marginal and alternative framework and context. A framework in which the relationships between producers and consumers is blurred and reflexive and fixed primarily within a self sustaining local culture.

As the eighties progressed people with no formal training began to become involved in record and flyer design. Inspired by the existing Manchester network a new breed of designers realized that in this city not only did you not have to have formal training to become a pop star, or a bohemian you could also become a graphic artist as well. Salford born Trevor Johnson of Johnson Panas (who both started off under the Enterprise Allowance scheme) was one such self taught designer who had been incited by punk to experiment with illustration. ACR, Electronic and 808 State are some of the Manchester bands that Jonson Panas have designed for.

Perhaps the most striking example of Mancunian working class pop networking is the relationship between Central Station Design and the Happy Mondays. The Monday's Ryder brothers are first cousins to Matt and Pat Carroll of Central Station Design. Both sets of brothers come from the same hedonistic working class background. Largely self taught Central Station design were to play a striking role in the Madchester phase of the city's pop design history.

The artistic entrepreneurial spirit within Manchester's pop infrastructure extends far beyond the bands, clubs and record cover and flyer design. There are a vast number of small scale fashion designers, which Sarah Purvis' chapter describes, based in Manchester who cater for the pop and club market. Again as with other aspects of the Manchester pop industry many of these fashion designers are self taught and retail from small outlets such as Church Street/Oldham Street's Afflecks Palace and Arcade and the Royal Exchange Design Centre. Particularly in the late eighties Bands such as the Inspiral Carpets and James designed their own band T-Shirts and took control of their own merchandizing. Leo Stanley built up an important fashion wholesale and retail business which was very much contingent on 'Madchester' and in particular he was responsible for the Manchester 'pride' T-shirts (Born in the North ...) which he claims(5) were developed as an ironic response to London tourist souvenir T-Shirts of Tower Bridge and Beefeaters.

From the examples given above we can see the extent to which production and consumption became increasingly intermeshed within the Manchester pop scene. People found careers within the sphere of their social life and leisure time — they had and have a great deal of power in dictating what they consume. Pop culture helped to renegotiate Manchester's cultural identity. Most importantly, at one and the same time, young people were able to make money and create places to go out to. Manchester is not the only regional site where this process has happened. I now want to look at two other prominent examples of this process.

The dawning of a new era

Coventry and its Two Tone bands and label is a strong example of a provincial city which attempted to break away from the monopoly that London had on the British music industry. As Frith points out, the legacy left by the Sex Pistols, where they had demonstrated that a record company cannot necessarily call all the shots, gave a certain degree of confidence and empowerment to would be pop stars:

> The Specials were in a seller's market and, as a post punk band, were more interested in control than cash. What they wanted was their own record company: not an Apple (the Beatles hippy fling) but a Motown, a label name to guarantee a sound (1988, p.78).

Jerry Dammers, the founder of the Two Tone label and the band The Specials, had been a well known figure on the Coventry punk scene and it is clear that the whole ethos of punk had inspired him. Most of the people Dammers collected together to form his first band — the Automatics — were already involved in some sort of musical activity in the Coventry area.

Jerry Dammers did not have the finance to set up the record label single-handedly and a series of events occurred before the founding of Two Tone: — Dammers borrowed some money to record 'Gangsters', Rough Trade distributed the record and it was phenomenally successful. This success allowed a deal to be made with Chrysalis records in which the Two Tone musicians and directors had almost total control over the label's output and the traditional power relationships between the major record company and the musicians had been shifted. Although Two Tone drew heavily on Ska and other earlier musical genres it was not a pure revivalist movement, it had its own coherent identity in terms of music, fashion, dance style, and 'corporate' image. As the bands publicist Rick Rogers recalls in George Marshall's book *The Two Tone Story*:

> The first thing he wanted was a definite sound, a definite identity for 2 Tone, a definite sound that would be identified with the label. He wanted 2 Tone to become the British equivalent of Stax or Tamla. He was still finding his way about the business, but that's what he was aiming for (1990, p.15).

The black and white two tone label echoed the ethnic mix of the bands (apart from Madness) and the blending of black and white musical styles. Most importantly, compared with more recent so-called revivals of previous subcultures, much of the music put out on the Two Tone label was original. The distinctiveness of the music and its impact on the national music industry generated talk of a 'Coventry sound' and engendered a sense of local pride. Also from Coventry were the Swinging Cats and the Selecter . The majority of the line up of the Selecter had been involved with various Coventry reggae and soul bands throughout the 1970s. The exception to this was Pauline Black who originally came from Romford but who ended up in Coventry to do a degree at Lanchester Polytechnic in biochemistry. Other Midlands bands, although not from Coventry, were associated with Two Tone, included The Beat who briefly joined the label in October 1979 and Dexy's Midnight Runners who toured with the Specials and Selecter. The popularity of Two Tone came and went — in a way it was a victim of its own success, constantly monitored and analysed by the music press and other media forms and as Hebdidge points out the Two Tone emblem was ripped off and mass produced by outsiders so that what had once been a symbol of exclusivity became mundane — or, as Hebdidge argues, Two Tone was in danger of becoming a culture of; 'Selector socks and Madness Tupperware' (1987, p.113). The heyday of Two Tone lasted about two years and although nothing remains of the record label, the movement paved the way for a series of other provincial music scenes to be taken seriously by the music press and the record buying public. During the 1980s a series of city specific music scenes gained a profile in the national and international music world including Sheffield (Cabaret Voltaire, Heaven 17, ABC and the Human League), Liverpool (The Farm, Echo and the Bunnymen, The Lotus Eaters, The Mighty Wah! and Teardrop Explodes) and Manchester (New Order, The Fall, The Smiths, The Stone Roses, The Happy Mondays, and 808 State).

A specific, direct attempt to use pop music as a way to stimulate economic growth was part of the motive behind Sheffield's cultural industries strategy and it is no coincidence that the strategy was developed just at the period when a number of its bands, such as Heaven 17, ABC and the Human League, were achieving national and international status. In this instance it was possible to try to learn from the mistakes that had been made by Liverpool with the Beatles.

During the 1970s Sheffield suffered over 50,000 redundancies in the steel and allied industries. Cultural industries were seen as something that could potentially be invested in to cope with this dramatic de-industrialization process that the city was suffering. The council attempted to formulate a policy which would both increase the number of voices heard in the media nationally and give more local people access to the means of cultural production. This was the thinking which lay behind the council's investment in recording studios for example; the facilities would enable all sorts of local people to make recordings and offer skill and training in the recording process. Part of the aim with the Sheffield strategy was to create a 'critical mass' — in other words to focus the cultural industries in a particular part of the city. At present this cultural industries quarter houses the Leadmill arts centre, Sheffield independent film cooperative, a gallery with dark room facilities, Red Tape studios and the Audio Visual Enterprise Centre. The process of development began in 1981 when the Sheffield city council strategy team identified the media industries as one of over 30 possible areas for intervention. Sheffield City Council formed a media policy unit in 1985 which recommended support for audio visual industries. Subsequently the Audio Visual Enterprise Centre was established. In 1987 plans to develop a 'cultural industries quarter' began. AVEC was officially opened in 1988 — by 1993 the complex housed 18 businesses with an approximate turnover of £6.5 million with 120 people being directly employed, plus a further 70 freelancers. The success of it led to a further 50,000 square feet being sanctioned for development. Red Tape Studios, which was opened in 1986, now has a 4, 8 and 16 track recording facilities and rehearsal space for community use. This was the first local authority music studio complex. The introduction of a wide range of training courses provides experience of sound engineering and media related technology for thousands of people each year. However central government restrictions on Sheffield City Council spending coupled with changing priorities for the eligibility for central government and European grants meant that the Workstation, a fairly recent addition to the cultural industries quarter, was developed by a private company. The Workstation is a managed workspace dedicated to the cultural industries. One of the spaces in the Workstation is occupied by the development office for the proposed National Centre for Popular Music. The director of this project is Tim Strickland (who, according to George Marshall's book, was involved with the early Two Tone movement) who is awaiting news from the National Lottery Department of the Arts Council to find out if adequate funding can be found. Funding is also expected to come from European funds. A feasibility study by Coopers and Lybrand estimates that the centre will attract 400,000 visitors per year. They also predict that the project will not need public sector revenue support. The plans for this centre include multimedia and interactive displays, exhibitions related to the history of popular music, and music and technology with both educational and entertainment purposes. The fact that places such as the Workstation and the proposed National Centre for Popular Music are, or will be, developed privately can be seen to demonstrate the success of the strategy — the local authority gave it a large kick start in developing an infrastructure and reputation and now private investors are convinced of the viability of Sheffield as a centre for cultural industries. Steve Redhead points out that although the local authority development of pop cultural industries has worked well in Sheffield such a strategy does not necessarily open itself to duplication in Manchester:

AVEC, and other aspects of the Cultural Industries Quarter,

clearly filled a requirement in the Sheffield region, once the bottom fell out traditional heavy industry there. Cultural industries tended to replace traditional ones. The Manchester music scene has evolved alongside the region's traditional industries and developing service sector, over a much longer period, and has characteristically displayed an independent entrepreneurship unmatched outside London. More importantly the intertwined relationships of the participants in the music industry in Greater Manchester meant that there was not the same need for bringing people together as there was in Sheffield. On top of this, facilities such as recording studios abound in Manchester (1992, p.50).

This is not to suggest that Manchester does not need any help at all from the public sector — the crash of Factory records is painful evidence of this. However, it is clear that Manchester needs a **different** type of strategy.

Contemporary regional pop cultural scenes continue to flourish and develop. Club nights such as Liverpool's Cream, Leeds' Back 2 Basics and Manchester's Flesh draw in crowds of pop cultural tourists from massive catchment areas. Managed workspaces for people working in regional pop cultural industries continue to be developed to meet the demand. Manchester has two large managed workspaces, Ducie House and the Beehive Mill, which both contain a large number of businesses which are specifically connected to pop culture. As we have seen Sheffield too has its pop cultural industry spaces as do cities such as Leeds, Birmingham and Liverpool.

Conclusion

In the quote cited at the beginning of this chapter Michel De Certeau refers to planners' misunderstandings of the 'ordinary practitioners of the city'. At different times and in different spaces there have been cases in the cities referred to in this chapter where the planners and other regulatory organizations have been out of time, out of tune with people involved in struggles to build civic cultures of creativity. At other times the planners and practitioners sing in a similar key. Disharmony and struggle do not necessarily have to be seen as being negative, struggle can bring about change. But, in the battles with

111

bureaucracy it would be refreshing sometimes not to have to fight too hard. To finish this chapter I would like to end with a quote by Stuart Cosgrove which, for me anyway, sums up why there is much to feel positive about with regard to regional pop cultural economies and scenes:

> ... one of the great conceits of modern day Conservatism is that socialism is a thing of the past, a thing of the North, an industrial thing, yesterdays news, an old tune that will never be revived. But one of the most reassuring and truly inspirational facets of the new music from the cities is the way sampled dance music reinvents bits from the past in presenting a regenerated future ... I'd rather be a rap star in Sheffield than bankrupt in Bournemouth (1991, p.190).

Notes

1. For example the following edited collections are focused around issues of place and identity; Bird, J., Curtis, B., Putnam, T., Robertson, G. and Tickner, L. (eds.) (1993), *Mapping the Futures*, Routledge, London, Keith, M. and Pile, S. (eds) (1993), *Place and the Politics of Identity*, Routledge, London and E. Carter, J. Donald and J. Squires (eds.), *Space and Place, theories of Identity and Location*, Lawrence and Wishart, London.

2. During the Two Tone and Madchester periods both Coventry and Manchester respectively were focused on by sections of the global media.

3. See for example *Land of a thousand dances: A history and geography of Northern Soul*, Hollows, J. and Milestone, K. Paper given at The Place of Music Conference, London, April 1993.

4. Bob Dickinson, *The Alternative Press*, M.Phil research ongoing at MIPC.

5. Interview with the author, February 1994.

References

Boon, R. (1992), 'Darling your Roots are Showing' in the *Sublime (Manchester Music and Design)* exhibition catalogue, Spinoza, A. (ed.) Cornerhouse Exhibition Publishing, Manchester.

Bourdieu, P. (1984), *Distinction. A Social Critique of the Judgment of Taste*, Routledge, London.

Chambers, I. (1985), *Urban Rhythms; Pop Music and Popular Culture*, Macmillan, London.

Chambers, T. (1985),*Leave the Capital*, Manchester Polytechnic, unpublished M.A. thesis.

Chambers, T. (1992),'Round Up the Usual Suspects:The Graphic Design Network in Manchester', in the *Sublime (Manchester Music and Design)* exhibition catalogue, Spinoza, A. (ed.), Cornerhouse Exhibition Publishing, Manchester.

Cosgrove, S. (1991) *Shaking up the city: Pop Music in a Moment of Change* in *Whose Cities?* Fisher, M. and Owen, E. (eds.) Penguin, London.

de Certeau, M. (1984), *The Practice of Everyday Life*, University of California Press, Berkeley.

Featherstone, M. (1991), *Consumer Culture and Postmodernism*, Sage, London.

Frith, S. (1988),*Music for Pleasure*, Polity, Oxford.

Frith, S. and Horne, D. (1987), *Art into Pop*, Methuen, London.

Hebdige, D. (1987),*Cut 'n' Mix; Culture, Identity and Caribbean Music*, Comedia, London.

Laing, D. (1985), *One Chord Wonders: Power and Meaning in Punk Rock*, Open University Press, Milton Keynes.

Lee, C. P. (1995), *And then there were none: Government Legislation and Manchester Beat Clubs, 1965-*. Paper given at the First Critical Musicology Conference, Salford.

Marcus, G. (1989), *Lipstick Traces. A Secret History of the Twentieth Century*, Secker and Warburg, London.

Marshall, G. (1990),*The Two Tone Story*, Zoot Publishing.

Redhead, S. (1992), in *The Culture Industry*, Wynne, D. (ed.), Avebury, Aldershot.

Savage, J. (1991),*England's Dreaming* ,Faber and Faber,London.

Shields, R. (1991),*Places on the Margin: Alternative Geographies of Modernity*, Routledge, London.

Spinoza, A. (ed.) (1992), *Sublime (Manchester Music and Design)*, Cornerhouse Exhibitions, Manchester.

Straw, W. 'Systems of Articulation, Logics of Change: Communities and Scenes in Popular Music', *Cultural Studies* 5 (3), 1991.

4 The interchangeable roles of the producer, consumer and cultural intermediary. The new 'pop' fashion designer

Sarah Purvis

> Building a career now requires flexible thinking, the ability to manage opportunity and, sadly often the ability to manage adversity (David Jones, Fashion Business Consultant).

> Those who are capable of reacting and adjusting and have the right attitude stand a far better chance of success. Let's stop pretending. This is the Nineties and the fashion world needs to stop dreaming (Fiona Cartlegde, 'Sign Of The Times'. Both from *The Face,* September 1994, p.109).

This chapter seeks to discuss many of the related themes inherent in a discourse about contemporary socio-cultural change associated with debates around postmodern theorizing. It will look at the way in which the fashion industry and more specifically the 'popular' fashion industry has been transformed through issues concerning the continuing commodification of high and popular culture, the changing nature of production and consumption within the realms of the fashion industry, the destabilization of the boundaries between culture and the economy and finally the changing nature of the roles of those people working within the fashion industry; the designers themselves.

The above dicussion will be contextualized within a wider framework of the emergent economies of the cultural industries and will be based around intensive research into Manchester's popular cultural fashion businesses. Of importance to this debate will be the suggestion that Manchester is one example of the transformations occuring in contemporary society under the auspices of a 'postmodern society' and that, in many other cities nationally and internationally, these changes can be observed.

Manchester's flexible 'pop' fashion designers

This ethnographic research concentrated on the small producer often working in units of ten or less employees. Phizacklea argues 72% of the women's fashion market is now produced in units of ten or less and this marks a radical shift in the production processes and organizational structures of contemporary fashion production (Phizacklea, 1990, p.12). These designers work with symbolic capital in the production of specialist, small run, fashion garments. They comprise of a multi-skilled and highly networked operation and in many respects this mirrors the framework theorized in the post-Fordist/flexible specialization model (see Mole, this volume). These activities challenge many of the working practices and production processes inherent in Fordism and so leads us to believe that there is a post-Fordist shift occurring in the pop fashion industry in Manchester and the cultural industries in general.

The pop fashion businesses are involved in fashion production in three areas; design, manufacture and retailing. This vertically integrated system is characteristic of processes within the post-Fordist model whereby all areas of production are undertaken by a core of workers and specialized activities will be sub-contracted out. Of the businesses studied, two types were found to be the norm. There were those who designed and manufactured from their own workshops and retailed from their own premises and there were those who designed, manufactured and wholesaled from their own workshops and only on occasions retailed through other peoples premises. As will become clear, the reasons for these two scenarios are not always clear cut and it is not always the case that the most established own their own premises.

These small and often 'one man bands' are interesting in so far as they share many common characteristics entailing the formal make-up of their business, i.e. organization, working practices, business and working relationships, etc. Also the informal make-up, i.e. informal business ties, their networking arrangements and lifestyles they lead.

In Crewe's (1992) research paper entitled, 'Markets, design and local firm alliances in the Nottingham Lace Market: possibilities and problems', much of the information she documents of the working practices of the cultural producers in Nottingham echo the characteristics of the cultural industries examined by Wynne (1991; 1992), and are pertinent of the flexible specialization thesis more generally. Crewe argues that certain characteristics provide important clues to successful restructuring within the textile and clothing sectors.

These characteristics include; the 'adoption of flexible, versatile work practises', which involves manufacturing, fabric sourcing, flexible production; with shorter lead times and smaller batch sizes, and flexibility in the work force and multi-skilled seamstresses. Second, the 'recognition of the importance of design and quality'. Third, 'the development of local networks and inter-organizational alliances', exemplified in the soft management hierarchies and the informal labour relations within each firm. Fourth, the 'adoption of collaborative, non adversarial relationships between firms' and finally the 'co-operation between individual firms in terms of design, marketing and sales'.

This chapter focuses on the working practices of these pop fashion designers, manufacturers and retailers in relation to a new type of economy emerging in the pop fashion industry and to the cultural industries in general. These working practices can be understood and examined fully in the context of the post-Fordist, and more specifically, the flexible specialization model. In a close examination of Manchester's pop fashion industries, one can document these working practices and show how they have changed in line with recent developments of structure and composition within the fashion industry in particular and the overall changing nature of an emergent postmodern economy in general. Points (i) and (ii) will look at the changing working practices in pop fashion design.

Changing working practices

Retailing has come to assume a leading role in the economic change process, and is at the cutting edge of Britain's new postindustrial era, characterised by flexibility, rapid response, new subcontractual arrangements, and new employment practices. Retailing is, in many ways, 're-defining the economic and cultural horizons of contemporary Britain' (Mort 1989 p.168), (Crewe and Forster 1993 .p3).

Similarly Murray (1988) suggests that retailing not only provides a post-Fordist vision for industry, as retail investment was a dynamic area of the financial markets and retailing itself could be seen as an innovative and very profitable sector. It was also involved in the restructuring of the economy in the direction of flexibility, in which the retail sector could be seen to be spearheading a move towards new 'flexible' economic relationships throughout the supply chain. Thus he claimed that 1980s retailing in Britain was one of the 'commanding heights' of the economy, and that:

> ... the revolution in retailing reflects new principles of production, a new pluralism of products, and a new importance for innovation. As such, it marks a shift to a post-Fordist age (Murray, 1988).

Adoption of flexible, versatile work practices

Manufacturing

All of the businesses interviewed were involved with their own manufacturing of garments. They either had separate workshops and retailed through their own shops, e.g. Vicky Martin, Heyday, Holder and Pennington, Lily Wittingham, Bayliss and Knight, Brittain and Wear It Out. Or they manufactured in their workshops and retailed through other outlets, e.g. Consalvo Pellachia, Lyssistrata, Hayley Kato — these designer's sold through Big Banana or Wear It Out. There are many issues and problems which become manifest for the cultural producer with the manufacturing of pop fashion.

Not all the designers wanted to manufacture their garments as well as design and retail them. It was out of necessity that many of these designers entered into manufacturing. The most common complaint was that of the inflexibility and unreliability of manufacturers when they first started out:

> *We had made a conscious effort right at the very beginning never to manufacture, that was our philosophy, that we wouldn't*

manufacture ourselves. So we found a factory in Reddish to do our clothing for us and they were alright at first, but we realised through the economy of scale and finance and through experiencing the quality of the finished garments that we had to go back and make it ourselves ...I t was hard enough finding a manufacturer who would produce such small batches as we wanted and when you are dealing with high quality design for a market which dictates a high level of quality also but at relatively cheap prices, we could not afford to take chances on wasteful and damaged stock. We soon realised that by manufacturing ourselves we could keep an eye on what was going on at every stage of the production process ... outworkers were definitely no good because although their quality may have been up to scratch the deadlines were often late, and that was no good to us (interview with Lisa).

Many of the designers believed that the small batch orders, which led to shorter lead times and more frequent but smaller orders, underpinned the success rates of these small pop fashion designers. However the manufacturers were still associated with the more inflexible and mass production techniques of the Fordist past and often refused to accept small batch orders. This led to a conflict of interests between the small pop fashion designers and the manufacturers.

I went and put £500 of fabric into a manufacturers, this was about five years ago, it was the beginning of September and he (the manufacturer) told me I could have my jackets in two weeks time. I got forty of them without the collars, the linings or the buttons on Christmas Eve and the other forty I received in March. When I rang up he swore at me and told me to come and pick them up even though they were only half made. At that time it was my whole capital, I nearly had a nervous breakdown over it ... Another time I used a different company to dye my jeans, the same thing happened. I had to go and pick them up, fifty miles away and they weren't ready. Then when I went they'd dyed them the wrong colour, then they bleached them and dyed them again and then the zips had all rotted, this went on for six months (interview with Dosh Clothing).

Some businesses in their very early stages even had to lie to gain access to the manufacturers in order to buy materials. One such firm was a T-shirt printing company which designed prints and logos to put onto T-shirts. Andrew stated that they 'blagged' their way into one of the manufacturing companies around Cheetham Hill to buy a small batch of T-shirts. He argued that, 'as soon as they know the quantities you want they automatically become suspicious'. Other reasons included receiving bad quality garments back from the manufacturers because they believed they were too young and therefore the quality needn't be as good as an established and more traditional fashion chain.

In effect the reasoning behind the growth of the designer, manufacturer and retailer all in one is not surprising considering the demand that the market dictates for a rapid turnover of styles and the inability of the traditional manufacturers to offer this velocity. What the small autonomous (i.e. those not tied to a manufacturer) pop fashion designer excels in and is successful in doing, is creating a market of high quality, innovative and cutting-edge designs for a rapidly changing market, and is able to produce that supply without the constraints of large batch sizes and only two orders per year, which is a problem that many manufacturers face. Exclusivity can only be attained with rapid response, and in the case of the pop fashion designers they have the flexibility and the creativity to provide this new and novel fashion production process.

Fabric sourcing

The problems faced by the designers in this area of the business are widespread and exacerbated further by the old traditional values and inflexibility of the fabric merchants and wholesalers. All but two of the designers sourced exclusively from Manchester. A point which many theorists on the flexible specialization debate argue is crucial to the survival of these micro industries (Piore and Sable, 1984; Crewe, 1992; Magatti, 1993). This was not always through choice, as will be explained below, and there were complications which ensued from this scenario. Problems which arose from designers working with the same fabric sources in Manchester are self evident as the need for exclusivity in design also relates to fabric. As Sally indicated:

... it's difficult not to end up with the same fabric. There are a

couple of wholesalers that we all use. You end up buying something and then see it hanging up all over the place. You try to avoid it at much as possible and it's got to the stage now that the wholesalers do give you a bit of insight into what others have bought, there isn't really enough choice.

Other problems stem from the traditions inherent within the fabric wholesaling industry. Such chauvinistic attitudes, for example controlling the accessibility of the wholesalers to women and young people (some argued 'if you looked scruffy'), make themselves apparent and causes problems for the designers. It was only after they had purchased fabric three or four times that they started to accept them as business people and not students looking for off-cuts. Even at the trade fairs the small designers came up against some discrimination:

We went to a cloth show in London and they were totally unhelpful. They were only interested in how many thousands of metres you wanted. They were not bothered about small designers. Basically they didn't want our business. Which is really stupid, we now import from Spain (interview with Darren and Dennise).

However even the more established and financially stable designers who could afford to travel abroad to find new fabrics as a way of determining exclusivity, find that there still remains fundamental problems with sourcing abroad and these contradict the way their businesses are organized. Overseas sourcing makes flexibility in production very difficult as the lead times are extended, the wholesalers and fabric manufacturers only want to sell in large batches when all efforts are made to keep them at their minimum, so as to be one step ahead of the rest. They find that they have to stretch out their resources to buy larger batches and less frequently. As Crewe notes the lace market has similar problems:

Although many firms had no problems with sourcing trims, the problem of fabric sourcing emerged as a major problem. The message seems to be that fabric manufacturers have not adapted to new demands for flexibility, to shorter lead times and smaller batches. This creates sometimes fairly serious bottle-necks in the smooth-running of production. This is particularly the case for firms with small average batch sizes (Crewe, 1992, p.36).

Alison believed there were problems in the batch sizes that they wanted and that it did cause problems in some instances:

I don't like buying fabric from the bigger places where you have to send off for it, this occurs normally with fabric agents ... I'd rather be able to pick fifty metres up and get it straight away. You can only do this at places which keep stock lines, basically all that means is that they have a huge selection and keep all their fabrics. If you get made to order not only is there often problems with quality but you have to order huge amounts ... and wait for ever for it to be delivered.

However attitudes are slowly beginning to change, as Crewe explains above, many of the old traditional merchants and manufacturers are having to change their practices to accommodate the new wave of consumers who are becoming more interested in and demanding quality and design in their consumption. This leads to a demand in more flexibility and radical change in the production processes. However it is not just the consumers who are directing this change. The growing numbers of small producers are also involved in this transformation:

When the Manchester scene was very popular and when the independent music industry set up, a lot of these large companies were knocked off their thrones because it made way for a lot more independent retailers and a lot more independent manufacturers ... it is not the taboo activity it once was to demand short runs and more frequent orders because that is the way the industry is moving (interview with Kate).

Similarly Crewe found the Lace Market dictated a move for change, albeit a slow one, because of the growth in these small businesses. The increasing demand for more flexible arrangements in fabric manufacturing to accommodate changes in the market is apparent. Crewe states:

There is hope, however, as quality fabric agents and

124

manufacturers are becoming more used to dealing with small quantities. One manufacturer using silk stated, 'We use an agent in London. They have extensive stocks and there is no problem with small quantities, they are used to it'. Other silk garment manufacturers confirmed this attitude. Another argued that suppliers had changed their attitudes because of the predominance of small firms, 'manufacturers have rethought their attitudes. In this area there are so many small designers they have to'. The problems of firms in this area are also minimised by help from local government. Many facing these problems use the Fashion Centre, 'there is help here with swatches and the library." It seems that the centre is quite effectively overcoming these problems (Crewe, 1993, p. 37).

Unfortunately for the Manchester pop fashion designers there is no Fashion Centre for them to utilize either in sourcing new materials or sharing technology (see below), and they have had to struggle with what they have got.

Flexible production — lead times and batch sizes

The small pop fashion designers can offer the consumer something that the larger firms cannot, that is decreasing the lead times that garments are available in the shops. As they are small and very flexible and because batch sizes are very much smaller than the medium and large stores, they can distribute a new idea or collection in as little as two or three weeks.

In some cases, as with Consalvo's Ted Jackets, they were in the stores within a week. The lead times vary from only half a day to cut out the fabric to two or three days to have finished sixty pairs of trousers ready to be sold. As Lisa stated, 'It is in our interest to keep things very tight, that's why we can survive because the main stream shops cannot compete with our time-tabling'.

With a yearly breakdown of up to six 'seasons' (mainstream retailers in medium and larger outlets rarely have more than four seasons), the small designer does not need to produce large batch sizes. They can filter the stock over a period of time into their retailing outlets. The largest batch size was often about 500 garments, but this was more often in their capacity as wholesalers and not retailers and they would have more time to prepare the garments for the buyer. For example Consalvo's current collection included trousers, dresses and skirts in which he produced thirty two of each garment, including three colours and sixteen in each size, in the space of two to three weeks.

Flexibility in the work force - multi-skilled seamstresses

The notion of flexible specialization and numerical flexibility is widespread in the make-up and organizational structure of these businesses. The internal structure of the businesses correlate with many of the issues surrounding the flexible specialization debate such as having a core of skilled workers who often have a multitude of skills in the fashion industry and a periphery of workers who are also skilled machinists but are used in a part-time capacity. In terms of numerical flexibility they sub-contract to certain skilled workers in the pattern cutting and pressing departments, and also use temps or agency workers in times of deadline requirements, like Christmas. They utilize the flexibility of home workers although it is in their interests to keep this at a minimum because of the lack of control over quality and keeping them to deadlines. In some cases they sub-contract to local manufacturing firm CMT (Cut, Make and Trim), if the batch size is large enough and the design is simple (they cannot afford to rely on the manufacturers to make-up complicated garments and prefer to do it themselves).

The core workforce of many of the designer businesses rarely exceeds five full-time machinists. The more established designers and those with their own retailing premises have a core work force of about five people. Lisa has five full-time machinists and three part-time machinists. Most of their sub-contracting occurs when deadlines are imminent and they need to bring in skilled pattern cutters and fabric cutters to relieve the pressure on the core workers who are too busy making up, fitting and finalizing garments ready for distribution. As Peter argued:

It was Christmas when we employed six machinists, a cutter, a presser and a student from the University (Manchester Metropolitan University), and then we had all the extra shop staff. But it's quiet now and we don't need all those staff at the moment. Normally we have ten staff including ourselves, but we always have a pool of part-timers who are ready and willing to come in when we need them ... The cutter was employed full-time for a few weeks before Christmas but normally we employ a woman part-time who comes in three days a week ...We are very lucky in this respect because most pattern cutters are male and they want full-time work, it is just not possible because we are so small and cannot cope with employing one full-time.

Sally took advantage of the sub-contractors more widely because of the small core workforce. She employed only two full-time machinists and much of her periphery workers were targeted from local agencies specializing in the textile and fashion industry. One such agency in Manchester is the company 'Menswear/ Womanswear', a nationally based recruitment agency focusing on the fashion industry specifically. It is through such agencies that Sally relied for the periphery pool of labour, one where, 'we can dip into and out of at random'. However as she argues, '... quality of work is very uneven and it is much better if you can arrange part-timers who are available on a permanent basis so I can keep an eye on their progress and their ability.'

As already noted, another way sub-contracting is used on occasion is by 'farming' work out to CMT. Both Lisa, Sally, Consalvo and Alison had used sub-contractors to manufacture certain garments but as stated above the main reservation in this instance was the fact that the quality may not be the same as the rest of their products:

We have farmed out for CMT in the past, when we did a trade show in London. The orders were quite large and at the time we were not really ready to cope with all the extra work it entailed, that's where the CMT came in. About half of the orders we received from the trade show we tendered out to sub-contracters but in the end we lost money from it because the quality wasn't good enough and it was expensive (interview with Consalvo).

Alison had also sub-contacted out but again they came across the same problems in quality. However they stated that there were some cases where sub-contracting was a better option than doing it themselves:

At the moment we have got a manufacturer to make up some rubber garments. I did try to do it myself but it was a complete

127

pain, you need specialist equipment which we don't have so it was much more beneficial for us to sub-contract (interview with Alison).

Many of the owners/designers were involved with nearly every stage of production and they had to become proficient at all aspects of the business, including accounts and finance, if they were to survive, although in some cases it was beneficial to the designer if he/she could rely on the machinists and the cutters to be able to get on with their work so they could be left to design.

Darren and Dennise who had five full-time machinists and one part-time presser did not have any strict rules on who used which machine. They were in the process of training the young student presser to be able to pattern cut also because it was something which they realized took up too much time. By the time they had searched for fabric and threads and cut out materials and pattern there was little time to spend on the design which they thought was a vital component of their business. Multi-skilling in their business was a common theme for all the designers, and their talents included having a 'hands on' approach themselves: from days spent in the workshop using the machines, to spending time in the office keeping up to date with tax returns and accounts.

Similarly Vicky, who has four full-time machinists, an assistant who worked as a cutter or presser in the workshop, her sister who helped design the collection, the part-time girls who worked in the shops (one in the Royal Exchange, Manchester, and one in Hyper Hyper, London) and herself working in the business, felt that time spent in all areas of the production process not only kept her informed with what was going on in a very non-heirarchical way, it promoted a good relationship with the employees:

> *Yes I suppose I am quite multi-skilled and I don't think I could ever go back to doing just one job. I think it's very difficult after this amount of time because of the control thing. To me being in control of my life is very important, especially because I have two small children ... I have a very varied day as you can imagine. I'm buying fabrics and trimmings, going to shows, I'm in the Royal Exchange making sure the shop is running smoothly, I'm going to London every three or four weeks to see buyers and journalists, I'm designing and cutting, its a bit of everything ...*

For a long time, certainly for the first year I was actually doing a lot of the machining myself, and even today I still spend time in the workshop especially if someone is off or we need a bit of an extra kick in production, I'll be there doing some sewing or cutting, I always have done...whatever needs doing I will do ...

In all of the designers' businesses the production processes varied to fit in with the orders they had at the time. However, on average they preferred to allow the machinists to make up a whole garment from start to finish. Consalvo was very flexible in the tasks and jobs that his machinists would be involved with in any one day:

We arrange our production processes in order so that the machinists get a sense of fulfilment in finishing a garment, having said that it is much easier, I know that we are small and that we can allow this to happen ... but it makes for a higher quality garment in the long run.

Alison also believed that quality was enforced when the employees could complete a whole garment from beginning to end:

Not only do they enjoy it much better, instead of doing the same repetitive job all day they are able to use all the machines in the workroom, there are not certain people using certain machines ... it's never a production line we don't need one because our market dictates that we supply small runs with a high design content and exclusivity ... it just doesn't work like that for us.

Design and technology

A vital component in the equation which gives firms the competitive edge in the new market climate is design. It is generally acknowledged that the way forward for UK textile manufacturing is to move away from standard designs which can be easily and cheaply reproduced in low wage countries, and to move towards quality production of design based garments produced in quick response to current fashion trends (Crewe and Forster, 1992, p.31).

In Crewe's study, one of the categories she documented in the lace market included: 'small manufacturers/designers who operate as retailers or independent retailers who have manufacturing facilities and who produce their own designs'. Crewe identified this correlation to be 100 per cent. Similarly all the pop fashion designers who were interviewed stated categorically that design and innovation in design was one of the most important factors in their business. Sally argued that:

> We used to serve the alternative crowd who wanted something completely different from the high street. It was an easy job to come up with different designs to that of the mainstream standardness of the Top Shops of the fashion business. But in the last fifteen years things have changed so much and design and innovation is imperative to keep ahead of the Top Shops ... It isn't good enough to be different you have to be new and I think that is where we come in.

Similarly Dennise argued that:

> ... you can't compromise on design ... although things have changed on the high street and they are designing for a more design conscious market, we need to be one step ahead of them because our customers want that extra bit of individuality which we can provide because we can get a design made up and in our shop in less time.

Questions directed at where they got their inspiration from heralded very diverse responses although many had common and related themes. For example all of the designers interviewed at one stage believed that they got some inspiration from the club scene in Manchester and supported the contention that Manchester had a very strong sense of identity in the clothes that people wore, and that there was a large population of customers who were prepared to pay extra for exclusive, even outrageous, designs.

Darren and Denise were just two of the designers that had 'a fabric first approach', and they, 'let the cloth dictate the style', however there were problems with this process which resulted from, again, the manufacturing side. Fabric sourcing was a constant problem to the designers because of the lack of merchants and stock lines in

Manchester and the amount of designers looking for interesting and new fabrics.

In any debate surrounding the post-Fordist argument, the notion of new technology and high tech innovation is always at the fore. In one respect the pop fashion industry or indeed the majority of the fashion industry does not lend itself to high tech production processes. As Wilson (1985) argues, the fashion industry has always been labour intensive as opposed to capital intensive.

Likewise the pop fashion industry is not very technology intensive and all of the designers interviewed started their business on a domestic sewing machine. In most of the interviews the designers did know about new technologies but they were realistic in their aims and abilities and believed that such innovation was not needed in their set up. However this is not to say that technology does not exist to aid the production process or more particularly the design process. It is more a question of the initial outlay of expenditure being far too great for the small designer. Such technology includes Computer Aided Design or Computer Aided Manufacturing, but on the whole, nearly all the designers did not have any association with new technologies.

One business, was in the process of computerizing much of the office administration. However it was stressed that it was more the result of Denise's boyfriend being a computer 'whizz kid', and being able to set it up for them, and not because it was a concerted effort to make their business more technologically friendly.

It is interesting to note this contradiction in the lack of technology in these micro businesses, as the most flexible and arguably most post-Fordist example documented, the Benetton firm, has high levels of technological innovation providing market information by computer. The Benetton example, exemplified by Murray, explores the way in which clothing retail has been transformed by the Electronic Point Of Sale (EPOS), in which centralized distribution outlets can keep a record of local and regional variations and fluctuations.

However the contradiction lies in a major difference between the Benetton example and the pop fashion designers. That is size, both in the firm and their markets. As Urry and Lash (1994) argue:

Benetton itself is basically a manufacturer and an information system whose central Ponzano headquarters exercises control over the outsourced production and retailing. As Manufacturers the firm is involved in design, size grading, cutting, dyeing, quality control, warehousing and delivery ... they subcontract labour-intensive sewing (Urry and Lash, 1994, p.177).

I have already documented that the pop fashion designer is involved with all of these production processes listed in the Urry and Lash quote, from the design to the warehousing, albeit on a micro level. The reason why technology does not play a large part in the production of these small producers is precisely because they are small and their markets are minute compared to the markets of the globally advertised Benetton. Surely then, this does not mean that they are any less post-Fordist or flexibly-specialized because of this. In a way it is arguably the opposite, that the small firm has the opportunity to remain flexible because they consciously keep their operations small.

Changing attitudes to work

What an examination of the working practices can also show is how attitudes and lifestyle choices have influenced the way working relationships, especially between management and the workers, have changed. For example in Manchester's pop fashion industry, entrepreneurship is not solely concerned with the bottom line, with cut throat business attitudes, with profit-maximization, and absolute authority, which one would have traditionally associated with this business. What is important to these people is business cooperation and producing networking patterns of friendship ties within the business framework.

The development of local networks and inter-organizational alliances

Within the discourse surrounding the Fordism and post-Fordism debate there is the idea that business in a post-Fordist society is not based solely on the bottom line, on profit maximization, and that worker relationships are important to those who work within the business. The owners/designers of this novel business organization were very intent on making the attitude and atmosphere for their workers a more egalitarian one. Peter stated; 'It's not a kind of

Victorian mill owner mentality, we try to be fair ... it's a lot more egalitarian I think'. Similarly Consalvo argued:

> *It's quite informal, we are all friendly with each other. I don't like the idea that 'I'm boss and you will do as I say' attitude, I like to keep it friendly and then if there are any problems they can tell me about it. Everybody has off days and I like to think that I'm flexible with them. There has not been many problems really and if there has they have been quickly solved because people feel they can come and discuss things and we can sort them out.*

There were close friendship ties with many of the people who worked for them for example Vicky argued:

> *It's very informal because most have worked for me for a long time. So you tend to find someone, and if you like them and get on well, keep hold of them, that's why many of my machinists have been here from the start more or less. They've seen me go through two pregnancies so yes it's very informal and we have a good time together in the workshop whenever I'm there.*

However there was a big difference in the friendship patterns with the machinists and those with the shop assistants. On the whole the machinists were older (for reasons I will explain later), and although they worked in a very informal and friendly way there were distinct generational differences. So when asked if they socialized with the seamstresses, they all said they did not. What is apparent is that this was not some kind of conscious labour relations activity, it was merely that, socially, they were incompatible. As one seamstress argued, 'my days of hitting the night-spots are over'.

On the other hand, however, those employees who worked in the retailing outlet, the shop assistants, had a different relationship with the designers. They were much more likely to socialize together and often had been friends with the designers for many years before they worked together.

Although relationships in the workshop was very informal and friendly there had to be someone organizing the tasks to be done. However there was no formal hierarchy and organization was often left up to whoever was there at the time. Whilst some would argue that this was impractical for a business to run smoothly, it was very practical because most of the employees were trained in all aspects of the job and did not need someone constantly checking their work. They were very much left to their own devices.

Other designers had similar stories about the way their machinists related to them. But what they stressed was that it wasn't just a one way street, although friendly there was, on occasion, some formality in the relationship, and the machinists themselves often dictated the way the relationship was to be enforced. There would be, in some cases, a lot of respect for these often older machinists. This was because the designers knew that 'machining' is a dying industry, and these women had often been involved in the industry a lot longer than they had and had vital experience which they could pass on to the designers when initially starting out on a new design.

In effect the industry has an ageing population of skilled workers and the designers know from the experience of finding good quality machinists that once they find someone they must hold onto them. Alison saw this problem as very serious indeed:

> *Finding good quality machinists is a bit of a nightmare really. At the moment is not so bad because we've found four brilliant full-timers and our part-time staff are very flexible which is definitely what you need in this business. We have a brilliant position on Great Ancoats Street and we have a lot of space...but by far the biggest benefit to us and our location is that the machinists who are all older women can get to us really easily ...These are little things that many people forget about ... many of these woman don't have access to a car or they can't drive, and having a cheap factory in the middle of nowhere is no good to us. Central location is imperative really.*

The adoption of collaborative, non-adversarial relationships between firms

In Manchester's pop fashion industry, friendship ties and business contacts are inextricably linked. They have survived commercial activity and competition, which one would think would be the poison which killed any friendship, whether formed before or after the business was established. The informal relationships which the designers have created are unique in any business, but none more so than the fashion industry — where cut-throat tactics and underhand business activities were once seen as the norm and to a certain extent still exist in parts of the industry — especially in Manchester, as Philipa Grant (1994) recognizes:

> The north of England, particularly, is a magnet to original ideas due, in the main, to the thriving club and bar scene but also to the community spirit among designers who frequently help each other out (Grant, 1994, p.22).

Many of the pop fashion businesses interviewed had started out sharing workshop locations and work spaces. The reason for this was a financial one at the outset because most of the designers did not have the capital to fund an individual work space:

> *I started off in Tib Street with my own premises together with Sally and Sarah ... We would have stayed there if it was not for the fact that the building was sold and the new owner, Leo Stanley from Identity who was already manufacturing his own label in Manchester wanted us out to turn the building into a warehouse. In the end that was a blessing in disguise because it forced us to find new premises and because we had found it productive working in close proximity to each other before, we carried on. The new workshop was a huge 40,000 sqare foot warehouse on Dale Street and too big for just the two of us. So Jackie Haynes a friend of mine from college and Simon Belcher also from college decided to move in ... Not only did it keep the cost down it was a breeding ground for cross germination and many of the ideas that people had were interpreted and used in their designs. Two others moved in just after that, Holder and Pennington who started by designing for Lysistrata before moving on to their own label and Big Banana. At that time the notion of cross germination wasn't really a problem because we were all starting up and the social thing was brilliant ...we really had a certain Manchester style at the time which was funded in part by the whole Madchester scene, they were good times* (interview with Lisa).

In the mid-80s, designers such as Alison Knight and Sandra Bayliss from Bayliss and Knight, Abigale Porter from Britain, Sue Barnes from Swell Guy and a graphics company called Johnson Panas all rented premises in Bloom Street in the centre of Manchester but found that the work area was too small. Bayliss and Knight then moved to Sackville Street which was, at the time, an area of Manchester where many fabric wholesalers were situated and buying fabric was not a problem. However that area was designated as part of the Central Manchester Development Corporation regeneration corridor and they had to move out of the building. Alison Knight remembered working in the area and believed it was not only very productive but it promoted a sense of togetherness and community.

> *I don't want to sound like it was **all** fun then, it wasn't, we still had problems, but working with other people was great fun and it did give you a feeling of heightened creativity because there were always ideas floating around the place.*

Cooperation between individual firms in terms of design, marketing and sales

Similarly on the retail side there was emerging a close network of co-operation between very small micro businesses just starting out and the more established firms. Although still micro themselves they did have some confidence in their ability, and they would become the most crucial part in the promotion of the small Manchester pop fashion scene. They invested their success in others by allowing designers space in their units to display their stock. Two such people are Ursula Dorrigan from Wear It Out and Fred Royal from Big Banana:

> *That was always a passion of mine to sort of give people who are starting out a chance to perform in a commercial market ... you know, people who might take their clothes to a bigger shop and they'd say, 'no, you've got threads here or whatever' ... or ... 'I don't know your name ... so we don't want your designs'. I always wanted to give people that chance because it doesn't take much to make a space in your unit and all the garments are on a take back arrangement, if they don't sell we return the garments ... everybody is happy really. A lot of the designers who started*

136

through me have got their own units now ... they are doing really well, people like Heyday, Consalvo Pellachia, all very well established Manchester and national designers. Don't get me wrong I don't just do this for their benefit I get a lot out of it also, it keeps me on my toes to see all the talent (interview with Ursula Dorrigan).

The designers themselves who traded then, and still trade from there today, realize the benefits that Wear It Out offered to them at the very beginning. As Sally acknowledged:

I knew about Wear It Out ... and that used to be the initial place to sell in Manchester ... It was held in quite high esteem and it was a huge step up the ladder if you could sell through them because there were a lot of designers at that time ... Even today Wear It Out has a good reputation because a lot of buyers go directly to them and it is through the shop that they get in contact with the designers.

From an industry with a strong historical link to underhand, secretive working relationships with others in the field, this novel example of cooperation is quite unique and works very well. Of course there are problems in some cases where people are protective over their designs and try to keep the new fabrics a secret, this is 'par for the course', in such a dynamic and high profile industry as fashion.

This friendly and cooperative way of working is not just something which is common in new businesses, although this is a feature of young firms, as many of the designers have been associated with this way of working after they had established themselves and moved onto to bigger things.

Interpretations and explanations

In conventional economic terms, these 'businesses' look both ephemeral and peripheral, unlikely to expand or consolidate, and equally unlikely to survive the ups and downs of the business cycle, recessions, and local and foreign competition. They may be just an alternative to a 'proper, full-time job', which the fashion and clothing industry has been unable to provide in recent years; that these people are in an apprenticeship for the full-time jobs which the industry will eventually want filling. In other words they are 'no choice' jobs and are not taken seriously by themselves or others.

My research has challenged this kind of critique, in showing dense networks of friends and business associates which sustain both the lifestyle patterns as well as the productive capacities of these fashion designers. The smallness and informality of these enterprises is a choice, not a fate, which permits them to anticipate or react to changes on the streets or the clubs sensitively and quickly. They successfully create and occupy their market niches precisely because they are small and informal.

Vicky agrees with this scenario. Probably the most successful of all the designers in Manchester she believes that to keep a certain level of uniqueness you have to, 'limit the distribution of the garments within the community that you design for'. In her case it is the club community. It is after all a small or niche market that would buy these clothes but she admits that it's better for her customers '... I think exclusivity to a certain extent is what these people want, and by keeping small I can provide this service'.

The pop fashion designers have illustrated the ways in which we can identify their post-Fordist qualities. From versatile and flexible production processes, sub-contracting, and a flexible workforce, they exemplify the need to stay small in a self-limitation process, including both products and size of organization, to ensure exclusivity. They are involved with a diverse range of products, which often entails making whole garments, manifesting itself in the fashion industry by increasing 'seasons', due to their reduction of lead times and batch sizes. As such we can look to the pop fashion designer working in such a way as to herald the shift to a flexibly specialized production process and ultimately a post-Fordist economy.

Bibliography

Crewe, L. and Davenport, E. (1992), 'The puppet show: Showing buyer-supplier relationships within clothing retailing', *Transactions of the Institute of British Geographers: New Series: 17.*

Crewe, L. and Forster, Z. (1992), *Markets, design and local firm alliances in the Nottingham Lace Market: possibilities and problems.* Final research report to the University of Nottingham.

Crewe, L. and Forster, Z. (1993), Markets, design, and local agglomeration: the role of the small independent retailer in the workings of the fashion system. *Environment and Planning, D: Society and Space: 11.*

Grant, P. (1994), 'Sorted Styles' *Fashion Weekly,* February 17, p.22

Lash, S. and Urry, J. (1994), *Economies of Signs and Space,* Sage, London.

Magatti, M. (1993), 'The Market and Social Forces.' *International Journal of Urban and Regional Research.*

Murray, R. (1988), 'Life After (Henry) Ford', *Marxism Today,* October.

O'Connor, J. and Wynne, D. (1993), *From the Margins to the Centre: Cultural Production and Consumption in the Post-Industrial City,* Working Papers in Popular Cultural Studies, MIPC, Manchester.

Piore, M. and Sabel, C. (1984), *The Second Indusrial Divide,* Basic Books, New York.

Phizacklea, A. (1990), *Unpacking the Fashion Industry — Gender Race and Class in Production,* Routledge, London.

Wilson, E. (1985), *Adorned in Dreams: Fashion and Modernity,* Virgo, London.

Wynne, D. (ed.) (1992), *The Culture Industry,* Manchester University Press, Manchester.

5 The ecstasy of urban regeneration: Regulation of the night-time economy in the transition to a post-Fordist city

Andy Lovatt

For at moments like this the city goes soft; it awaits the imprint of an identity. For better of for worse, it invites you to remake it, to consolidate it into a shape you can live in (J. Raban, 1974).

Introduction

For many cities the post-industrial landscape offers an opportunity to re-invent themselves as places of consumption of popular cultural forms based in the night-time economy. A new economy of pleasure linked no. longer to repression but to proliferation and multiplication within a new wave of commodification — of pleasure and desire, evasion and of transgression. This is a liminal economy where boundaries between legal, illegal, formal and informal are blurred to such an extent that they retain little meaning.

The post-industrial landscape presents both problems and opportunities for the enhancement of the urban public realm and for the local state charged with its governance. This chapter will attempt to place some of the more theoretical accounts of global economic and political transformations, notably the supposed shift from a Fordist to a post-Fordist regime of accumulation, in a local context. Specifically we will focus on the cultural and political negotiations surrounding the night-time economy which emerged in Manchester at the beginning of the 1990s and which continue there and in other UK cities today. We will move on to argue that developing theories of social, economic and political regulation of the urban realm should not only place greater emphasis upon the deliberate rule making of the local state but also pay closer attention to cultural negotiations currently emerging in revitalized city centres. To do this I will utilize the language of The Regulation School(1) although some distance will be maintained from their particular methodological stance.

Whilst calling for more 'nuanced and detailed accounts of particular modes of regulation' (p.290) in order to assist the development of this relatively new theory, Painter (1995) and others insists upon strict adherence to the initial conceptualization used by the French economists Lipietz, Aglietta and Boyer. They eschew the 'deliberate rule making of *réglementation* and the auto-regulation of the body or the individual agent and rely solely on 'the kinds of regulation of economic life which are neither wholly deliberate nor automatic' (p.277). It is difficult to see how the implied accidentalism of global economic shifts can be applied to the urban realm without reference to local state management, and the making and unmaking of political-legal regulation therein. It is here that the deliberate rule making of the local state **and** individual agency interact in a complex set of negotiations to distort global configurations at the local level. In this call for a more detailed exposure of regulation theory to local conditions Regulation Theorists must accept a more open, complex and meaningful interpretation of the initial concept which recognizes local political, cultural and economic configurations.

Indeed Lipietz, one of the founders of the Regulation School acknowledges that any materialization of the regime of accumulation must incorporate a complex set of interrelations, habits, political practice and cultural practice. Indeed it must take '... the form of norms, habits, laws, regulating networks and so on that ensure the unity of the process ... this body of interiorized rules and social processes is called the *mode of regulation*' (Lipietz, 1986 p.9). Here we attempt to expose this broader regulationist approach to developments in the governance of the night-time economy in Manchester where macro-economic and cultural shifts have to come to terms with a specific political-legal entity and local cultural practice.

Regulation

For the purpose of our research we separated 'regulation' into three aspects:
i) Firstly, the organizing dynamics of the complex whole of which

142

the night-time economy is a part;

ii) secondly, the conscious application of legal-political rules to specific cultural configurations ;

iii) and, thirdly, the internal and specific 'regulation' of these configurations by those involved in its operation and those who use its services. All of these have both macro and local-specific dimensions which need to be addressed in any case study.

In relation to the night-time economy we must look at the more specific notion of regulation — the political-legal regulatory regimes which cannot be reduced to epiphenomena of 'economic demands' but which are of course implicated by them. The night-time economy has been heavily regulated in a deeply embodied legal/political/moral structure and finds itself open to a number of competing claims. Given the complex set of discourses at work in this field it would seem that a regulationist approach utilizing a more complex framework provides a useful heuristic device when analyzing the urban realm in relation to wider economic shifts to global regimes of accumulation.

The night-time economy

The night-time economy represents an object of dispute between a number of competing agencies — economic, cultural, political and 'moral' — and stands to illuminate the changing structure of the (post)modern city and some of the stakes involved in the current social structural transformations. However as an object of policy the night-time economy has been strangely marginalized. Until recently it seemed that the night-life of a city was not a legitimate object of attention for the local state other than as something to be regulated and contained.

Since its emergence with the invention of gas street lighting in the 18th century, the night-time economy has **shadowed** the 'normal' business of the city. It came to represent less a suspension of work but the clicking into gear of a new economy. Yet many of its associated activities remained marginal, and those associated with it, as both producers and consumers, regarded as dubious (Seigal 1986; Clarke 1985). But it did interact with the daytime in that it represented not just crime and sin, secret pleasures, obsessions and obscurity, but also an extension of the public realm, a new space and time of consumption and socialization. This sense of schizophrenia, of choice, of fascination and anxiety was present then and has persisted to this day (O'Connor & Lovatt 1995). This **otherness** presents both national and local state government with a series of strategic challenges as they adjust to a new regime of social and economic regulation designed to facilitate local economic development within a 'globalized space of flows' (Lash & Urry 1994).

Development of strategies designed to enhance the night-time economy can be seen to focus attention upon attempts to re-imagine the city as a place of spectacular, hedonistic consumption and an exciting cosmopolitan location for footloose global capital. It is the night-time economy which provides the location for much of the activity around which the post-industrial city has attempted to re-imagine itself. Despite its inextricable link with the image of the vibrant city it has remained primarily an object of attention for agencies concerned with licensing, health and safety, planning and policing. It has been, and to a certain extent still is, a heavily regulated zone of space and time which represents the worst aspects of Fordist bureaucratic control and zoning. Until recently it was a location for transgression conceived in terms of social dysfunction (O'Connor 1994). Nevertheless the increasing presence of the night-time economy on policy agendas — when even a decade ago it was the province of police, magistrates and social workers, and where those operating within it represented marginal economic, moral, social and cultural figures — points to a fundamental shift in the dynamic of the city and the discursive parameters which policy makers now engage.

The night-time economy has become a central cultural and economic issue — crucial to many cities urban regeneration programmes, if not for the image of the contemporary city *per se*. In Britain especially it is also the most controlled; bringing together defining aspects of legal, political and moral codes and competing discourses of the city, youth culture and the new middle class. With the global expansion of consumption of leisure and cultural goods and spaces, some locales have experienced a concurrent growth in production and consumption in the night-time economy and have begun to deploy policies aimed no longer at its repression but designed to secure its proliferation. It is in the night-time economy that the generalities of macro-regulation theories have to come to terms with the complexities of a specific political-legal and cultural entity. Whilst presenting new challenges for local economic

144

governance, debates around the night-time economy also challenge those theorists who exclude deliberate rule and law making of the local from the regulationist approach.

Re-inventing the urban

The 1980s saw the re-emergence in of a concern with city centres as focal points for and symbolic of, a specifically urban way of life which had somehow been eroded in the 70s. Cultural questions were pushed to the fore and while city governments were keen to re-orientate policies around cultural production and consumption they were also faced with ever changing notions of what culture was. Its very fluidity stood out in stark contrast to the stasis of regulatory structures and embedded bureaucracy of the local state. At about the same time local government had to adapt to social and economic transformations caused by the processes of global and national economic restructuring (Harvey 1989; Sassen 1990; Lash & Urry 1994). This transition was complex but we would highlight five main features.

i) The first aspect is the de-industrialization of older industrial areas which left large sections of many city centres derelict. The consequent shattering of local and regional identity brought on by this economic crisis — and which this dereliction powerfully symbolized — form the backdrop to negotiations about restructuring which have dominated regional politics in this country for the past 12 years.

ii) The second aspect of this shift is the re-valorization of city centre sites in the development boom which began in the late 70s and early 80s. Areas adjacent to the Central Business Districts (CBDs) were invested with a 'cultural capital' represented by 'downtowns' which was subsequently recouped by developers eager to create a new urbanity centred around leisure and upmarket consumption (Bourdieu 1984; Harvey 1989; Zukin 1981, 1991).

iii) The third aspect is the emergence of city to city competitiveness at a national and supranational level where the management of the local image was deemed to be crucial in an increasingly globalized market place. This image was tied to the cultural facilities and 'vibrancy' of the city centre. If the processes of de-industrialization led to the abstraction of production from place, and if the 'post-industrial' economies needed to attract footloose global capital, then cities with a bad image would lose out.

iv) The fourth aspect was the reorganization of city centres around consumption rather than production. Planners now became faced with an emphasis on urban culture and space which demanded more fluid approaches to regulation. Yet the more immediate and powerful pressures for a retreat from regulation stemmed from the market — often backed up by political expediency. Forced to relinquish control of local economic systems by the deregulatory ideology of the Thatcher Government, their inclination to step back from regulation due to other factors was severely muted as the local state desperately clung to their already diminished legislative powers.

v) The fifth aspect, following on from this shift from the city of production to the city of consumption, involved the more central role ascribed to leisure, the arts and culture, but also to that re-invention of urbanity which had been evoked by urban regeneration projects. However superficial and spatially circumscribed, the emphasis on play, (the carnivalesque, the festival, the fair), strolling and idle socializing could be seen to have wider effects. These activities, which had previously been regarded as secondary or marginal to the 'real' business of the city began to question what the city (both universal and particular) could and should be (O'Connor & Wynne, 1994).

A further aspect of this transition refers to those complex shifts out of which this latter process emerged. The definition of culture was in flux under the impact of its massive commodification and the radically transformed lifestyle patterns that had emerged since the late 60s. In this context national and local state subsidy for culture could not stay the same, neither with respect to its objectives, to those activities it funded, nor to the form in which it was given. Cultural policy in this context demanded a complete rethink. This rethink not only implicated those directly involved in 'culture' but also began to ask question of those involved in urban design and planning, and of those agencies concerned with local economic development. As these latter groups began to look for something called 'culture' the very processes which were compelling them to search for the beast had changed shape. The night-time economy is one of these strange beasts (O'Connor & Lovatt 1995).

Cultural policy and urban regeneration

In the light of these changes local government has sought new political strategies which enable the shift to a 'post-Fordist' economy where legitimation is sought through the enabling abilities of a streamlined bureaucracy and where social provision is subordinated to the needs of economic competitiveness and place marketing (Jessop, 1994). Some theorists have characterized this as a shift from the organizing principles of the Keynesian Welfare State (KWS) to those ascribed as the Schumpeterian Workfare State (SWS) (Jessop, 1993; Painter, 1995; Goodwin, 1993).

In this environment, and in line with the neo-liberal strategies deployed by most western governments, a degree of legitimation is sought by supply-side intervention. As Jessop notes that the SWS would:

> ... promote product, process, organizational and market innovation and enhance the structural competitiveness of open economies mainly through supply-side intervention; and to subordinate social policy to the demands of labour market flexibility and structural competitiveness (1993, p.19).

Though initially resisted by local authorities traditionally dominated by the political left this ethos has been adopted or forced through in the absence of other coherent political strategies. Urban policy and urban political processes increasingly became dominated by the need to deal with economic restructuring and the shift from an industrial to post-industrial economy (Painter, op cit). Indeed, just as earlier in the 80s local government had to learn the language of the market economy, by the late 80s there were pressing reasons for them to adopt the language of 'culture' (Fisher & Owen, 1991). If, as Lash asserts, the 'cultural' has become the most decisive moment in the economic and social life of the city, then the pressures to recognize the place of culture in the urban environment came from local producers and consumers who, until this time had been excluded from the processes of urban governance and the 'grand compromise' of Fordism[2].Under conditions that can be broadly characterized as post-Fordist, new alliances must be sought if the local state is to continue to secure an acceptable level of legitimation.

For many cities, including Manchester, this involved the

appropriation of policies designed to enhance cultural production and consumption in the city. These policies would aim to emulate strategies used with varying degrees of success in other European regional cities. In Manchester and other regional cities this has involved complex and often competing negotiations with the national state and networks of cultural producers and consumers in the city. For the cumbersome and detached bureaucracies of the local state this has proved problematic. Where negotiations have involved anachronistic cultural legislation imposed by central government (liquor licensing) and the competing moral codes implicit in the night-time economy, they have often proved intractable.

The dichotomy of competing regulatory narratives is complicated further when the dominant cultural production is not the relatively safe controllable output of so called 'high culture' — concert halls, opera houses, International Arts festivals — but the rhizomic impulses of popular culture often rooted in the spatial and temporal ghetto of the city at night and with feet placed firmly in both the formal and informal economic practices. The splicing of an explicitly Fordist bureaucracy with an essentially post-Fordist leisure economy, where the former attempted to facilitate the latter, not only highlights problems of embeddedness in the local state, but also a continued ignorance and fear of urban popular cultures, even when those cultures have been seen as the engine of many urban regeneration programmes. The relationship between cultural policy and urban regeneration has been well documented (Bianchini & Parkinson, 1993), though the difficulties of establishing an economy which is essentially post-Fordist in character, utilizing a system of governance or mode of regulation which has all the embedded characteristics of Fordism has, until recently, avoided scrutiny. In Manchester, the regeneration programmes and an apparent shift in their respective mode of regulation have co-habited similar time spans: their stories are recounted in the following narrative.

In Manchester, economic restructuring and the consequent revalorization of the city centre around 'upmarket' consumption was, as with many regional cities, delayed (see Mole, this volume). However city governments eager to secure this transition have begun a process of restructuring in order to facilitate this proliferation. The activity surrounding this shift from city of production to city of consumption was initially focused on the 9-5 retail economy. Recently however, emphasis has been refocused towards the night-time economy where cultural policy, urban design, economic initiatives, begin to occupy an orbit previously filled by the police, health and safety officials, etc. To this end policies of deregulation and active strategic intervention through economic incentives or marketing strategies have begun to repackage the centre as 'Fun City'. Implicit in these strategies is the notion of informalization in the social life of the city and a tacit 'decontrol of emotions' by both the regulators and the consumers. This restructuring has led to a re-assessment of groups and activities previously seen as peripheral to the main business of the city. Formerly marginal groups have become central to the city and have made the city central to themselves (O'Connor 1994).

Nevertheless the liminality of night life resists 'planning' in its traditional sense, local authorities now need to deal with people previously excluded from the management of the city. As in Manchester they must begin to talk to producers and consumers in the night-time economy, not as the regulatory authority but as partners in the regeneration process. This will be both difficult and frustrating and will involve a drift away from the tacit implementation of strict legal and bureaucratic codes towards an assumption of a new role for urban governance.(3) This will involve a more reflexive approach to the regulation of urban culture and will need to responded to the challenge of specific regulatory practices and a rapidly changing relationship between law, state, culture and the economy.

Regeneration (stage 1): shiny happy buildings

During the past ten years Manchester city centre has undergone a transformation from a dour, derelict working class city which represented the very worst aspects of the desolation brought about by political and economic restructuring from central government to the threshold of an Olympic millennium. This renaissance was achieved in part by the building-led regeneration projects orchestrated by the Central Manchester Development Corporation (CMDC), the country's first urban development agency, in partnership with private capital and the initially reluctant cooperation of Manchester City Council (MCC). It attempted to use private developers to transform the landscape of the centre towards consumption of its historical and (high) cultural values. This included not only the usual symbols of civic aplomb such as a new Concert Hall, exhibition space, and heritage parks but also the conversion of Victorian warehouses into city centre apartments.

The promotion of Manchester was implicitly tied to these building led projects and the image of Manchester as a lively, vibrant and cultured place in which to live and work was pursued by local agencies (O'Connor & Wynne, 1994). The many strategies and initiatives aimed at bringing people back into the city (whether as producers, consumers or merely spectators) either incorporated or pointed to the cultural facilities of the centre. The city was promoted as a culturally vibrant realm and many strategies, explicitly or unconsciously, incorporated the idea of the night-life in their formulation.(4) The night-time city began to be re-packaged as a realm of play, of socialization, of encounter and of the carnivalesque whereas before it had been the object of repression and regulation. The link with image and culture was reflected in sickeningly sycophantic and distorted City Council literature promoting the city to potential investors:

> Manchester marries the panache of a cosmopolitan city with the informal fun of a friendly town. And knows how to enjoy both ... Lifestyle Manchester is all about choice, lived in your own style at a pace that gives you time to spare (MCC, 1992).

Symbols of civic boosterism such as the long awaited Concert Hall and exhibition spaces, heritage trails and museums may have satiated the formalistic desires of the business suits at the state sponsored development corporation and the Town Hall, but did little to accommodate the nascent decontrolled desire within the city's bohemian pop culture. Like any attempt to simulate global cultural and economic shifts in the local arena these spaces did little to resolve the contradictions of a working class city without work.

Provicilaism and the politics of pleasure

Behind the glossy brochures very few changes had been made to the city's cultural or political infrastructure. Cultural producers and consumers were still excluded from the decision making process and the city's pop culture was continually shunned by the city's grandees.

By the late 80s the regulatory structures which shape the night-time economy of the city had changed little; either at the national or local state level. Indeed it has been argued that the Fordist structures of the local state were embedded deeper than those of the centre due to a combination of accumulated resistance to the deregulatory ethos of the Tory Government, a dogged provincialism and a puritanical regard for culture, fun and hedonistic pleasure (Montgomery 1990; Mole 1995). In a taped interview on 12 May 1993, Acting Head of Environmental Health (at the time responsible for Entertainment and Cafe Licences), Mike Ankers stated that although in principle he agreed with expansion within this sector his department would continue to object to new licences until the existing market was satiated. Late night cafes were refused licences 'because they attract the wrong sort of people into the city' and because 'the police do not have the resources to police them' (ibid). Similarly the leading licensing solicitor for Manchester regretted the closure by the police of clubs in Moss Side because the Afro-Caribbean community would be tempted into the city centre(5).

It was a Fordist zoning system gone mad; with powerful, unelected individuals expressing their personal prejudices to eliminate 'undesirables' from the city's streets: echoes of the spatial, temporal and racial zoning experienced in New York and recounted by Chevigny (1992). In *Gigs* he outlines the history of attitudes towards popular culture and bohemian mores and law's place in both creating prejudice in the first place and occasionally eradicating it. Personal and institutional prejudice in Manchester manifested itself in an almost baroque regulatory regime with a consequential ecomonic and cultural stagnation. For a time during the 1980s boom years inward investment in this area slowed to a trickle as local and specific intervention deflected a global cultural flow and the possible transition to a post-Fordist cultural economy.

Cultural production and consumption in this field was confronted with deeply embedded planning restrictions and bureaucratic practice characteristic of Fordism. Spatial and temporal zoning was enforced with vigour. Detached officials, who had little regard for the creative potential of the city's cultural production, enforced laborious planning strictures; a place for everything and everything in its place. It seemed that the city council could always find a new way to say 'no to culture' and little or no effort was spared to facilitate cultural creativity in the city. Legislation, planning practice, bye-laws, licensing restrictions and overbearing policing all mitigated against cultural production in the night-time economy of the city.

It seemed little had changed since J. B. Priestly had visited Manchester in 1930. Here he recalls an encounter an acquaintance had with Manchester's contrary relationship with entertainment:

> This man's firm runs cafes and Dance Halls in various London suburbs and provincial cities, so that you may say he makes his money out of the new frivolity of our age, which we so often hear condemned by peoples who do not happen to like cafes and dance halls themselves and do not see why others should. He goes round visiting these places from time to time, had just inspected their Liverpool properties and now wanted to have a look at their big cafe in Manchester. He did not like Manchester. It seems that when his firm decided to open the cafe on Sunday evenings, they asked Manchester City Fathers if they could provide their patrons with music, a little orchestra and a singer or two. The City Fathers said: 'No we can't allow that sort of thing in Manchester.' So they asked if the cafe could have gramophone music. The fathers replied promptly 'certainly not, no gramophone music on Sunday'. Could they install a (radio) loud speaker in the cafe, and thus entertain their patrons with the programmes that John Reith himself passed for public consumption on the Sabbath? Again Manchester refused permission. So now, he informed me dryly, the cafe is open on Sunday evenings, and generally full, but nothing happens in the way of entertainment and his firm is spared the expense of providing it. The people are only too willing, on winter Sunday nights, to go in and stare at one another. It is a change from the streets or back bed-sitting rooms up the Oldham Road. There was a time when Manchester was known as the 'home of living causes', but exactly what living causes are finding their home there now I do not know (1932).

By the 1960s, although alive with the sounds of British Beat groups and American dance music, most venues were unlicensed and frequently faced harassment or were closed. Yet night-clubs and late-night cafes once again proliferated in spaces vacated by the diminishing cotton and textile trade. Just as London was swinging so too were Liverpool and Manchester. There are many who remember cities like Manchester in the 60s as exploding with bars, clubs and cafes — rooted in the lives and works of a wealthy industrial city. But the unease with which a city of production regards the role of fun was evident then in the Chief Constable report of 1965:

> 'Young people danced to beat music or sat about and were known to lie on the floor kissing and petting' he went on '... generally adults are not acceptable at these clubs, but there was some evidence that prostitutes, homosexuals and thieves visited some clubs though not necessarily to ply their trade' (*MEN* 31/10/65).

Later that year local legislation was introduced to close most of these clubs while the rest found their demise with the development of an enclosed shopping mall known as the Arndale centre. De-industrialization and the lack of entertainment spaces in the 1970s led to a desertion of the centre by all but residual groups. Women and older people avoided the city centre through fear of (male) violence. In this context the police and regulatory authorities increasingly saw the situation as one of crime and disorderly behaviour. In short a problem.

By the late 1980s little had changed. There were artificial limits placed on the number of licensed premises allowed to operate in the city centre (by the police as well as the city council) which harked back to the pathologization of the city at night which developed in the 70s. In the absence of a demonstrable 'need' for a new licensed premises magistrates, on the advice of either the police or the local authority, would refuse any new licence application. The city at night was still regarded in terms of social dysfunction; every bar was seen as a potential trouble spot and a stretch on police resources. The limit on licensed premises imposed by a triumvirate of GMP, MCC officers and local magistrates prevented new investment in this sector as potential owners were asked to purchase existing but redundant licenses for up to £10,000, the nominal cost from the magistrate is £12.(6)

By 1992 tables and chairs were still banned from the city's streets and squares in an attempt to prevent public consumption of alcohol. As with other provincial towns night-clubs were forced to close at 2.00 am on Sunday morning and owners were still being prosecuted under the 1780 Sunday Observance Act. If people were found dancing after this hour they and the owners were liable to prosecution and the club threatened with closure. In one prosecution brought against the owner of a gay night-club later that year, the case dissolved into farce as the police were asked by defence lawyers to define 'dancing'. The officer contrived to come up with the definition as 'moving the feet and body in time with amplified music'. Asked to demonstrate before the court, the officer declined(7).

Attempts to organize one-off events were foiled by one of several city council departments, who all had an input into the regulation of the night-time economy. All this operated within the framework of a moral authoritarian discourse from central government; where restrictions on licensed hours were and are completely incompatible with new flexible lifestyles and consumption within a post-Fordist leisure economy. Embedded Fordist regulation could accommodate 'high' cultural investment in a building led regeneration programme funded by global capital which produced questionable economic and cultural returns, but was continually found wanting when confronted by the demands of popular cultural production located in the night-time economy of the city.

Regeneration (stage 2): shiny happy people

By 1990 the then 'Acid House' or 'rave' scene had gathered momentum through the informal networks in operation within the city's popular culture. These networks began to work around regulatory and bureaucratic obstacles to continually find (illegal) space for expression. Vernacular gay and pop cultures struggled to re-appropriate the revamped city spaces from which for so long they had been excluded through the combination of over zealous policing and embedded planning regimes(8). By this time the impact of the Rave scene of the late 1980s, and a new found confidence of the considerable gay community completely re-drew the cultural landscape of the city and the relationship of the local agencies to it. As O'Connor notes:

> Whilst looking to the cultural flows associated with Olympic bids and 'international' concert halls Manchester was briefly thrust into the very centre of the global information flow in the guise of 'Madchester'. Almost invisible to the developers and local

politicians looking at one source of cultural capital, journalists, commentators and consumers headed for the city. They poured over its spaces as a new pop vernacular exploded in the city celebrating the intersection of global and local, a local production out of a global cultural flow (1994).

This cultural and technological flow may at first seem marginal, but in the UK the formal rave or house economy is conservatively estimated to be worth at least £2 bn p.a. (Henley Centre For Forecasting, 1994). It is now a major cultural industry with significant influence in fashion, design, pop music, festivals and creative new technologies. In Manchester it was the local configurations developed out of this pop cultural phenomenon which demanded to be recognized and which, perhaps inadvertently, secured a shift in the regulatory stance of the local state.

Almost by accident and despite the best efforts of regulatory systems rooted in the notion of city of production, Manchester had become 'Madchester' a Fun City where it was cool to be. Manchester made the cover of *Time* and *Newsweek* in the US; 40% of New Yorkers voted Manchester as the place in Britain they most wanted to visit. This also applied to students with applications to its three universities: up by 30%. Applications through the UCCA and PCAS admission systems were topped by Manchester University and Manchester Polytechnic for three years in succession. The wider economy also benefited as Manchester secured the relocation of governmental departments and major corporations. During the period 1988-1991 whilst traditional industries continued to fail MCC actively sought inward investment initially utilizing tired global formulas of 'place marketing' but eventually realizing the potential of the city's pop cultural production.

Anecdotal evidence suggests that Manchester's image as an exciting creative city led directly and indirectly to many relocations[9]. Tabloids, broadsheets, the music press and style magazines all revelled in the appropriation of the 'Madchester' theme, heralding each and every no hope 'scally' band as the next big thing and celebrating the city's new found *joi de vivre* at any given opportunity. Yet behind the media hyperbole the city centre was in the middle of a real transition of the cultural economy and the spatial arena in which it was situated.

The initial activity around the rave scene became focused in and around two clubs in the city centre one of which, the Haçienda, has become one of the city's most significant landmarks and major tourist attractions: 'Manchester's Eiffel Tower' according to lead singer of local band James (Redhead, 1993).

Unlike London where the rave scene flourished in the re-appropriated disordered spaces of warehouses and the orbital motor way system, Manchester's illegal rave scene was quickly corralled into the city centre by effective intelligence and surveillance by the police and the territorialized violence of organized criminals. Attempted suppression of this scene by implementation of explicit legalism focused this energy into a tightly policed city centre, traditionally the space of surveillance and demographic control. Yet instead of repression we found proliferation both in terms formal investment into the night-time economy and in the tactics of evasion, transgression and subversion utilized by consumers within it. Proliferation of consumption within this field can be read as an expression of deregulated desire which defies the ability of a regulatory system characterized by stasis to repress both the desire and the proliferation (Stanley 1995). It is the failure of this suppression, both nationally and locally, which forced the regulatory authorities to reassess their regulatory strategies **and** the object which they sought to regulate. In the process they opened the door to a re-evaluation of what the post-industrial city centre could and should be.

Despite the embedded planning regime club nights came and went in wave after wave of rhizomic activity. Producers and consumers staying one step ahead of both the surveillance of the police and the violence of organized crime. Each club changed its music and its appearance almost every night. Communication was and still is carried out using 'flyers' with a high design element which again fed into and out of Manchester's pop culture and its cultural industries (see Mole and Purvis this volume). This (pop) 'cultural capital' (Bourdieu 1984) was accrued by the consumers and producers in the night-time economy and its value redeemed and reconverted into economic value via a series of direct and indirect routes both in the formal and informal sectors.

'Going out' and taking Ecstasy became part of the everyday life for a significant section of the population(10). It was an everyday life of invention which in countless ways poached on the property of others (De Certeau 1989) — the regulatory authorities, property owners and the dealers. Through excess consumption was driven production. Minor shifts towards spatial deregulation facilitated proliferation of productive space and further productive consumption(ibid). For a moment it seemed the city was awash with new urban *flaneurs* eager to consume 'a fantastic melange of fictions and strange values' (Chambers 1987) in a movement which went beyond individualism towards the fluid *comunitas* proffered by Maffessoli's post-modern tribes (1988).

The move towards deregulation

During this time the city council was caught between several competing narratives. The repressive narratives of the police force with whom they were 'partners' in the complex and overlapping licensing regime and with whom their own officers were closely aligned, were counterposed by competing economic, functional and aesthetic narratives of a faltering regeneration programme. This had been kick-started by deregulation at the local level through the intervention of central government and CMDC but was now seen to be stalling in part due to embedded regulatory structure and practice in the Town Hall. Distinctly political-legal processes, designed to have a direct and consequential effect on the management of the economy at a local level, could be seen to be interacting with, but mainly opposing, global shifts associated with post-Fordism or a more flexible regime of accumulation.

Shifts in the discourses around the (de)regulation of the night-time economy and of the concrete policy coalitions and networks out of which local regulation arises become central to the function of this cultural economy. The new social, political and cultural networks that emerge with the shifts to the 'post-industrial', 'post-modern' or 'post-Fordist' city are crucial to the understanding of that process. Legitimacy gained under the 'grand compromise' of Fordism had been eroded and new strategies and alliances needed to be built. In contrast to the broadly Keynesian Welfare State indicative of Fordism, Jessop characterizes the would be post-Fordist state as one in which the local state would: 'promote product, process, organizational and market innovation and enhance the structural competitiveness of open economies mainly through supply-side intervention' (Jessop p.19). As Painter observes, this implies a shift in urban policy away from explicit concern 'with social and spatial equity' (p.286) towards initiatives which promote economic competitiveness of the private sector. These pressures were certainly apparent to the city council as they began to re-assess its relationship to the night-time economy in the run up to the Olympic bid of 1993.

Further pressures for deregulation were being exerted by the formal and informal networks of producers and consumers within the night-time economy. Political-legal deregulation would eventually entail the acceptance not only of a new mode of regulation for the city, which relied heavily in the spectacular and informal consumption in the night-time economy, but also an acceptance of the liminal and transgressive practices which it implicitly incorporates.

Popular culture, regeneration and political-legal deregulation

In Manchester the shift to a more flexible and indeed more reflexive regime of accumulation at the local level generally and the night-time economy in particular can be traced to a series of events and negotiations which centred around the future of a night-club, and arguably Manchester's most famous cultural artefact. The Haçienda by this time had come to represent a many sided free floating sign — of folk devils and moral panics, of organized crime, of ecstatic carnivalesque celebration, of global media flows, of artistic creativity, of tourism, as representative of cultural and economic transformation and as the site of competing regulatory discourses.

Given powers recently secured under the Entertainment's (Increased Penalties) Act 1990, the police could have permanently closed the Haçienda and every other club in the city where Ecstacy was being consumed and sold. However, caught between competing discourses of repression and proliferation, the police — now with a more enlightened Chief Constable — in consultation with the city council opted for the latter. The council leadership entered the debate with direct and public support for the Haçienda's Liquor and Entertainment's Licence. Almost overnight and despite the tragic deaths of two young people from Ecstacy use, implementation of political-legal regulation was reversed. Concurrently the city council began to reassess their own role in the licensing regime by bringing licensing officers, under the auspices of the Leaders office, where greater political control could be exercised. Regulation of

Manchester's Entertainment economy moved from the margins to the centre of the political debate in the city and became increasingly referenced to global economic shifts, de-industrialization and the reorganization of the city centre towards consumption in the night-time economy. Pat Karney, the (Labour) Chair of Arts and Leisure at MCC, stated that:

> ... we have to make this city attractive to potential investors in the area, we have a responsibility to the people of this city and to the people of the region to revitalise Manchester's economy. In the absence and continual decline of traditional industries jobs and wealth have to be secured from other sectors. Those jobs are gone forever, they are not coming back. The city's cultural and entertainment industry can not only provide new jobs but also make Manchester a better place to live, work and play. Expansion of this sector will allow us to compete for inward investment on a global stage ... it is central to the future of this city.(11)

This statement and the subsequent drive for deregulation in this field shows not only an awareness of the changing role for the local state in the management of the economy, but also how fragmented cultural production and consumption in the city was seen to offer a degree of economic stability while at the same time offering the city council a new role as 'enabler' of private consumption rather than 'provider' of collectively consumed goods and services. As the emphasis of urban policy shifted from the provision of these 'social goods' to the need to deal with economic restructuring, new political strategies were sought, not only to deal the social effects of de-industrialization but also to attempt to secure a new identity for the city and a sustained period of growth in this sector. Policies of political-legal deregulation in the night-time economy and the reorganization of local bureaucracies to facilitate inward investment can be read as a significant and symbolic attempt by the local state to come to terms with not only this new role, but also with wider economic and political realities.

During 1992-3 Manchester, along with Beijing, Sydney and Berlin, was bidding to host the Olympics in the year 2000. The (cultural) image of the city became all important as Manchester was thrust into a global media circus. Old practices associated with Fordism were swept aside, new licenses were granted to entrepreneurs, limits on the hours clubs could open were abolished, at first during the week and then into Sundays. Tables and chairs were allowed in the streets outside pubs, bars and cafes. Informal networks and policy forums were established in an attempt to formalize and legitimate rave culture and its supporting activity in the night-time economy.

The police dropped closure orders against the Haçienda after the installation of increased security, although the management of the Haçienda themselves closed the doors on the club for 6 months in May 1991 due to increased harassment of their door staff by organized gangs eager to control this prestigious and lucrative site. It was the violence surrounding drug distribution rather than drug use itself which closed the Haçienda and it is a violence which has now been incorporated into the formal economy of the city and its regulatory structure (but therein lies another story).

Is this the dawning of a 'New Era'?

Since this change of policy inward investment into the night-time economy has flourished. Club capacity has risen from 8,500 to 26,000. The past 3 years has seen the creation of 25 new cafe bars, 8 new night-clubs and numerous new restaurants[12]. Employment in the city centre night-time economy is estimated to be between 4 and 5,000[13] and for the person on the street Manchester has become a lively, vibrant and cosmopolitan place in which to spend their leisure time. A recent female interviewee remarked that despite continued restrictions imposed by national liquor licensing restrictions:

> Manchester offers so much more than it did a few years ago. There seems to be a more relaxed, convivial, 'European' flavour to the city at night. I feel safer in the streets and the new bars are so much more welcoming than the smoky old pubs we used to go to (13/5/95).

The city council now have monthly meetings with the Pub and Club Network which includes bar and club owners, DJs, promoters and artists. They liaise frequently with Lifeline, a pro-active drugs support agency and with other groups in the field. For the past five years they have operated a Safer Dancing Campaign which acknowledges widespread use of recreational drugs in clubs but aims to minimize the risk to the consumers by insisting on high health and safety standards within clubs and access to water, fresh air and first aid facilities. Through negotiations with club and pub owners they have recently initiated a Registration of Doorstaff Scheme which has attempted to reduce the violence in and around bars and clubs, most of which stemmed from the door staff themselves.

Various other formal and informal networks are involved in some way or other in the production and consumption of this economy. In an apparently post-Fordist settlement these networks will be implicated in the conflicts around new forms of political-legal regulation in this highly contested area. Though these negotiations are new and ongoing and have begun to throw up their own contradictions, it is clear that the hierarchical and embedded structures associated with the Fordist regulatory regime have begun to give way to a flatter, more responsive system of urban governance in the city. As Featherstone has noted:

> ... the 'decontrolled control of emotions pursued by the individual, the relaxation of codes that accompanied the informalization process are also favoured by organizational structures which shift towards 'management through negotiation rather than management through command (Featherstone, 1992, p.45).

It is clear that this ethos has been delayed in the UK and it is only now, with a shift towards a post-Fordist cultural economy, that the benefits (and problems) of these shifts are becoming clear to the local state.

Conclusion

Deregulation of the night-time economy represents not only a policy of informalization which has facilitated proliferation in this new city of pleasure, but also a search for legitimation by the local state through the provision of cultural space and an ongoing courtship of cultural producers and consumers. It serves notice of a recognition on the part of the local state of shifts towards the city as a place of consumption and a new public realm of socialization. Yet it is still unclear whether negotiations around the night-time economy in Manchester, which demonstrate the ability of the local state to adopt post-Fordist forms of governance, signal a wider acceptance of post-Fordist structures **within** the local state. Negotiations in the night-time economy were forced through more by political expediency and strategic failure rather than any macro-economic foresight or planning.

Negotiations currently under way in Manchester and other British cities surrounding the regulation of the night-time economy present a raft of new and difficult challenges for those charged with the governance of this restructured urban realm. They ask questions about whether this civic space of the late twentieth century can be made to work in the flesh, on the streets, or whether this is merely nostalgia for some nineteenth century city that never was (O'Connor and Lovatt, op cit). The night-time is a liminal time in which the world of work is seen to lose its hold. A time for and of transgression, a time for spending, a time for trying to be something the daytime may not let you be, a time for meeting people you shouldn't, for doing things your parents told you not to, that your children are too young to understand. This is now being promoted as vibrancy. But this invitation to transgression, marginal in the Fordist city of work is now central to contemporary consumerism. Its success depends as much on curbing the intolerance of the 'respectable classes' — who include the regulatory authorities — as it does about accommodating the needs and desires of living expressive popular cultures.

In Manchester this new form of governance has demonstrated some of the characteristics ascribed to post-Fordism. Cultural negotiations have been pushed to the fore and cultural producers and consumers have become, nominally at least, partners in the regulatory and regeneration strategies of the city. This shift is demonstrated by the recognition on the part of the regulatory authorities of marginal practices in everyday life and the incorporation of marginal groups into the regulatory structure of the city. This signals the recognition by the formerly hierarchical power structure of the centrality of informal and even extra-legal activities within the city's night-time economy and a marginalization of law to facilitate political, cultural and economic objectives. This in turn will have its own repercussions. Nevertheless the local state tactics still continually resort to the safety of Fordist practice — there is always a new way to say no.

The deliberate law-making (regulation) and law-undoing

(deregulation) in this terrain challenge those regulation theorists who eschew local negotiations and the 'conscious and active intervention by the state' (*réglementation*) (Boyer, op cit) in favour of a more abstract notion where the 'regulation of economic life is neither wholly deliberate or automatic' (Painter, op cit) to adopt less rigid interpretations. Without detail of local and specific political and cultural conflict which frequently results in political-legal adjustment in the process of urban management, regulation theory can justifiably fall victim to charges of teleology and functionalism caught up in its own logic of development from one regime of accumulation to the next.

Whether the emergence of these new cultural and regulatory networks signals the emergence of a new post-Fordist settlement is open to question, particularly given the embeddedness of local practice and the lack of political will within local authorities to dislodge it. What we can see is the emergence of 'competing political strategies in response to the decline of Fordist arrangements' (Painter, op cit). These competing strategies are present at the political, economic and cultural level and come into clear focus when set out in relation to current revitalization programmes. What has been seen however is that when a system of local governance adopts the characteristics of post-Fordism, and where the local state becomes sensitive to the language of (popular) culture, real benefits can be accrued with the creation of a new vibrant and **inter**active public realm.

Notes

1   Here we understand 'regulation' as the organizing dynamics of the economy, which are neither wholly deliberate nor automatic; the economy as a complex whole of which the night-time economy is a part. A change in the order of intervention here designed to facilitate greater flexibility in the regime of accumulation; the relationship between investment, production and in this instance, cultural consumption stand to reflect possible wider societal changes.

2   According to Lipietz, the 'grand compromise' of Fordism is achieved through social democratic political settlement. Here a degree of political power is offered to certain (organized) sections of the working class in exchange for a degree of toleration of capitalist relations of productions (Painter).

3   'Governance' draws on Foucault's more positive, constructive notion of law; a law that forms part of a complex set of institutions, discourses and practices through which power operates (*Discipline and Punish*, 1982; *The History of Sexuality*, 1978).

4   Manchester's Olympic Bid and its cultural strategy 'Manchester First' incorporated a safe notion of the city's NTE, preferring to cite the grandeur of the Palace Theatre or Opera House rather than its pop culture. Nevertheless both incorporated a sense of the NTE which could be used to sell the city.

5   Interview with J. O'Connor and K. Milestone, 1993.

6   This figure was quoted by Carol Ainscow co-owner of Manto's Bar and Paradise Factory night-club in an interview with the author on 28 June 1993. It was later repeated to the *Manchester Evening News*. Without objections from the police or city council, licences would be issued by the magistrate for £12. After a concerted press campaign this practice has now ceased.

7   Case of GMP vs. Michael Snailham witnessed by the author November 1992.

8   Whittle, S. *The Margins of the City*, 1994. For a critical account of Manchester's accommodation of the gay community within a revitalized city centre.   Also, Milestone, K., *Pop Cultural Tourism*, PhD. Thesis, MIPC, 1995.

10   Interview with Steve Carr, Principle Officer at Economic Initiatives Group at Manchester City Council. Here he recounts how the British Council made their decision to relocate to Manchester after an oblique pitch by council officers about Manchester's youth culture and consultation with their siblings (March 1993).

11   Taped interview 8/6/93.

12   Figures supplied by police and City Council Licensing departments, December 1994.

13   Data obtained in a survey of all Manchester's licensed premises late 1994 during a period of intense debate on the future of licensing in the city. We received a 40% return of our questionnaires.

References

Aglietta, M. (1979), *A Theory of Capitalist Regulation: the US Experience,* Verso, London.

Bianchini, F. & Parkinson, M. (1993), *Cultural Policy and Urban Regeneration,* Manchester University Press, Manchester.

Bourdieu, P. (1984), *Distinction,* Macmillan, London.

Boyer, R. (1990), *The Regulation School: A Critical Introduction,* Columbia University Press. New York.

Chambers, I. (1987), *Popular Culture: The Metropolitan Experience,* Routledge, London.

Chevigny, P. (1992), *Gigs: Jazz and the Caberet Laws in New York City,* Routledge, New York.

Greater Manchester Police, Chief Constables report of 1965

Clarke, T. J. (1985), *The Painting of Modern Life,* Thames Hudson, London.

De Certeau, M. (1988), *The Practice Of Everday Life,* California University Press, California.

Featherstone, M. (1992), *Consumer Culture and Postmodernism,* Sage, London.

Goodwin, M. (1993), 'The City as Commodity: The Contested Spaces of Urban Development', in G. Kearns and C. Philo (eds.), *Selling Places: The City As Cultural Capital, Past And Present.* Pergamon, Oxford.

Harvey, D. (1989), *The Condition Of Postmodernity,* Blackwell, Oxford.

Jessop, B. (1993), 'Towards a Schumpeterian Workfare State? Preliminary Remarks on Post-Fordist Economy', in *Studies in*

Political Economy, No.40 (Spring).

Lash, S. & Urry, J. (1994), *Economies of Signs and Space,* Sage, London.

Lipietz, A. (1992), *Towards a New Economic Order: Postfordism, Ecology and Democracy,* Polity, Cambridge.

Manchester City Council (1992), Economic Initiatives Brochure.

Mole, P. (1995), 'Fordism, Post-Fordism and the Contemporary City', in J. O'Connor & D. Wynne (eds.) *From the Margins To the Centre,* Arena, Aldershot.

Montgomery, J. (1990), *Manchester First.* MCC Cultural Policy Document, MCC, 1993.

O'Connor, J. & Lovatt, A. (1995), 'The City and The Night-time Economy', in *Planning, Practice and Research,* Vol.10, No.2

O'Connor, J. (1994), 'Whose City, Whose Civilisation?' in *Regenerating Cities,* No.5.

O'Connor,J. & Wynne, D. (1994), *From the Margins to the Centre,* MIPC Working Paper.

Painter, J. (1995), 'Regulation Theory, Post Fordism and Urban Politics', in D. Judge, G. Stoker & H. Wolman (eds.) *Theories Of Urban Politics,* Sage, London.

Raban, J. (1988), *Soft City,* Harper Collins, London.

Redhead, S. (1993), 'The Politics of Ecstacy', in S. Redhead (ed.) *Rave Off: Politics and deviance in Contemporary Youth Culture,* Avebury, Aldershot.

Sassen, S. (1991), *The Global City,* Princeton University Press, Princeton.

Seigal, J. (1986), *Bohemian Paris,* Viking, New York.

Stanley, C. (1993), 'Repression and Resistance: Problems of Regulation in Contemporary Urban Culture (Part I: Towards a Definition)', in *International Journal of the Sociology of Law*, No.21.

Zukin, S. (1981), *Loft Living*, (2nd. Edition), Hutchinson/Radius, London.

Zukin, S. (1991), *Landscapes of Power: From Detroit To Disneyland*, California University Press, California.

6 The space that difference makes: Negotiation and urban identities through consumption practices

Jenny Ryan and Hilary Fitzpatrick

Introduction

The debate on changes in urban culture and the city in late (post)modernity is one which has become focused upon trends in consumption practices, lifestyle and lifeworld interests, and a re-conceptualization of the processes of individualization and community. The study of consumption rather than production has come to the fore through the recognition of fundamental changes in how work and non-work activities figure in the ways in which individuals locate, and identify, themselves in their social world(s). Consumption in/of the city carries therefore resonance of the negotiation of identity, and of a sense of belonging, which generate the meanings of space and place. The ways in which the individual makes sense of the city draws upon reservoirs of meaning, cultural resources for reading its spaces and places, which themselves are products of this negotiation. At the level of the individual and of cultural formations, the meanings encoded in particular spaces and places are thus contingent upon the specific ways in which space is produced. At the same time the cultural resources available for this sense making operation embed the cultural (structural) changes at work in a more global sense. Consumption in/of the city has to be located within the patterns of global economics, communication and commodification characteristic of late (post)modernity. Translated into particular locales these wider processes impact upon local patterns of consumption; in particular upon the ways in which desire and wants become packaged for lifestyle projects in consumer goods or consumption spaces. The global and the local interpenetrate in the meanings that are embedded in the everyday lifeworlds of the city.

The purpose of this analysis is to ground this perspective of consumption and the city in such lifeworld experiences, to explore how it can be useful for explaining the production of spaces in the city. It draws upon research into the production and consumption of sites of leisure in the city of Manchester, England; sites which can be seen as catering for specific groups of young adults previously marginal in cultural terms to the city's pattern of leisure consumption. In the process these spaces become inscribed and encoded with meanings which are constantly renegotiated in the social practices of both those who 'produce' and those who 'consume' them. These social meanings are further stretched over time as differential social usage over day, evening and night-time creates a temporal ordering and negotiation of their cultural significance for different groups of urban consumers. In analysing the social construction of these sites of consumption as 'contested spaces' in the city, the chapter argues that this enables a reading of how 'difference' and 'identity' are constructed and regulated within urban culture, with a particular focus on gender and sexuality. This perspective suggests that the social construction of difference can be seen as a process which stretches over time and space, involving the manipulation of the resources that particular sites of consumption afford for the negotiation of identities in the city.

Space and identity in the city

Given the preoccupation of geographers with the 'spatial' it is not surprising that contributions from within that discipline have been central to the constructions of the 'spatial' within the modernity/postmodernity debate. In particular the work of Harvey (1989) and Soja (1989) provided new ways of critiquing the importance of space and time in the project of modernity at societal/global levels whilst also re-emphasising the importance of their 'local' articulation in specific forms of social, economic and political relations. The social construction of space in terms of the exercise of power is recognized by Harvey within a Marxist problematic in which:

The common-sense rules which define the 'time' and 'place' for everything ... are certainly used to achieve and replicate particular distributions of social power (1989, p.227).

This formulation directs attention to how the production of space and time enters into the processes of capital accumulation and the reproduction of the capital formation. The social struggles through which this exercise of power is resisted are recognized by Harvey but, as his critics argue, within a frame that prioritizes the power relations of capitalism as crucial to spatial practices, rather than elaborating the spatial and temporal dynamics of other power struggles (Massey, 1991; Deutsche, 1991; Morris, 1992; Ryan, 1994). Similarly the work of Soja (1989), another Marxist geographer who defines spatiality in terms of the inscription of relations of power and discipline, has recently been described as economic reductionist in his approach (Keith and Pile, 1993).

It is therefore within the transcendence of purely Marxist questions in the analysis of the production of space that cultural geographers are linking spatial practices to those of wider questions of identity construction and power struggles in local arenas (Keith and Pile, 1993; Duncan and Ley, 1993). This work has particularly drawn attention to the urban landscape as constructed through competing spatialities — social meanings inscribed in space. These meanings are invoked in the use made of the physical spaces of the city, in a process in which the multiplicity of spatialities (meanings) and the power relations of which they are constituted (relations) give rise to struggle over what is termed 'the politics of identity' (Keith and Pile 1993, p.38). It is such a struggle over the construction and negotiation of identities that makes the sites chosen for this analysis especially relevant. The meanings that are being constructed of these spaces constitute a cultural struggle in terms of issues of marginality and centrality of different identities and of the crossovers between different cultural formations in the city.

The concern of cultural geographers to map out the meanings of places and spaces in this way demonstrates the cross over of ideas between this discipline and that of sociology. In particular, within social theory, the contribution made by Giddens (1990; 1991) to the modernity/postmodernity debate about identity has been to stress that a defining feature of (late) modern subjectivitys is that of the condition of reflexivity. For Giddens the process of self identity becomes 'a reflexively organised endeavour' (1991, p.5) in which the individual constructs a self narrative to give coherence and account for 'the finite lifespan given changing circumstances' (1991, p.215). In this chapter the notion of reflexivity is employed to characterize the ways in which negotiations of spatial meanings are embedded in the constructions of urban identities. What is challenged however is the idea that there is, as Giddens suggests, a 'self' that is being 'authenticated' by this process of reflexivity. We follow Kellner (1992) in suggesting that the possibility of individuals pursuing multiple identities invokes a different construct of 'self' as 'more multiple, transitory and open' (Kellner, 1992, p.158). This construct allows for the process of ambiguity and contestation in spatial practices as individuals simultaneously seek to sustain different identities. But we would not go as far as Kellner does in the degree of autonomy he ascribes to the individual in this process of self realization. He argues:

> In contemporary society it may be more 'natural' to change identities, to switch with the changing winds of fashion ... one can always change one's life, that identity can always be re-constructed, that one is free to change and produce oneself as one chooses (Kellner, 1992 p.154).

Our analysis suggests a more stressful and contested struggle over identities; who, where and when, one is free to express oneself is located within wider ideological constructions of what are marginal and central identity formations. Reflexivity is a construct that can usefully be employed to analyze how individuals position themselves, not only in relation to multiple identities, but in relation to this ideological struggle. That struggle is also about a sense of belonging, of appropriating space for oneself and others, of being 'at home' in the city.

The spatial referent of this process is contained in the notion that the fracturing and fragmentation of identities is lived out within the definition of different spatial locations — both in a physical and social-spatial sense. This is suggested, for example, by Mort (1988) and Holland (1994) in relation to young men experiencing the shifting relations between work and consumption, and by MacRobbie (1994) and Miles (1993) in describing the position of young women within youth cultures. Our interest is in exploring how particular social spatializations are produced as individuals negotiate their multiple identities in their spatial practices. The consumption practices with

172

which we are concerned are theorized within the debate about cultural consumption, consumption aesthetics and the construction of lifestyles (Jameson, 1984; Bourdieu, 1984; Featherstone, 1991; Lash and Urry, 1994). The opening up of new life spaces through the material conditions of consumer culture, through commodification, finds particular expression in the urban spaces with which our analysis is concerned. That these life spaces are also sites of, and cited in, cultural struggles over hegemony is a crucial part of our story.

Sites of meaning and city spaces

Our use of the construct 'social spatialization' follows that of Shields (1991), although our analysis moves away from his in significant respects. Shields draws from Lefebvre (1991) the insight that spatial meanings are constituted within a dialectical process in which spatial practices, representations of space and representational spaces relate in a state of perpetual tension to one another. This provides a way of juxtaposing the 'lived' spaces of existing social practices with different kinds of social practice; what Lefebvre termed the knowledge (meanings) and practices of space embedded in the power structures of (capitalist) society (representational spaces) and that knowledge (meanings) and those practices which arise out of challenges to hegemony (spaces of representation). In the latter Lefebvre draws attention to the ways in which spaces become 'imagined' as different by individuals and groups, and thus their spatial practices can contest and subvert dominant meanings. Shields uses Lefebvre, but also Bourdieu and Foucault, to frame his analysis of the dynamics of place — mythologies that are constructed through this dialectical process. In the particular work being referred to his concern is with how places become lived, represented and 'imagined' in terms of cultural and physical marginality (Shields, 1991, p.4). It is the place mythologies themselves that become the focus of each of his case studies.

By contrast our analysis attempts to first of all understand how previously 'marginal' spaces become 'central' in urban culture, and secondly how urban experience of this centrality is constructed through the on going negotiation of identities in particular spaces. This involves us in, first of all, describing the physical spaces upon which we focus, their physical location as sites within the (city) centre. Secondly we locate these physical sites within the cultural changes taking place in how the consumption of pleasure in the city is organized; the focus upon particular spaces as central sites of pleasure. Our third concern is with the centrality of particular spaces as sites of identity formation. The multiple meanings given to the term 'space', and use of spatial constructs in this way, enables us to explore the construction of spatiality as a dynamic process of contested meanings and actions.

The particular space being analysed here is a cafe bar in the city centre of Manchester: in the text given the fictitious name of 'Otto's Bar'. The bar is located in what is known, locally, regionally and nationally as the 'Gay Village'. This area, together with other parts of the city centre, has become 'central' to the strategy of urban revitalization through the promotion of cultural industries (O'Connor and Wynne, 1995).(1) Hence at one level the spatial significance of the bar can be read within the physical and cultural centrality of the area within which it is located as a site of cultural consumption in the city. The meanings encoded in this process have become part of new place mythologies surrounding Manchester as a post industrial city.

> Manchester marries the panache of a cosmopolitan city with the informal fun of a friendly town. And knows how to enjoy both ... Lifestyle Manchester is all about choice. Lived in your own style at a pace that gives you time to spare (Manchester City Council, 1992).

Youth culture is defined as central within this siting of Manchester city centre as consumption space.

> All over Europe Manchester is idolised by young people as the centre for music, fashion and style. From clubs like the Hacienda to the seminal sounds like Simply Red and Happy Mondays Manchester is the culture of a generation (Manchester City Council 1992).

This sense of the cultural centrality of Manchester city centre, as not only where things happen but as showing the way to other cities in the region, is echoed in the sentiments of the cultural intermediaries who have been responsible for setting up new bars and clubs in the city centre.(2)   How different definitions of this centrality develop and change over time is illustrated by how three competing, but inter-penetrating and in some sense inter-dependent, spatializations are invoked; Manchester as Madchester, Gunchester and Gaychester. Talking about the introduction of gay spaces in the club scene of the early 1990s:

> *The thing about Flesh* (a monthly gay night at a Manchester club) *is that it had a fantastic media profile right from the   start because it came right after Madchester, Gunchester.   And Gaychester fitted really nicely into a new story for Manchester. So it* (Flesh) *got a news coverage out of all proportion to what a normal club might get.   You know we had the Observer, the Independent, The Guardian, all the serious papers doing articles on Gaychester, right?*(3)

The emergence of Manchester as the Gay Capitol of the North has been documented elsewhere (Hindle, 1994; Whittle, 1994; Evans, 1994).   The building up of a critical mass of gay culture is also associated with the earlier prominence of the city in the mid-1980s with the new youth music from which the Madchester image emerged (Brown, 1994; Redhead, 1993; Rietveld, 1995).   Both imaginings of the city became also juxtaposed with its other, darker image as Gunchester, to the notoriety of the city for violence and access to weapons.   The city of pleasure evoked by these three spatializations emphasizes both the dark and light side of the consumption of desires. It is within this cultural context that the sites of consumption with which our analysis is concerned emerged.

Otto's Bar provided from its inception a new gay space in the city. In describing the emergence of the Gay Village it is credited with a special significance:

> *I think Otto's helped a lot and I shouldn't leave them out of my story because actually, 1991, I think Otto's opening did make a big difference because although it wasn't a club space, it provided a meeting place for alternative gays around to come together and that obviously was when we started to launch Flesh, it gave a meeting place and a promotion to people that they wouldn't otherwise have had.*(4)

175

The importance of this kind of space, at this time, lies in the struggle and contestation over what the club scene in Manchester signified, and whom it catered for.

> *Although in 1988, and into 1989, the straight scene was fantastic in Manchester, it had by the early 1990s settled into what became known as Gunchester, em, from Madchester to Gunchester in two short years really and the clubs had become extremely straight, sort of mixed crowds that, compared to the early acid house parties, has a vaguely intimidating atmosphere.*(5)

Bars, such as Otto's thus provided an opening up of gay spaces in the city centre but, as we emphasize in our analysis, within an overall cultural context where the juxtaposition of interests of straights and gays in the consumption of the scene was always a feature, even if this accommodation is at times tense and stressful. Part of this cultural equation lies in the way in which gay culture in the nineties has become a part of the mainstream cultures of consumption.(6) In Manchester gay culture, to some degree, submerges into what is taken to be 'trendy urban living'. This facilitates, but does not necessarily account for, the transformation of its spaces from 'marginal' back street, seedy venues to the new, liminal, public spaces that celebrate diverse post-modern architectural aesthetics.

Otto's, as a bar space demonstrates this new aestheticization of gay spaces. It was set up in 1991 for young gay people disillusioned with the given scene and who where tired of being classed as either 'clones' or 'camp'. It was also seen as a space for lesbian women whose participation on the scene had been marginal, catered for by 'private' support networks and groups and space within the alternative political cultures of student and feminist politics.(7)

The architecture and interior design of Otto's, as a bar space, set a precedent for the creation of gay spaces in the Gay Village. Its physical location in the city centre is made more visible by a glass frontage which allows direct visual access from the outside to the activities within, and from the inside to the city outside. The design and furnishing of its interior celebrated Italian post-modern style incorporating an 'art' gallery that also serves as a 'gazing' space onto the open plan ground floor below. This is laid out, and functions as, a 'catwalk' display arena surrounded by more discrete tables and chairs. Visibility and the expressivity of performance are thus stressed in the ambience created which satisfies both the commercial demands of niche marketing of consumption and makes a statement about gay culture in its movement from the margins to the centre.

Because it is both 'trendy' and 'gay', the space it provides makes visible the potential tensions between different groups of urban consumers. As such it is inherently then a contested space that has to be managed by rules of inclusion and exclusion operated by both the 'producers' and 'consumers'.(8)   For example, the employment of doormen and door policies operating at particular times of the day or week focus the bar for its gay consumption, whilst the customers themselves seek, not always necessarily successfully to apply their own moral pressure to appropriate the space for themselves. The conflicts that both kinds of activities can generate will be returned to later.

To some degree the social regulation of space, and the containment of conflict, is accommodated within the temporal ordering of its significance for different groups of consumers throughout the day. The central location of the bar attracts a day-time custom of lunch customers and coffee drinkers from the surrounding offices, shops and businesses of the city centre. This usage stretches into the afternoon without any particular significance in terms of either sexuality or gender, but is class defined. In this temporal phase it becomes a comfortable, trendy, relaxed space to drink coffee, read newspapers, play chess and generally observe and be observed in the city outside the glass frame. By early to mid evening the atmosphere changes; it becomes more sexually loaded and more determinedly gay as the space becomes transformed both as a 'cruising' space and into a pre-club venue for gay men and lesbian women. On evenings towards the end of the week, and over the weekend, it also becomes charged with the ambiguities resulting from its use by straight clubbers, faghags and urban voyeurs. At these times the intervention of those managing the bar, their operation of inclusion and exclusion rules is crucial. The way liminality is negotiated at these times is particularly interesting because it affords insight into how the two scenes of gay and straight culture relate together. The locking in of the bar with the future of the gay club scene in the city is illustrated with the recent provision of a (non-alcoholic) 'Breakfast Bar', opening after the clubs close to provide a space for clubbers to prolong their pleasure in the city. It can be anticipated that this will require particular effort to preserve it as a gay space, given its potential attraction to straight clubbers.

As a mixed space the cafe bar is also charged with the ambiguities that arise from the shifting temporal ordering of space for consumption by different types of customers. This can be illustrated in the growing popularity of the bar, between 5-8 pm weekdays, for 'straight' men using it as a drinking place after work. Bar staff are drawn into conversations with such customers in which the customers straight domestic lives are discussed sometimes at length. This causes some mirth for the (gay male) staff concerned because they sense that the customers don't realize that 'they are discussing their straight lives with gay men'. This inability to 'read' the identities of others is part of not only the changing nature of the bar's space within the two cultures (gay and straight) in the city, but also of the fluidity and flux within which these identities are constructed and expressed in dress codes and other signs. The ambiguities created make the transformation of liminality into known, stable spatial meanings more confused and confusing for all concerned. The possibilities of a mild flirtation with the Other (gay or straight depending on whose perspective is being addressed) may be opened up by this liminal consumption space in the city.

The dynamics of the appropriation of space by different groups are further revealed by the ways in which the internal design of the bar is used for opportunities to observe and be observed by different consumers. The gallery space overlooking the central floor area below provides a natural surveillance site recognized by both those doing the observing and those being observed. It provides a vantage point for the spectacle of the presentation of 'self' (Goffman, 1956, 1963). What is critical for the meanings encoded in the use of this vantage point is who appropriates it and who is marginalized by this appropriation. Both observational and interview data confirms that it is young gay men who monopolize the frontal balcony area, with older gay men standing by ground floor doorways, and lesbians occupying the more backstage tables and chairs outside the central floor space, outside of the glare of the 'catwalk'. As a gay space in the city the bar is also a contested space in terms of gay and lesbian identities, a theme to which we shall return later. This kind of understanding of centrality and marginality is a significant feature which has to be unpacked in order to understand the spatial politics of the gay scene in the city.

Reflexivity, consumption and identity

The tensions observed in Otto's Bar also echo the problematic relationship between gender and sexuality as identity formations. The relevance of differences between gay and lesbian spatialities is discussed in other literature (see Winchester and White, 1988; Adler and Brenner, 1992; Valentine, 1992, 1993; Bell et al, 1994; Whittle, 1994; Bell and Valentine, 1995). We discuss these issues in relation to the production of the bar space by both the bar management staff and the customers. In the case of the former it is suggested that those who work behind the bar may be perhaps more typically carriers of the 'post-modern' cultural concerns with aestheticization and lifestyle than found in other similar bar work settings. In their pursuit of identity they blur the distinction between work and consumption, as one of our interviewees expressed it 'to me leisure time is work time, and vice versa. If I didn't enjoy it I wouldn't do it'. Our interviewees who worked the bar defined themselves very much as part of the scene they serviced.[9]

> R: *Well, as a student, and not having any money I knew I'd have to get a job. I had been thinking about Otto's for ages, and it seemed like the logical choice. I was in there all the time anyway spending a lot of money.*
> I: *What, so you could still be there by earning money instead of spending it?*
> R: *Yeah, exactly, and also it seemed the only way to meet lots of other gay women. Manchester is good for its social scene but sometimes it can be cliquey and pretentious and you don't really want to walk up to people out of the blue and start chatting. Standing behind the bar you can talk to whosoever you want and can definitely make a lot of friends. I met my girlfriend in here.*
> I: *So what's happened to your social life since you started working here?*
> R: *Oh God, it has exploded. You know it's the only way to do it.*
> I: *Could you see yourself working in a straight bar now, or in the future?*
> R: *No, I can't because in Otto's it's not like work. Well, yes it is, because I'm earning but all my friends come in and the rest of the staff are great.*
> I: *Is Otto's your place as such?*

179

R: Oh yeah, of course it is. It's my second home!

This convivial work atmosphere is reinforced by the ways in which the staff of the bar socialize after work, at the very clubs for which the bar serves as a pre-club venue. The introduction of the Breakfast Bar extends both work opportunities and pleasure time for the staff as well as the space it creates for the clubbing customers.

However this out of work socializing is framed within the negotiation of the difference between a gay men and a lesbian woman.

R: Oh yeah, after we finish we all go to Paradise together.(Paradise is the name of a club). We'll all hang about together for a bit and have a drink and then the women go upstairs to the women only bit and the men stay downstairs.

Attention needs to be drawn to the positioning of gay men and lesbian women in analysing the contested spaces of gay culture. To further this argument we explored how the customers of the gay bar defined, and negotiated, their interests within the city's gay scene. In particular, unlike Whittle (1994) who analysed the scene from the viewpoint of gay men, our focus is upon exploring the spatial meanings and practices of lesbian women. In the sense that they are defined as 'Other' in relation to both gay men and heterosexual men and women, their multiple positioning affords particular insights into the processes both of hegemony and resistance.

As also described by Valentine (1992, 1993) our analysis suggests that in 'coming out' as lesbians, our interviewees put a geographical distance between the location of their new identities and their old. In addition however the attraction of Manchester as Gaychester evoked a sense of safety and 'home' within which to establish the roots to sustain the new identity and lifestyle as lesbians.

I: Could you have come out in ... (names place where brought up)
R: You must be joking! No, Manchester seemed the perfect place to do it, you know, the Gay Village and all the different sorts of people. No (names birthplace) would have been a nightmare!
I: Why in particular?
R: Because like these bars there are not like Otto's or whatever. The lesbians and gay men they attract are like real clones. You

know, men with leather jackets and caps and handle bar
moustaches. and the women with skinheads and beer bellies. Oh
God, it was awful. Real stereotypes of what straights think of us
gays.
I: So you felt intimidated then?
R: Oh yeah, (names birthplace) would have been a scary place to
come out in. I had to go to Manchester.

The lesbian customers and staff of the bar identified themselves
within what has been described elsewhere as the growing diversity of
the lesbian subculture. Up to the late seventies the depiction of
lesbian identity as either 'butch' or 'femme' mirrored the hegemonic
discourse of heterosexual patriarchy (Martin and Lyon, 1983 quoted
in Valentine, 1992). The creation of a more politicized androgynous
style of the eighties, as a resistance to this hegemony, has itself been
superseded by the emergence of yet further performative styles
through which to express multiple lesbian identities (Bell et al, 1994).
Our interviewees, in their discussion of their own spaces within the
lesbian scene, locate the problems and troubles of constructing
identity within this more fluid and fragmented cultural formation.

In talking about the one gay, women only, club she had previously
visited and in which she had felt uncomfortable one of our
interviewees felt:

R: You know, when you're there, you feel quite different from
them. They're quite tough and well look like dykes. My
girlfriend and I prefer feminine women. Well, that's what we are
after all!

The troubled relationship between hyper heterosexual style and
gay/lesbian identities is analysed by Bell at al (1994) in relation to
Lipstick Lesbianism and the London Skinhead look for gay men. How
hyper feminine lesbian style can be transgressive, and can carry the
opportunity of destabilizing heterosexual spaces is witnessed in the
inability of straight people to read lesbian identities in unproblematic
ways. Not only is this seen as troublesome for heterosexual men but
it has implications for heterosexual women also (Bell, 1994 p.42).

'Lipstick style' therefore has the potential to make heterosexual
women question how their own appearance is read, to challenge

how they see other women and hence to undermine the production of heterosexual space.

Without going here into the argument about whether this process of destabilization does in fact undermine patriarchy the significance of this analysis for our purposes is in the raising of the troubles of reading identities from performance to which it gives rise.

In particular this refers for us to how lesbians negotiate their multiple identities of sexuality within the dualism of gender identities. Our analysis suggests the importance of both processes in relation to the gay spaces with which we are concerned. The struggles within Gaychester, for spaces by gay men and lesbian women, is therefore more than just evidence of the contestation created by gay male culture being absorbed and made more central within hegemonic heterosexual city culture. The focus of struggle is also upon lesbians attempting to appropriate space as both 'lesbian' and 'women' within both the discourses of the gay male culture and of the heterosexual culture of the city.

The spatial problematic through which to understand gay culture was first raised by Adler and Brenner (1992) in their response to Castells' (1983) assertion that gay men and lesbian women have different spatial interests. According to Castells gay men seek to dominate space (because they behave as 'men') whilst lesbians do not have the same territorial aspirations (because they behave first and foremost as women). Adler and Brenner challenged whether this was accountable for as a cultural difference, or one located in the different material resources that gay men and lesbians had access to because they were (also) men and women. However cultural difference was attributed to the differential access to public space that being men or women afforded gay men and lesbians. This for Adler and Brenner explained why informal friendship networks and 'private' spaces were especially crucial for lesbians as access to sociability and relationship formation.(10) Our data also confirms the conclusions of earlier research that 'safe' gay spaces are particularly valued by lesbians now more than ever before. This can be attributed, in part, to the greater difficulties of reading off lesbian identity, what our interviewees referred to as 'dyke spotting', from clues of dress or body language. This is made more difficult when both systems of signs are now much more fluid and liminal across both heterosexual and gay culture.

Our argument here is that these tensions are heightened as public spaces become more significant for lesbians in terms of both their sexuality and their gender identities. New battle lines over the appropriation of space are being drawn up because of these changes. In Manchester in a gay scene that is acknowledged as being dominated by gay men, this creates particular tensions as lesbians struggle for their own space. Our data however suggests that this is not reflected in any simple constructions of what this means in terms of either gay men and lesbians sharing spaces or of lesbians, gay men and 'straights' occupying the same space. The meanings given to the tensions are diverse and problematical for the lesbian women we interviewed.

> *I: Do you think there are any tensions between the gay men and women in Otto's?*
> *R: (lesbian bar worker) Well, I can only really speak for myself. I don't have any problems with gay men. I know some gay women who do, you know the radical political lot who want to separate. And I know some gay men who hate lesbians, well hate women, in general but in Otto's I don't really come across that. But I'm sure it happens in the Village.*

For others the tensions are more apparent. For another of our (lesbian) interviewees the high profile of gay men within the gay community, and the greater amount of respect they were shown was evidence, she felt, of a greater legitimacy for men to express their sexuality. In her eyes this was a reflection of the straight world where 'all girls are slags and all boys heroes'. As a result lesbians tended not to be so demonstrative and were more passive in their use of the spaces. This confirms our earlier ethnographic observations of the backstage position of lesbians in occupying the Otto's bar space.

The potential conflict of interests between gay men and lesbian women is also referred to in our data in accounts of particular incidents that happen in the bar. In one such incident, much to the consternation and annoyance of the gay women concerned, some gay men starting using the facilities of the women's toilets in the bar. This was interpreted in accounts of the incident as a real infringement of 'women's' space at Otto's, and evidence of the marginalization of both sexual and gender identities for women customers of the bar.

This fear of marginalization, and the anger expressed towards it, is also reflected in the observations of yet another of our interviewees (a lesbian customer of the bar) who shared her feelings about the unequal spatial positioning, in relation to both sexuality and gender, within both the gay scene generally and the Otto's bar space in particular.

Recounting the lesbian baiting that she and her girlfriend had experienced outside Paradise Factory (renowned as a gay club venue) by men she identified as 'straight' she went on to deplore their behaviour in particular.

> R: And then they actually went in the bloody Paradise Factory ... at the door they thought they were being quizzed about their sexuality so they pretended to be gay to get in the place.

The attitude amongst straight and gay men in general towards 'lesbian only spaces' and her feelings about being in male dominated spaces is discussed by our interviewee.

> I: Hang on, this (Paradise Factory) is a women only space?
> R: No, the women only space is on the third floor, and like, they don't half get their knickers in a twist don't they, you know, as soon as we (emphasis) have got a (emphasis) third floor of a bloody night-club for one night of the week (laughs) and you know, you'd think we were taking over the entire town, or something. Oh God we're not even allowed to do that, they just, like, they have to hassle us and have to take the piss and have to like, if they can't go somewhere. And like there's loads of places we can't go, there's loads of places that are male dominated, but if they can't go somewhere, oh my God!
> I: This is with heterosexual men? But you also talked to me before about conflicts with gay men?
> R: Yeah, (about walking through the Gay Village) that struck me, I don't know whether this was this summer or last, it was just like, it was a summer's evening, it would have been about 5 o'clock right and em, and it was a nice evening and for some reason .I was walking through there and like it seemed to me like a whole street full of guys all sat there outside Otto's and I thought, like, there's no way I'm walking down there. Yeah, it did seem really intimidating, I don't know why it should be,

perhaps it's because they're all there, like looking at you. Maybe it's because it's so trendy there as well, you know, I don't know.
I: It is called the Gay Village, but you, being gay, do you feel it's your Village?
R: No, not as a lesbian. I think we're on borrowed space all the time really. It's usually dominated by men. I think, you know, those ·little back streets around Cruz, I find them quite intimidating but, you know there's lots of guys (gay) out, they're quite happy with it, it is their space. No. I mean I feel quite happy going to somewhere like Otto's, which is mixed, than I do going into somewhere like the New Union.
I: Which is all gay?
R: Well, eh, a lot of what I would call an old gay scene like drag, leather ... Otto's, well, is very fashionable, it's this thing again it does have to be institutionalised, (gay culture she was referring to gay spaces in general, and lesbian spaces in particular) *otherwise there would be no space for women on their own, and it's only because Otto's is prepared, the woman who owns Otto's is prepared to do that. It shouldn't be necessary but ...*
I like women only space because I can do what I want, I can be myself.

In the course of this interview it became clear that the 'mixed' environment to which she referred was where gay men, lesbians and straight women, but not straight men were found together. The presence of straight men was seen as troublesome because of the threat to safety that they represented. It is in this sense of safety that the ways in which gay spaces are often defined as comfortable for straight women is understandable. The identity women share, because of their gender, can override their differences in terms of sexuality in how they ascribe meanings to spaces. But this sense of safety and comfort can itself be very differentially experienced, as with the cases of some interviewees who commented that even gay male spaces can be threatening, and thus lesbian only spaces preferred.

Particular mixed gay spaces can be problematic for lesbians if they feel that they are being marginalized within them. This to some extent was confirmed by our observational data, and interviews in the gay bar we are studying.

I: Are you aware that you're different in, can you see different groups in Otto's?

R: What in Otto's? Not in Otto's (not different) but yeah, I can see different groups of gay men, different ages and groups of lesbians and I would identify heterosexual with students.

I: Yeah, but last time I was in there were all these gay women at the top of the stairs, it just seemed like they were pushed into this corner whereas all the gay men were all round the ...

R: Yeah, round the balcony. That's cos they're 'looking' isn't it, a lot of it's whether you're there with your mates or whether you're there looking at what other people are doing ... that's what they're doing, they're out for shallow meaningless sex, that's a very male thing isn't. It's not something that women are into on the whole.

This constant tipping backwards and forwards between responses, meaningful in terms of gender typifications and in terms of different sexualities, is a key feature of our interviews with lesbian women. The gay men we interviewed were more likely to stress their gay identity, and responses drawn from it, first and foremost, and their identity as men second. Their reactions to who dominates (and should dominate) spaces reflects their positioning both as 'Other' within heterosexual culture but also in another sense as dominant (as men) within that culture. They are both marginal and central at the same time, whilst for the lesbians interviewed they viewed themselves as marginal to public spaces as both lesbian and woman. In the dynamics this situation lends to the overall juxtaposition of the gay scene within the emergence of a consumption led city centre revival further aspects of the liminality and closure surrounding notions of cultural centrality and marginality can be explored.

The difference that space makes and the spaces that difference makes

Our analysis is located within an understanding of how different place mythologies depicting Manchester have developed over time; Manchester as Madchester, Gunchester and Gaychester. In many ways these discourses, and the social practices they signify, have become incorporated into the meanings of the urban regeneration strategy being pursued in the city.(11)   In particular the

186

commodification of gay culture, and its incorporation into the image of Manchester as a cosmopolitan and European city of cultural consumption, can account for its fashionable status, referred to in our data and elsewhere (Hindle, 1994; Whittle, 1994). The cross-over between the 'straight' and 'gay' cultures has been, and continues to be, a key ingredient of cultural change in the city. This is seen, for example, in the significance attributed to particular club spaces in the history of both Madchester and Gaychester

> *The role of the Haçienda in all of this (the emergence of gay culture in the city) as with other cultures that its stimulated is very important to observe because, obviously, as with Madchester, the Haçienda provided, continues to provide Manchester with a fantastic focus for cultural scenes to develop.*(12)

In the emergence of a critical mass of gay culture in the city, links between the emergence of such physical sites of consumption, the space provided by a particular type of popular music (house) and the development of a drug culture surrounding the use of Ecstasy, are accorded special significance. The point at which there was a cross-over between drugs, music and the gay scene may have helped open up a wider range of identities within gay culture itself making it more emancipatory in the negotiation of multiple identities.

A wider debate therefore is about how far this opening up of life spaces is, or is not, empowering to those whose sexual identities previously made them marginal in cultural terms. Whittle (1994) argues that the spaces for 'difference' that cultural centrality affords has an effect of disempowering gay people. It represents a governance and regulation of gay culture as it becomes absorbed into mainstream, hegemonic cultural practices. For him a key issue of this movement to the centre is that (1994, p.31) 'Being gay has moved from being dangerous to being safe, not just for gay men and lesbians but also for the State'.

This focus, on the interests of the State in the transformation of gay culture into safe culture, provides the framework from which Whittle explores the problems arising for gay men. These come from the translation of gay spaces into places for urban voyeurism in the new consumer culture. He argues that this deprives gay men of safe spaces, and creates what he sees as a fictitious tolerance of gay

187

lifestyles. These become, he argues, 'within, but not part of the law'. This movement to the centre signifies for Whittle (1994, p.29) 'that as a group moves into the centre it is not tolerated — it is merely not expelled'.

For Whittle, the incorporation of the Gay Village, in Manchester, into the life of the city symbolizes a process which is not only disempowering but which also depoliticizes it (the Gay village) as a space for gay resistance to hegemony. Thus the movement of gay culture to the centre is dismissed as 'a post-modern acknowledgement of alternative lifestyles with their varying truths'. This represents for Whittle the spatial expression of how the 'gay body' has become the increasing focus of surveillance and control by the State so that 'difference' becomes constructed and thus depoliticized within hegemony (sic Gramsci and the ethical project of the State).

We find Whittle's approach problematic on a number of grounds, the full exploration of which goes beyond the scope of the present chapter. It raises for us issues of both the theorization of hegemony and of practices of resistance. His definition of the interests of the State in the process of the cultural inversion of gay lifestyle from marginal to centre needs further attention. What does the State gain from such a culture becoming 'fashionable' in consumption terms?

Is Whittle perhaps arguing that it is in the challenge to hegemonic masculinity that gay culture posed the greatest threat to the State? Is it in the depoliticization of that culture, through its commodification as fashionable consumption practices, that this challenge to the State is defused? We presume this is what Whittle means by the 'fictitious tolerance' given to gay lifestyles. But how is such tolerance 'fictitious' except by some notion of a 'false' construction which serves to mystify the 'real' intolerance? Without such a notion of 'false' and 'true' tolerance, which itself is problematic, it is difficult to define what is fictional about the tolerance that is currently expressed towards gay culture. What also requires further exploration is how far the tolerance towards gay culture may itself be destablizing the practices of hegemonic masculinity and thus have political implications as a site of struggle. This is not to deny that the expression of this culture through spatial practices does not become more ambiguous and perhaps problematic for gay men themselves. What is being questioned is how this process of cultural change is being theorized.

It is also difficult to see how this incorporation, through changes in consumption practices, actually does make 'the State' safe from the subversion of gay (male) culture. After all the defining act of that culture, sleeping with other men, must be deeply subversive of hegemonic heterosexual masculinity. On one definition of 'the State' (as patriarchal, heterosexual), gay men's lives are thus subversive regardless of whether in consumption terms their 'culture' becomes fashionable. It can be argued however that the significance of this process of centrality (in consumption terms) is perhaps more clearly shown in the ways in which it benefits capitalist economic interests in cashing in on the consumption of pleasure in the post industrial, service structured political economy of the city.

What we do draw benefit from in Whittle's analysis is his focus upon the inscription of power relations in space in terms of consumption practices. This is in line with new ways of exploring the spatial in terms of popular, urban, culture.(13) However insufficient acknowledgement is given to how this spatial expression of power is both structured and experienced differently in the lives of gay men and lesbians. Whittle appears to imply that, whatever is happening in terms ·of the incorporation of gay culture(s) into fashionable culture, this raises the same issues of governance and resistance for all gay people. Our research suggests that these issues may be both perceived and responded to differently by gay men and lesbian women precisely because they (gay men and lesbians) are located differently with both the hegemonic heterosexual practices and within gay cultures.

Thus moving to the centre may not have the same consequences for lesbian women as Whittle argues it does for gay men. Admittedly he acknowledges that he is only talking about the urban lives of gay men, but nevertheless, and perhaps unwittingly, the overall conclusions he draws about these lives gives the impression that this voice is being made to speak for all gay experience. Our argument in this chapter is precisely the opposite; that because both gay men and lesbian women occupy multiple identity spaces in urban culture, they are in a position of struggle both as men and women, and in terms of their sexuality. We suggest that, as a further stretching of this focus, the location and interpenetration of these struggles within the experience of race, ethnicity and class needs also to be studied.

The urban spaces within which these conflicts are situated are thus contested spaces in terms of both sexuality and gender. Resistance to hegemonic practices is thus constructed in more complex ways than suggested by Whittle. The potential for challenge to these practices in the development of new representational spaces of lesbianism is directed to both the hegemony of heterosexuality, and the positioning of lesbian culture within the gay scene. As oppressed 'Other' in both cultural locations lesbians are placed differently to gay men in relation to negotiating their multiple identities. This is the 'difference' that both gender and sexuality make in the movement from the margins to the centre.

Our discussion focuses primarily on the experience of lesbian women to shed light on the complexities of experience grounded in this difference. This complexity can be demonstrated, for example, in the ambiguous responses that lesbian women make to the presence of 'straights' on the gay scene. In talking about the segregation of the gay and straight worlds, one of our interviewees remarks

> R: I have a lot of straight friends and go out socially with gay men so for me it's difficult to say. It's obvious that some women do need women only spaces where they can express themselves but I need somewhere where I can meet all my friends. Yes, somewhere like Otto's or Paradise Factory.

It is perhaps in the way in which lesbian identity is constructed biographically in relation to other sexual identities, as well as in relation to gender, that this response is intelligible. This interviewee was conscious, in other parts of the interview, of the ways in which she was negotiating her current identity as a practising lesbian within a chronological ordering of her sexuality first as practising heterosexual, then bisexual and (presently but still with some feeling of ambiguity) as lesbian. For her the Gay Village, as a cultural, lifestyle enclave is problematic within terms of providing spaces that can leave people unprepared for the (hostile and bigoted) conditions of 'real life'. But it is a place where she feels safe as both a woman and a lesbian, even though recognizing its points of cross-over between the gay and straight cultures of the city. It may be that for women like her it is the location of the Gay Village, within fashionable urban consumer culture, that neutralizes the impact of the hegemonic masculinity of gay men, whilst at the same time it is a space for her to safely challenge hegemonic heterosexuality through lesbian practice.

This complex negotiation of multiple identities can be further demonstrated in another aspect of our data; that which suggests a more ambiguous response by lesbians to the existence of straight women on the gay scene. Whittle concludes gay men are, on the whole, hostile to the invasion of gay spaces by straight men. A different response made by some of our lesbian interviewees is summed up in one kind of comment:

> R: I can immediately spot who is gay and who isn't, so problems of a sexual nature do not arise (despite presumably the more free floating sign system of gay identities) ... I feel it is good for everyone to explore their sexuality and this doesn't cause me a problem in having straight women in the clubs, bars.

Other lesbians are not so tolerant of the cross-over however. One of the lesbian bar staff interviewed recounted an incident in which the liminality of a mixed space, like Otto's bar, caused problems for lesbian staff and customers.

> R: (Another lesbian bar worker) ... was walking around and collecting glasses last week and there was this group of girls in, and they said to her 'Oh, where can we go on after this?' (...) suggested another (gay) bar. The girls exploded 'OH, God it's full of poufs in there!'

For our interviewee this signified that the space Otto's provided was no longer recognizable as a gay space because of the number of straights around, and that this could frighten 'our crowd off' and lead to everyone staying in their own territory. In other interviews we also came across this reference to the problem of managing mixed spaces so that a 'critical mass' of straight users did not subvert their meanings for both gay men and lesbians. In the case of Otto's door policy this has been discussed in terms of maintaining the right percentage balance of gay and straight customers, and through expression of conflict over what that balance should be quantified as. Lesbians seem, however, to have a greater threshold of tolerance to diversity to what is acceptable before that position was reached.

The social regulation of gay space, by closing it off through exclusion practices, was seen by our interviewees to be the responsibility of those who control initial entry to it as bar management and doormen. How these gatekeepers interpret their role is crucial to the tensions this could give rise to. This was evidenced in the incidents reported to us of straight male doormen of the Bar allowing in crowds of good looking straight women. This was interpreted by the lesbians concerned as the straight doormen satisfying their own heterosexual interests in 'copping off' rather than heeding their (lesbian, gay) interests in the space.(14) This inclusion of straight women can, for some of the lesbians we talked to, transform space into more 'male' space, and make it more difficult to read and feel comfortable in as a lesbian. Our data suggests that gay men do not experience the presence of straight women as threatening or subversive to their space.

Straight women who were welcome by the gay women we interviewed were those who had the right attitude, and who were aware that it was a gay bar by being told this by the doormen when they came in. This recognizes that a cultural line needs to be drawn in how the space is negotiated between the gay and 'trendy straight' cultures of the city.

> R: I don't mind at all the idea of straight people coming into Otto's. Otto's is a young, trendy bar and as such is going to attract straight people. The problem lies with the bouncers I think. They need to tell people before they get through the door that it is a gay bar. A lot of people don't know. They come in, order a drink and then they suddenly realise, I suppose, because from the outside it looks like an ordinary cafe bar. The bouncers won't let in groups of young blokes but they let in young women and 'faghags'.
> I: How do you feel about 'faghags'?
> R: Well it seems like they're out to try and straighten their gay male friends. It's like a competition and sometimes I also feel they're here to tease us lesbians and take the piss. And you know sometimes in gay bars there's more heteros getting off with each other than gays.

The ambiguity towards other (straight) women is nicely summed up in the following quote from another interview:

> R: I think that some of them really want to straighten our scene in a strange sort of way.

The tolerance of difference is thus tinged with uncertainty about its consequences for lesbians who themselves find it more difficult, for reasons given earlier, to read off lesbian identity from performativity and dress codes. The dilemmas of negotiating the two identities of being lesbian and woman are echoed in the resonance of mixed feelings about the spaces that the new cultural centrality affords in terms of both gender and sexuality. We suggest in this chapter that unpacking what this means in terms of the cultural significance of different spaces in the city sheds light on the different ways in which marginal sexual identities and gender issues are moving to the centre. The spatial dynamics of how spaces are constructed as meaningful for social action is a complex interaction of these practices of negotiating multiple identities in the city.

The construction of identities, grounded in experiences of sexuality and gender, through particular consumption practices in the city neither exhausts the exploration of the multiple character of urban identities nor that complex variety and shape that consumption takes in the post industrial city. Rather we have been proposing, through the frame adopted, and the ethnographic data analysed, a particular theorization of identity and consumption in urban culture and the city.

One of the spatial dynamics upon which we have focused is that of what can be termed the process of cultural inversion; the movement from the margins to the centre of those consumption practices, identities and values which have made certain groups in the city more central to it culturally, and it to them. In the context of the wider transformations of urban culture this is suggestive of a further new problematic; that of how the movement from the margins to the centre takes different shape and has different resonance because of the different locations of those who effect it and whom it affects.

This wider problematic of 'difference' affords the opportunity to study 'difference' in relation to other negotiations of identity, and the processes of liminality and closure at other sites of identity formation. The wider significance of viewing contested spaces in the city in terms of identity construction and consumption practices is made apparent.

These practices must be located within the discourses of cultural, economic and social change in the city which frame the struggle over hegemonic control. The need to critique the constructs of hegemony and resistance has also been raised through this focus upon contested spaces. Mapping the spatial meanings of cultural changes, and deciphering the spatializations through which they are rendered intelligible, is a process of mapping out power relations in the city. The understanding of urban experience with which this is concerned has been explored here with particular reference to the power relations of gender and sexuality. Equally crucial is the need to explore how other 'differences' inter-penetrate gender and sexuality; in how the experience of social class, race and ethnicity is also constructed, regulated and resisted in the space(s) of the city. These are the spaces that difference make in the negotiation of urban identities.

Notes

This contribution to the present volume of work is a substantial re-working of a paper presented to the 1995 Annual Conference of the British Sociological Association, 'Contested Cities', Leicester, April 1995. Our appreciation goes to those who made comments on this earlier version and stimulated our thinking afresh of some of the issues with which it deals.

1   In their paper entitled *From the Margins to the Centre* the authors discuss three themes within which this change is located: the process of gentrification of previously marginal residential areas, the re-structuring of activities once deemed peripheral to the 'productive' or Fordist city and finally, the theme with which the analysis in this chapter is concerned; that of the process whereby previously 'marginal' groups have been made central to the city, or made the city central to themselves (see O'Connor and Wynne, 1995).

2   For definitions of the term, and discussion of the role of 'cultural intermediaries', see Bourdieu, 1984; Featherstone, 1991, Bovane, 1990; O'Connor and Wynne, 1993. For example Featherstone describes cultural intermediaries as 'the new petty bourgeoisie of producers and distributors engaged in providing symbolic goods and services ... fascinated by identity, presentation, appearance and lifestyle and the endless quest for new experiences' (Featherstone, 1991 p.44). In their construction of stylized drinking spaces, and their concern with the aesthetics of the spaces they produce, our analysis depicts the bar managers of the sites studied in the research as 'cultural intermediaries'. The term, however, may not be relevant to describe both sets of bar staff working in these venues. It may be more significant to describe the staff of Otto's bar in these terms, than those of the **in** 89 bar. Just because an individual helps produce a physical/cultural space, through working in it, this does not necessarily signify that s/he can be described as a 'cultural intermediary' in the sense defined in the above debate.

3   Taken from a transcript of a presentation given to the Manchester Institute for Popular Culture seminar series,

November 1994, by the manager responsible for founding and running the gay night at the club concerned.

4   Transcript referred to above

5   Ibid.

6   Whittle (1994) accounts for this in terms of the incorporation of gay culture into the hegemony of dominant heterosexuality. As will be discussed later we raise issue with the manner in which this is formulated in his analysis.

7   Valentine (1992, 1993) and Bell et al (1994) provide an excellent synopsis of the transformation of lesbian culture since the 1970s and of the subsequent transformation of the spatial dynamics of lesbian experience.

8   The terms 'producers' and 'consumers' are being used to describe respectively the managers and bar staff of the cafe bar (producers) and the customers (consumers). This usage carries no theoretical weight since in terms of the framework being developed in this chapter both categories are theorized as both producing and consuming the space concerned. However the need for textual reference of material sources makes the use of the descriptive terms necessary but hopefully not too confusing to the argument.

9   Some of those interviewed have however stressed that more gay couples use the bar during the day. This suggests the need to further investigate whether the temporal ordering of the space within the gay cultures of the city is not itself mediated by the location of gay people as single or as part of a couple within the scene. Whilst gay couples may use the space during the day-time, there may be different usages by both single and gay couples in its evening and night-time transformation. This speculation is to some extent borne out by the data which suggests that the bar has a particular significance at night for single gay men 'cruising' the gay scene.

10   Valentine also suggests that the lesbians with whom she

discussed these issues relied on established gay social relationships as a source of first time lesbian contact (Valentine, 1993, p.110).

11   Different aspects of both the changing political economy of Manchester, and of the regulation and control of its forms of popular culture, are discussed in the other contributions to the present volume.

12   The fact that the speaker here is also successfully managing the club is of significance for the understanding of how the commercial interests of niche marketing and the 'cultural' role of the intermediary interpenetrate.

13   Grossberg, in his presentation of the Annual MIPC Lecture in Manchester, October 1994, put forward this position as a new direction for cultural studies. That is the study of how power relations are constructed in the spatial practices of everyday life and inscribed in the spaces of popular culture.

14   The verb refers to the pursuit of sexual liaisons — either same or opposite sex.

References

Adler, S., Brenner, J. 'Gender & Space: Lesbian and Gay Men in the City', *Journal of Urban and Regional Research*, Vol.16, No.1, 24-34,1992.

Bell, D., Binnie, J., Cream, J., Valentine, G. 'All Hyped Up and No Place to Go', *Gender, Place and Culture*, Vol.1, No 1, pp.31-48,1994.

Bell, D., Valentine, G. (1995), *Mapping Desire*, Routledge, London.

Bourdieu, P. (1984), *Distinction*, Macmillan, London.

Bovane, L. 'Cultural Intermediaries: a new role for Intellectuals in the Post-modern Age', *Innovation*, Vol.3, No.1, Interdisciplinary Centre for Comparative Research In Technology and Social Policy, 1990.

Brown, A. (1994), *Democratising Popular Culture: Comparing Contrasting Some Cultural Industries*, PhD. Thesis, MIPC, Manchester Metropolitan University.

Castells, M. (1983) *The City and The Grassroots*, Edward Arnold, London.

Deutsche, R. 'Boys Town', *Environment & Planning Design: Society & Space*, Vol.9, 1992.

Duncan, J., Ley, D. (1992), *Place, Culture & Representation*, Routledge London.

Evans, K. *Tolerance and Diversity in a North of England City: a study of Manchester's Gay Village*, Paper presented to the British Sociological Association Annual Conference, Preston, Lancashire, 1994.

Featherstone, M. (1991), *Consumer Culture and Postmodernism*, Sage, London.

Giddens, A. (1990), *The Consequences of Modernity*, Polity Press,

Cambridge.

Giddens, A. (1991), *Modernity and Self Identity*, Polity Press, Cambridge.

Goffman, E. (1956), *The Presentation of Self in Everyday Life*, Anchor, New York.

Goffman, E. (1963), *Behaviour in Public Places*, Free Press of Glencoe, New York.

Harvey, D. (1989), *The Condition of Postmodernity*, Basil Blackwell, Oxford.

Hindle, P. (1994), 'Gay Communities and Gay Space in the City', Whittle, S. (ed.), *The Margins of the City: Gay Men's Urban Lives*, Ashgate, Aldershot.

Holland, R. (1994), *Geordie Youth Cultures and the City; Restructuring Work, Home and Consumption*, paper given to the City Cultures, Lifestyle and Consumption Practices Conference, Coimbra, Portugal.

Jameson, F. 'Postmodernism or the Cultural Logic of Late Capitalism', *New Left Review*, No.146, 1984.

Keith, M., Pile, S. (1993), *Place and The Politics of Identity*, Routledge, London.

Kellner, D. (1992), 'Popular Culture and the Construction of Postmodern Identities' in Lash S. and Friedmann J. (eds.), *Modernity and Identity*, Basil Blackwell, Oxford.

Lash, S. and Urry, J. (1994), *Economies of Signs & Spaces*, Sage, London.

Lefebvre, H. (1991), *The Production of Space*, Basil Blackwell, Oxford.

Manchester City Council (1992), *Manchester IS the City of the*

Future Manchester City Publications, Manchester.

Martin, D., Lyon, P. (1983), *Lesbian Women*, Bantam Press, London.

Massey, D. 'Flexible Sexism', *Environment & Planning D: Society & Space*, Vol.9, 1991 (also reproduced in Massey D. (1994), *Space, Place & Gender*, Polity Press, Cambridge).

McRobbie, A. (1994),*Postmodernism & Popular Culture*, Routledge, London.

Miles, C. *Spatial Politics: A Gendered Sense of Place*, MIPC Working Paper in Popular Culture Series, No.4, 1993.

Morris, M. 'The Man in the Mirror; David Harvey's condition of postmodernity', *Theory, Culture & Society*, Vol.9, 1992.

Mort, F. (1988), 'Boy's Own: Masculinity, Style and Popular Culture' in Chapman, R., Rutherford, J. (eds.), *Male Order: Unwrapping Masculinity*, Lawrence & Wishart, London.

O'Connor, J. and Wynne, D. (1995), 'From the Margins to the Centre: Cultural Production and Consumption in the Post Industrial City' in Sulkunnen et al, *Constructing the New Consumer Society*, Macmillan, London.

Redhead, S. (1993), *Rave Off: Politics and Deviance in Contemporary Youth Culture*,Averbury, Aldershot.

Rietveld, G. (Forthcoming), *This is Our House*,Avebury, Aldershot.

Ryan, J. 'Women, Modernity & the City', *Theory, Culture and Society*, Vol.11, pp.35-63,1994.

Shields, R. (1992), *Places on the Margin: Alternative Geographies of Modernity*, Routledge, London.

Soja, E. (1989), *Postmodern Geographies*, Verso, London.

Valentine, G. 'Negotiating and Managing Multiple Sexual Identities:

Lesbian Time-Space Strategies', *Transactions of Institute of British Geographers*, Vol.18, pp.237-248, 1992.

Valentine, G. 'Desperately Seeking Susan: a geography of lesbian friendships', *Area*, Vol.25, No.2, pp.109-116, 1993.

Whittle, S. (1994), *The Margins of the City: Gay Men's Urban Lives*, Ashgate, Aldershot.

Winchester, H. P. M., White, P. E., 'The Location of Marginal Groups in the Inner City', *Environment & Planning D: Society & Space*, Vol.6, No.1, pp.37-54, 1988.

7 The city as a site of ethical consumption and resistance

Jonathan Purkis

It is becoming widely accepted that the global economic system should be able to pursue ethical as well as financial goals. In a world where people feel politically disempowered, and where governments are becoming less powerful than corporations, citizens are beginning to realise that their economic vote may have as much influence as their political vote. This is true both for individuals and for institutional purchasers (*The Ethical Consumer*, definition of terms, 1993, Issue 26).

Dramatic prelude

It is a slightly overcast Friday morning in the centre of a northern English city. Two of the major High Street Banks are going about their everyday business, dealing with a steady flow of customers and enquiries. At just after eleven o clock each building experiences a steady influx of young people, some of whom are dressed in suits, others who are garbed in brightly coloured T-shirts, leggings, and green wax jackets. In the space of five minutes several have attached themselves to walls or furniture using strong bicycle D-locks around their necks; others have hung large banners in the windows displaying messages such as 'Earth First! Profit Last' and 'Stamp out Third World Debt'; paying-in slips have been replaced with 'alternative' information sheets; and customers have been joined in queues and engaged in conversation. One of the activists dressed in a suit makes an announcement that the demonstrations are against the Banks' investment in ecologically damaging projects in Third

World countries which are set up to help repay enormous sums of money owed to the Banks at the expense of their people, many of whom are starving. The Bank staff are informed that the demonstration will not end until the Banks have confirmed in writing or by fax that they are involved in a number of specific projects; trained people are among the demonstrators to negotiate with the Banks. Initially the Banks respond by calling the police, who show no interest in moving or arresting any of the demonstrators, possibly because of the peaceful and largely non-confrontational nature of the protest. One of the managers becomes very irritated by this but is still prepared to be interviewed by regional television reporters when they arrive. The arrival of the media increases both the interest of the public and the tempo of the demonstration. Tribal drumming, the chanting of slogans and the occasional playing of a tape recorder containing a series of songs about money serves as an unusual backdrop for the negotiations which are taking place between a couple of the demonstrators, the Banks and their Head Offices. Eventually the negotiators are happy that the Banks have fulfilled all of the criteria of their demands, and that the information can be used in publicity for putting pressure on the Banks and persuading people to change their accounts to other institutions. The demonstrators leave the premises after ensuring that no damage has been done, and any items rearranged are put back in their proper places.

Earth First! — setting the scene

The above account describes a typical demonstration by the radical environmental group Earth First! active in the North of England over the period 1992-1994 . Using the action as a touchstone, this article sets out to examine the sociological significance of the city in terms of the philosophy and campaigning methods of Earth First! (EF!). It will show that, by theorizing the city in terms of a radical ecological perspective, it is possible to shed new light on three areas of sociological theory: consumption and cultural theory; the constitution of 'space'; and the characteristics and implications of postmodernist political practice.

EF! actions in the city are informed by a radical notion of consumption that questions to the core many of the assumptions which are held about lifestyle by inhabitants of the First World. The places which epitomize these assumptions, such as superstores or financial institutions, have become the focus for types of protest befitting the age of leisure economics and globalization. Rather than protest occupying public space, there is a 'colonization' of private space, done in a manner which fuses the real with the symbolic, and transcends normal notions of time and space.

EF! emerged in Britain in 1991 as a response to the steady institutionalisation of the radical green movements of the 1970s and 1980s (specifically Greenpeace and Friends of the Earth). Taking their inspiration from the North American Earth First! movement which has existed since the late 70s, a handful of individuals set about establishing a network of people willing to undertake direct action campaigns on a number of environmental issues. From a small network which comprised of only ten contact addresses in December 1991, EF! has grown to between sixty and seventy groups at the time of writing (Autumn 1995), with many more other organizations linking up for specific direct action campaigns.

In terms of its organizational structure, EF! is unlike any of the major environmental groups: it has no membership lists, no paid workers, no central office, 'only individuals united by the practice of putting the earth first'.[1] Each group is responsible for its own finances and agenda and the local autonomy of groups is strongly emphasized, although a national gathering happens two or three times a year at which 'policy' is discussed and formulated. According to their own literature, the aims of EF! — as drawn up at their first national gathering in 1991 — are:

(i) "To defend the environment".
(ii) "To confront and expose those destroying the environment".
(iii) "To realise a human lifestyle that exists in balance and harmony with the natural world that has respect for all".[2]

So, in the 'Bank action' described above, EF! are engaging within the parameters of aim (ii), and to do this are utilizing the political strategy of Non-Violent Direct Action (NVDA) — a course of action which advocates confronting allegedly oppressive behaviour at its source by breaking the law in a non-violent manner, usually with large numbers of people. Its basic premise is that if enough pressure is brought to bear on a company or a government ministry through the repeated breaking of laws, the actions will result in a change of policy or practice. Consequently, NVDA is seen by EF! as an effective way of creating change, not only because it interferes with the project which they are opposing and captures media interest, but because it requires very little training and deconstructs the idea of the environmental protester as elite expert. EF! regard hierarchies, be they corporate, governmental or environmental, as "the main cause of environmental destruction".(3) Such a view obviously has implications for the way in which EF! activists hope to actualize part (iii) of their aims, and I shall return to this in the third section, with respect to consumers, boycotts and lifestyle.

Historically, EF! are the first grassroots environmental movement to advocate breaking the law as part of their political strategy, and are mostly able to do so without fear of legal repercussions because of their unofficial and informal status. In keeping with the actions of other so-called New Social Movements (NSMs) such as the Peace and Animal Rights/Liberation movements of the 1980s, civil disobedience is often justified by appealing to higher moral laws, whether of their own invention or the more formal, such as a United Nations declarations or international conservation treaties.

In terms of their sociological composition, EF! activists are predominantly between nineteen and thirty-five years old, white, educated mostly to degree level and with a fairly equal balance of the sexes. Unlike their parents' generation, most EF! activists have lived their lives entirely in the post World War II era — a period which has seen more damage to the environment than previously in the whole history of humankind; an enormous proliferation of weapons of mass destruction; greater inequality between the First and Third World countries; and a growing disaffection with the benefits of growth economics. This, argues Eckersley (1989), has produced a different type of political psyche, one which, particularly since the late 1980s, has been at the forefront of political agenda-creation, alongside a media willing to broadcast or print information on topical features such as global warming, pollution, destruction of the tropical rainforests and animal rights.

Given this context, it is hardly surprising that some of the other usual targets for EF! attention have been:

* companies stocking mahogany or other endangered hardwood trees from the tropics (in particular Brazil, where indigenous peoples have suffered enormous social costs and even death in trying to resist

the multi-national companies;(4)
* superstores with a policy of building on 'green-field' sites;
* building contractors, local councils, or security firms who have in some way contributed to allowing unpopular, environmentally-damaging motorways to be built.

Other actions have included: opposition to chlorofluorocarbon-manufacturing companies such as ICI; solidarity actions in support of indigenous peoples' struggles against oil multinationals (Shell in Nigeria) or super-dam development projects (Narmada in India); and disrupting international conferences such as G7 which are seen to promote environmentally damaging economic policies.

The systematic nature of EF! campaigning reflects a belief that, in the global system, power is all-pervasive, and that, in order to change a process which is destroying eco-systems, this power has to be confronted wherever it manifests itself. So, in most of the aforementioned cases opposition to the particular project in question also extends to the targeting of subcontractors, financial backers, security companies and haulage firms, either through occupations or organized boycotts of the services in question. Sometimes protesters have even purchased a small number of shares in a company for the purposes of gaining access to shareholders' meetings.

Why the city as a site of struggle?

When describing environmental protest, it is not unusual for certain sections of the media to depict 'battles' over natural sites as archetypal struggles between (bad) 'society' and (good) 'nature', with the protestors heroically aligned with the latter. This kind of 'binary opposition' — to follow Levi-Strauss — is becoming increasingly irrelevant in this particular context. Indeed Beck (1992) and McKibben (1990) make strong arguments for the interdependency of the concepts of 'society' and 'nature'. The decline of truly 'natural' places — courtesy of increased transportation, mass-tourism and over-consumption — has become a fact of life. Consequently, it is consistent with the idea that 'society' and 'nature' are inextricably linked to claim that, within the contemporary city, there are important discourses of 'nature' taking place. In this respect EF! are interesting because their discourse involves the use of symbols and language which might create the impression that they are very wilderness-orientated and possibly even misanthropic in attitude. Conversely, their campaigning activities are in fact very urban-centred, and in circumstances like the 'Bank action' described above, undertake complicated negotiations with people in business, government and local communities (see Purkis, 1995). Furthermore, as has been suggested above, there are important interrelationships between local political cultures in Britain ('society') and the plight of indigenous peoples around the world ('nature'). The focal point of this relationship is the postmodern city.

First-world cities such as Manchester are gradually transforming themselves in a number of significant ways which are befitting of a postmodern age: firstly, it is an urban centre increasingly devoted to consumption- and leisure-based economics; and secondly it is a focus for new global networks of information and communication — processes which are rapidly replacing more conventional structures of dominance in peoples lives (see Lash and Urry, 1994, p.28). Both of these factors are crucial in the theory and practice of EF!, in the first instance because there are aspects of consumer culture which are profoundly problematic when examined from a radical environmental perspective; and latterly because these new communication networks are precisely the sort of mechanisms on which EF! relies for its information or its communication during the course of a demonstration. Moreover, in the course of this transformation to a leisure-based urban centre, cities like Manchester may well be contributing — either through major development schemes or by encouraging particular trade or consumption patterns — to the destruction of ecological systems and human communities. And, as Beck notes, in a hi-tech informational age, where there are 'long distance moralit(ies)' (p.137) in operation, information becomes axiomatic, as pressure groups engage in a battle for truth with governments and companies (1992, p.57). The city is pivotal in these struggles.

It should be said for clarification purposes that there are conceptual differences between what is usually refered to as 'the local and the global' in sociology — which in recent years has become something of a cliché — and what is meant in the following discussion. Generally speaking sociologists use this phrase to describe new economic and social phenomena **in** the world rather than as part of a philosophy **about** the world. As will become apparent in the following section this is a vital distinction in trying to understand the criteria by which EF! understand contemporary society.

Consumers, boycotts and ethical lifestyles

Since the late 1980s several cultural changes have occurred which serve as a backdrop to the activities of EF!: firstly, as a result of a new public awareness of environmental issues, the 'green consumer' is now a socially recognized fact (Elkington and Hailes, 1990), and one repeatedly used by advertisers with images and discourses of what is natural and therefore 'better' for consumers; secondly, the type of 'long-distance morality' noted by Beck, is becoming increasingly sophisticated. So, as a result of environmentalists' pressure, companies can expect to be challenged on more than just matters of whether they recycle their paper. The new 'ethical consumerism' of the 1990s applies at a far more systematic level: thus every aspect of a company's practice comes under scrutiny in terms of where it invests its money, its marketing strategy, its waste disposal, workers rights, possible expansion into the Third World, its animal rights record and so forth. It has become the job of some non-governmental organizations (NGOs) — such as the Ethical Consumer Research Association or the Women's Environmental Network — to monitor these practices and to facilitate public boycotts of goods and services until the businesses accede to consumer pressure. So, just as there is a continuum of 'green' and 'ethical' consumerism, with individuals expressing different levels of commitment to environmental issues, there is also a complex cultural network or milieu embracing the agenda, activities and philosophies of EF! and the NGOs. There are however, important distinctions to be made which mark the philosophy of EF! out as distinctive from that of other environmental and political organizations. In this respect I feel it is useful to make a distinction between what I have thus far referred to as 'green' and 'ethical' consumerism from 'anticonsumerism':

- *'Green consumerism'*: This is where people purchase or participate in goods or services which attempt to replace existing ones with something designed to be 'friendlier' and less damaging to ecosystems and natural planetary resources;
- *'Ethical Consumerism'*: This is a development of green

consumerism which considers a variety of issues beyond a product's green credentials, such as whether or not the manufacturer invests in the arms trade or has supported oppressive regimes. Through a comprehensive monitoring of the behaviour of modern business, ethical consumerism aims to encourage trade to be as 'fair' and responsible as is possible within the current economic system;

-'*Anticonsumerism*'(5) however, challenges many of the assumptions about what is actually needed in contemporary society. It takes the view that the rich nations of the world are fundamentally damaging the planet and themselves in the pursuit of material acquisition. Rather than just buying green or ethically produced goods, different ways of living, trading and working are advocated in order to 'live more lightly' on the Earth and to be less dependent on buying things to feel good about ourselves.

Another way of expressing this is through Dobson's (1990, p.13) distinction between **environmentalism** and **ecologism.** 'Green' and 'ethical' consumption are still really kinds of environmentalist managerialism, where the aim is to curb the worst excesses of capitalism and make it responsible without altering most of its basic structures. Ecologism however, favours the construction of a society based around ecological balance and diversity, sustainable levels of production and consumption, and non-exploitative human relationships or power structures. In order for this to happen, the unequal balance of the Earth's resources — most obviously realized through free trade (see Lang and Hines, 1993) — is seen as the biggest obstacle. There is then, clearly much in common with the notion of 'anticonsumerism', and this is the point where the third aim of EF! — that of realizing a lifestyle in balance with nature — becomes relevant.

Although EF! campaign from an 'green' and 'ethical' consumerist position, advocating putting pressure on companies through direct action and boycotts, in their personal lives activists within EF! are attempting to fulfil the 'anticonsumerist' ideal. 'Living differently' consequently, manifests itself in living and making decisions collectively, participating in alternative economic practices such as the Local Exchange Trading Systems(6), learning to make, grow or repair everyday consumer products or durables, using more sustainable methods of transport and attempting to encourage these activities in one's own locality. There is a strong emphasis on

210

'cultural' rather than 'economic' capital (see Bourdieu 1984) within the EF! network, as individuals use their resourcefulness, informal contacts and belief in cooperation to ensure that there are ways of surviving the harsh conditions which Thatcherism in particular has imposed on young people's expectations (see Mole, this volume).

The city, then, though profoundly unecological in terms of its encouragement of increased flows of consumer goods and services, is also home to a political culture, which on individual and collective levels offers resistance to the dominant systems of economic growth and material acquisition. Based on an 'anticonsumerist' philosophy, that links the local with the global, the EF! contestation of city culture and spaces has implications for three separate areas of sociological theorizing, which I will now outline.

Implications for cultural theory on consumption

During the 1980s, sociologists become less interested in analyzing patterns of production, and turned in increasing numbers, to the study of consumption (e.g. Campbell, 1987; Featherstone, 1987; Burrows and Marsh, [eds.] 1992). The credit boom of the Thatcher years, the decline of the old Left and the emergence of 'New Times' in the wake of the collapse of the Soviet Union, serve as a backdrop, if not an explanation for this seachange in sociology. Of particular importance has been the intellectual controversy concerning postmodernism, which has been informed both by these developments and the increasing interest in notions of identity within the realm of popular culture. The postmodern thesis crudely put, ventures the view that during the post World War II period — and certainly since the 1960s — there has been a cultural liberation from traditional patterns of work, leisure, social mores, and lack of mobility, the most important consequence of which has been that people are thinking and feeling differently about their identity in relation to consumption.

In the field of the sociology of culture, many of the influential theorists on the study of consumption come from a non-empirical tradition, which has frequently utilized concepts of a highly abstract nature. The big terms of cultural theory, which are applied to consumption and identity are: the 'spectacle' (Debord, 1987), the 'panoptican' (Foucault, 1977), the 'gaze' (Urry, 1990) and especially

211

'hyper-reality' (Baudrillard, 1983). The extent to which many cultural theorists have critically accepted these (mostly disempowering) concepts — set in the anything-goes world of post-structuralist relativism has rarely been commented upon, let alone challenged.(7) Many of these neo- or post-Marxist theorists of culture have subsequently tended to dwell more on the hegemonic implications for postmodern life of the aforementioned conditions, than asking whether or not people **are** consuming, for instance, in a visual rather than a practical manner (see Langman, 1992 for an example of this).

Furthermore, there has been a surprising lack of the kind of rigourness in understanding consumption which is now commonplace in the sociological analysis of audiences. In this field there has been a move away from the determinism associated with both Behaviourist and Frankfurt School Marxist understanding of audiences (see Modleski, [ed.] 1986, p.x) to prove that people can and do creatively consume, and even resist.(8) As a result of this, one would have thought that particularly since the boycotting or even trashing of consumer goods has had a long history (see ECRA, 1993), this would inevitably affect theorizing. But, as Abercrombie (1994) notes, the extreme positions within Postmodernism may well have something to do with the fact that consumption as an activity is dominated by **meaning** and because meaning in contemporary society is so associated with images, it is consequently tempting to opt for a deterministic reading of consumption habits.

The theoretical implications of this for understanding the kind of consumerism practised by EF! is that some contemporary sociologists are attempting to read NSMs in a similar fashion, particularly on issues of symbol and identity. Lash and Urry (1994, p.256) for example, appear to read NSMs as more involved in the transformation of culture in a symbolic than an organizational sense, particularly since, with the decline of the old style Leninist Party model, individuals are choosing a more individualized reflexivity of self. The NSMs are therefore seen as symbolic ways of recreating a sense of community. Apart from the fact that many NSMs — and EF! more than most — have deliberately set out to try and organize differently from the Left anyway, this position is generalized and ahistorical.(9) This type of theorizing treats 'culture' and 'society' as separate spheres, and to follow Eyerman and Jamison (1994, p.1), it is as if representations and symbols are somehow unconnected with material reality and social practices.   It is therefore important for cultural theory to engage with a sense of 'agency' in its reading of the practices of consumption; to recognize the capacity for resistance even within the most conservative and mainstream of contexts (see Davies, 1995).   The resistance of EF! activists in the city — both collectively and individually — is clearly saturated in symbolism but it is a symbolism which is engaged with a 'social' — albeit one occurring thousands of miles away.

The matter of distance leads on to the second area for analysis, that of 'space'.

Implications for theorizing 'space'

One of the developments in recent geographical and sociological theorising of 'space' is that it is no longer possible to conceptualize 'space' in terms of territory (see Keith and Pile, [eds.] 1993). Readings of particular spaces now exist from the standpoints of race, gender and sexual orrientation.   These often reflect a new sense of globalization that is a result of the decline of colonialism (ibid, p.17). Interestingly, these readings tend only to deal with cultures who have either been involved in migrations to the West, or form part of Western countries own histories of exclusions. To date there has been a negligible interest in indigenous peoples who do not yet have a voice in the First World societies.   In this respect the notions of the 'local' and the 'global' apparent in the discourses of nature utilized by EF! have yet to be fully realized in the theorizing of 'space' — possibly because they are not in any sense consumers but more the victims of consumerism. Similarly, there has been no spatial reading of the city itself from a 'green' perspective, and this also seems overdue. For instance, if we examine the 'space' called 'Manchester' from a radical green perspective, it is possible to describe it in a number of ways:

- Firstly, Manchester can be said to be spatially significant in its own right because it generates its own radical political culture based on specifically local conditions. As a consequence of this, the choices of activities are determined by factors specific to Manchester itself. The campaign to stop the destruction of Abbey Pond — a site of rare flora and fauna in inner-city Hulme — to make way for a Science Park building and car park in late 1993 and early 1994, would be an example of this.

- Secondly, Manchester is also representative of a 'standardized urban space' containing the same consumer attractions, retailers or banks as would be typical of any large urban centre in the UK. In this respect when we try to spatially theorize the targeting by EF! activists of a 'standardized' business in Manchester it seems that we have to do so differently from more spatially unique sites. It matters very little to the activist that they are in the **Manchester** branch of Midland Bank or Texas Homecare, unless there are particular local features — such as empathetic management — which differentiate them.

- Thirdly, for a limited time Manchester becomes a focus for circumstances which it is allegedly responsible for, but inevitably, at the distance of several thousand miles do not usually figure in its daily activities. This collapsing of normal spatial and temporal dimensions is most evident, when in order to placate activists in a 'Bank action', international telecommunications have to be made to secure the information that the protesters are demanding. If, as occurred during the Partnerships for Change conference in Manchester during September 1993, a major International Finance Office of a Bank is occupied, this is even more pronounced.

- Fourthly, in choosing to minimize purchasing goods or services from specific multinationals, and trying to live a more sustainable lifestyle at the same time, each EF! activist is working with a highly **individualized** notion of 'green space', even though it is linked to group thinking. Ethical decision-making on a daily basis is sufficiently complex for there to be very different 'boundaries' being drawn by each EF! activist.

- In addition, the above notions of 'space' may also be ascribed with different discourses of 'nature' dependent on their local or global circumstances. For example, Abbey Pond does not constitute a 'wilderness' whereas certain areas of Brazilian rainforest do. The city thus becomes the focus for the interweaving of different spatial and natural discourses during the course of an EF! action.

Finally, it is because the city is such a focus for different spatial and informational interests that EF! choose to concentrate on it, and this is one of the reasons why notions of 'space' are linked to the types of protest evident in the postmodern city.

Implications for theorizing postmodern politics

(a) Storming the temples of the twentieth century

For much of the twentieth century political protest has focused on identifiably 'public' notions of space — streets, military installations, embassies or other symbols of authority. Infringement on 'private or capitalist space' has usually been in the form of occupations of places where the people involved worked anyway. In many instances, particularly prior to the emergence of NSMs, the focal point for a demonstration was a clearly identifiable enemy usually in a fixed location — perhaps a boss who had sacked his or her workers. In the 1990s however, the production of goods and services can be scattered across countries or even continents, and pointing the finger is not quite as straightforward. However, given that the EF! critique identifies everyone connected to an ecologically unsound company as culpable, there is not usually a shortage of places to target. Indeed, the 'standardized' nature of many contemporary commercial and financial institutions means that activists do not have to necessarily travel to a major Head Office if they can just pop around the corner to their local branch!

It would be wrong to claim that EF! — by 'colonizing' private or capitalist space — are engaged in a completely novel tactic, rather that the manner in which it is done suggests a new configuration, combining tried and tested strategies of civil disobedience with a distinctive theatrical sensibility[10] Despite this, there are not many protest groups who make a habit of repeatedly taking the 'problem' in question to the very people involved in creating or perpetuating it, and neither are occupations so thorough as in the Bank action described above (at four hours quite a short one!). However, there are a number of significances of these occupations:

- The public can be directly reached in the very places which are normatively conceived of as safe from political agitation. The Bank, the superstore, indeed the very places which are supposed to feel unthreatening — the ones which are designed to put people at ease for the purposes of spending more time and money — becomes a site rife for symbolic attention and political agitation. The sense of perspective was nicely surmised by one EF! activist at this Bank action who said, it is "the temples of the twentieth century which are being invaded".

- 'Colonizing' private space immediately places the activist in a complex series of interactions between themselves, the staff, the interested and disinterested public, the police and the media. For a short period of time, the meanings ascribed to the 'space' are no longer fixed as each interested party attempts to place their discourse onto it.

- Once the problem of EF! leaving a Bank has been solved, the Bank then has to envisage how it might deal with a future scenario. The very existence of EF! thus ensures that Banks are constantly having to redefine their 'own' space in relation to the possibility of an incursion by those with a different spatial agenda.

- There is also an excellent chance of a good media story, mainly because the action is in the city and journalists and TV crews are able to arrival quickly.

The spatial complexities which can be inferred from the 'Bank action', demonstrates the extent to which, in the postmodern city, resistance to dominant economic and cultural interests can and does happen, regularly, effectively, imaginatively and in highly distinctive places. It is to the characteristics and wider implications of postmodern politics that the discussion now turns.

(b) Creating places in the ruins

The emergence of a new 'green' wave of protest — epitomized by EF! — during the 1990s has ushered in a different era of environmental protest from that of the 1970s and 1980s. Although many of its characteristics such as civil disobedience, media-friendly actions, use of theatre and commitment to working anarchistically, are not in any sense new, what distinguishes the 1990s movement is that it is rapidly becoming a **culturally-based** movement. If diversity and pluralism have become watchwords for postmodernism, then the 1990s has spawned an extensive series of resistances, which rather than being fragmented, has actually generated associations on issues such as roads, live animal exports and most significantly the Criminal Justice and Public Order Bill of 1994 (a piece of legislation designed to marginalize already marginalized groups).(11) Indeed as John Vidal observes, environmental protest itself is moving along:

There is a quietly growing public appreciation that the environment is only partly to do with cuddly animals, pretty countryside and Third World forests, and that the eco-agenda so single-mindedly pursued throughout the Eighties is now changing into one of values, culture and social responsibility in Britain (1994, p.7).

As protest issues pertaining to the environment broaden — including mass cycle takeovers of city-centres and self-declared car-free zones — so the sociological composition of the cultural milieu within which EF! is situated also expands. In cases where projected motorways have threatened existing communities — such as the M11 extension through Wanstead in East London (1994/5) and the M77 through Pollock near Glasgow (1995) — pensioners, school children, the homeless, and the unemployed have joined middle-class protesters in opposing the roads. Independent republics have been declared in both of these cases, as if to underline their desire for self-determination.

The political significance of these movements is only slowly being recognized by the British Establishment, and the news is not favourable. Indeed, the new so-called 'disorganisations' (Bellos, 1995, p.25) are marginalized, but on the offensive, and want a society which listens to and acts upon the green values of the 1990s. Whilst the decline of the Left in British Parliamentary politics has ushered in an era of reassessment and readjustment, the assumptions which nutured it in an industrial age are steadily being challenged by new and vibrant voices.

Conclusion

The EF! philosophical world view, based as it is on radically different concepts of 'progress' in contemporary society, is best understood in terms of the cultural and economic practises in the postmodern city. Highly critical of the Western consumerist lifestyle — for its debilitating effect on Third World natural resources and indigenous peoples — EF! are active both in collective and individual ways in contesting business practises which are deemed to be profoundly ecologically damaging. Frequently this takes the form of a colonization of a 'capitalist private' space, such as a Bank, by a significant number of people who aim to effect company policy and customer attitudes. Although this is only one type of action carried out by EF!, it does have implications for certain areas of sociological theorizing.

Firstly, it demonstrates that engaging in consumption is actually a more creative and active process in postmodern society than some cultural theorists would have us believe. Rather than challenges to dominant economic practices slowing down in an era dominated by images, they are in fact getting stronger, aided by information technology and a new generation of committed green activists.

Secondly, it is typical of an action which fuses different notions of 'space' onto a single event, thus 'local' definitions of the spatial constitution of, for instance, a financial institution, become inextricably linked with destructive economic practices happening elsewhere on the globe. By examining the different spatial discourses in operation, it becomes possible to understand how we may begin to conceptualize 'green' notions of 'space'.

Thirdly, 'ethical' type of actions illustrate the extent to which, Postmodernist political practice is becoming increasingly complex and frequently employs a variety of strategies to gain its objectives. The actions of EF! and other emerging groups on the environmental spectrum, are representative of new political sensibilities which current mechanisms are unable to deal with.

It is possible to see the actions of EF! as attempting rather than to turn back the wheel of 'progress' but to wrest it from those in control and set off on a different course altogether. Resistance to the dominant cultural and economic practices occurs in many different ways for those in EF! and this might be seen — to follow Habermas (1981) — as a way to claw back ground which the state and capital has ridden roughshod over in the past. There is certainly still hope, that in the streets, in the Banks, in the DIY superstores, and on many symbolic and spatial levels across the planet, there are moves afoot to claim back our future, our children's future and the future of indigenous peoples everywhere, before it is taken away from us all.

Methodological note/acknowledgement

In keeping with the sentiments expressed by myself and Andy Lovatt elsewhere in this book, it should be said that earlier versions of this paper and related papers have been made available or circulated to various people within EF! and I have received feedback and support on a number of matters. It is to these dedicated and inspirational people from Manchester EF! that I am most indebted.

This chapter is one outcome from a deeply rewarding three year project. During this time I could not have done without the support of James Bowen and Anna Thomas. I am also grateful to Paul Kennedy for his comments on earlier drafts. Thanks also (!) to Chayley Collis, Paul Fitzgerald and Bar the Shouting for extra lifelines.

Notes

1. Earth First! (1993), *What is Earth First!?* p1.

2. Earth First! (1992), *Action Update*, No. 3.

3. Earth First! (1993), *What is Earth First!?* p1.

4. EF! 'demands' handed to Texas Homecare, 12/6/93.

5. The term 'anticonsumerism' is gradually losing its hyphen! This is apparently to emphasize the reclaiming of the word so as not to be defining a philosophy in terms of negatives. Further information about anticonsumerism can be gained from 'Enough', c/o One World Centre, 6 Mount Street, Manchester, M2 5NS.

6. LETS operates on a non-profit basis, trading goods and services using locally determined 'prices', and is run by its account holders. Originating on Vancouver Island, Canada in 1982 as a means of helping communities survive a bitter recession, the system took root in the UK in the early 1990s, and in 1994 there were 200 such schemes in operation.

7. This has been the legacy of the then-named Birmingham Centre for Contemporary Cultural Studies.

8. The work of many feminist theorists of culture, particularly those articulating 'post-colonialist' critiques (e.g. hooks, 1991; Spivak, 1990) have been a breath of fresh air in this respect. Similarly see Grossberg, (1992) and Squires, (ed.) (1993).

9. This over-emphasis on the search for identity at the expense of motivation is also true of Hetherington, (1990).

10. There clearly are precedents to the colonization of private or capitalist space, such as the anti-apartheid groups in the 1980s. It was quite usual for groups to turn up at large supermarkets and do what has since become known as 'trolley runs', which involved activists loading up supermarket trolleys with goods

from South Africa, ringing them through the checkout counter and then refusing to pay, getting banners out, demanding to speak to the manager of the store, talking to the public about the issue etc. Also, in America in the late 1980s the AIDS awareness direct action group ACTUP (Aids Coalition To Unleash Power) invaded all sorts of respectable private functions, political conventions and sports games to put across their message that governments were turning a blind eye to the situation and companies were persecuting people with HIV (see Gamson, in Burawoy, 1992).

11. In particular, this Act criminalizes trespass, squatting, anti-motorway protest and itinerant lifestyles such as the New Age Travellers.

References

Abercrombie, N. (1994), 'Authority and Consumer Society', in Abercrombie, N., Keat, R., Whiteley, N. (eds.) *The Authority of the Consumer*, Routledge, London.

Anonymous, (1993), 'Earth First! — As much a way of life?', *The Ethical Consumer*, Issue 26, October/November.

Baudrillard, J. (1983), *Simulations*, Semiotext, New York.

Beck, U. (1992), *Risk Society*, Sage, London.

Bellos, A. (1995), 'Pieces of the action', *The Guardian*, 29 July.

Bourdieu, P. (1984), *Distinction*, Routledge, London.

Burrows, R. and Marsh, C. (eds.) (1992), *Consumption and Class: Divisions and Change*, Macmillan, London.

Campbell, C. (1987), *The Romantic Ethic and the Spirit of Modern Consumerism*, Basil Blackwell, Oxford.

Crook, S. et al. (1992), *Postmodernization*, Sage, London.

Davies, J. (1995), *Anarchy in the UK?: Popular Culture and Anarchism in 90s Britain*, paper given to MIPC Seminar Series, Manchester Metropolitan University, 16 March.

Debord, G. (1987), *The Society of the Spectacle*, Rebel Press, AIM.

Dobson, A. (1990), *Green Political Thought*, Harper Collins, London.

Durning, A. (1992), *How much is Enough?* Earthscan, London.

Earth First! (1992), *Action Update*, No. 3.

Earth First! (1991), *Action Update*, No. 2.

Earth First! (1993), *What is Earth First!?*

Eckersley, R. (1989), 'Green Politics and the New Class: Selfishness or Virtue, *Political Studies*, June, Vol. xxxvii, No.2.

Ethical Consumer Research Association (1993), *The Ethical Consumer Guide To Everyday Shopping*, ECRA Publishing, Manchester.

Ethical Consumer, (1993), No.27 — Special Anti-consumerist edition.

Eyerman, R. and Jamison, J. (1994), *Social Movements and Cultural Transformation: Popular Music in the 1960s*, paper at City Cultures Conference, Coimbra, Portugal, July.

Featherstone, M. (1991), *Consumer Culture and Postmodernism*, Sage, London.

Foucault, M. (1977), *Discipline and Punish*, Allen Lane, London.

Gamson, J. (1992), 'Silence, Death and the Invisible Enemy,' in Burawoy, M. et al, *Ethnography Unbound*, University of California, Berkeley.

Grossberg, L. (1992), *We gotta get out of this place*, Routledge, London.

222

Habermas, J. (1981), 'New Social Movements', *Telos*, 49, Fall.

Hetherington, K. (1990), 'On the Home Coming of the Stranger: New Social Movements or New Sociations?' *Lancaster Regional Group Working Papers 39.*

Hetherington, K. (1992), 'Stonehenge and its Festival', in Shields, R. (ed.), *Lifestyle Shopping*, Routledge, London.

hooks, b. (1991), *Yearning: Race, Gender and Cultural Politics*, Turnaround, London.

Lang, T. and Hines, C. (1993), *The New Protectionism*, Earthscan, London.

Lange, J. (1990), 'Refusal to Compromise: The Case of Earth First!', *Western Journal of Speech Communication*, 54.

Langman, L. (1992), 'Neon Cages: Shopping for Subjectivity', in Shields, R. (ed.) *,Lifestyle Shopping*, Routledge, London.

Lash, S. and Urry, J. (1994), *Economies of Signs and Spaces* Sage, London.

Luke, T. (1994), 'Ecological Politics and Local Struggles: EF! as an Environmental Resistance Movement', *Current Perspectives in Social Theory,14..*

McKibben, B. (1990), *The End of Nature*, Penguin, London.

Melucci, A. (1989), *Nomads of the Present,* Hutchinson/Radius, London.

Modleski, T. (ed.) (1986), *Studies in Entertainment*, Indiana University Press, Bloomington.

Pile, S. and Keith, M. (eds.) (1993), *Place and the Politics of Identity ,* Routledge, London.

Purkis, J. (1995), 'If Not You, Who? If Not Now, When? — Rhetoric and Reality in the Vision of Earth First!', *Alternative Futures and Popular Protest Conference Papers Volume II*, Manchester Metropolitan University.

Roberts, K. (1992), *Young Adults in Europe*, Mimeograph, Department of Sociology, Liverpool.

Scarce, R. (1990), *Eco-Warriors*, Noble Press, Chicago.

Spivak, G. C. (1990), *The Post-Colonial Critic: Interviews, Strategies, Dialogues*, Routledge, New York.

Squires, J. (ed.) (1993), *Principled Positions*, Lawrence and Wishart, London.

Urry, J. (1990), *The Tourist Gaze*, Sage, London.

Vidal, J. (1994), 'The Real Earth Movers', *The Guardian*, 7 December.

8 Capitalist enterprise as a moral or political crusade: Opportunities, constraints and contradictions

Paul Kennedy

Postmodern, consumer societies revolve around a fundamentally materialist culture; one where the possession of many goods and services is desired more for their capacity to hold and engender a symbolic character than, perhaps, for their intrinsic utilitarian qualities. At the same time, popular consumer images and signifiers have become the dominant mode through which the cultural aspirations and concerns of many people now resonate. Symbolic consumer values may primarily serve to facilitate claims to social status through competitive consumption, as Weber, Veblen and others argued. They may denote the possession of taste and so legitimate a distinctive way of life high in cultural capital (Bourdieu, 1984) or they may provide the means to achieve affiliation with favoured groups. Alternatively, they may provide the resources for the creative and narcissistic expression of personal identities (for example, Featherstone, 1987). It is this latter dimension of symbolic consumption that is regarded as especially significant by many writers associated with the theory of postmodernization (for example, Baudrillard, 1988; Crook, 1992, etc.).

What is different about postmodern consumer practices compared to earlier forms of capitalist societies is the sheer scale of production and commoditization required and engendered by the search for symbolic values through the capture, possession and assembly of a constantly shifting mass of inherently unstable images. The increasingly symbolic nature of consumption, however, with its powerful links to cultural experience should not blind us to the underlying materiality of the goods and services to which these meanings are attached. Nor should we forget the relentless, rising and parallel consumption of renewable and finite physical resources — alongside the generation of vast quantities of often hazardous wastes — that must take place in the supporting economic infrastructure in order to make such cultural and lifestyle practices viable. Thus, postmodern society with its capacity to enhance enjoyment and creativity through the power of symbolic consumption also incurs enormous environmental costs.

In the view of many environmental groups what is required is either less consumption rather than more, or, at the very least, the determined and progressive attempt to de-materialize contemporary economic life; to reduce the throughputs of energy, resources and wastes currently required in order to support contemporary production and consumption practices. Some attempts at de-materialization are already evident; for example, re-cycling, miniaturization, energy-conserving technologies, moves to reduce the impact of the car economy, the switch to full or part-time vegetarianism, and so on. Nevertheless, the proliferating and seductive nature of symbolic consumption practices remains a dominating force in capitalist economies and in ways that are much more environmentally destructive than the reverse.

Yet, the very power and ubiquitousness of symbolic consumption in postmodern society also contains the potential to neutralize or counteract some of these environmental dangers. Thus, material goods and services can also assume particular meanings that contain connotations of ethical or green correctness. Indeed, over the last two decades or so, there has been a remarkable propensity by growing minorities of consumers to consciously seek to moralize some aspects of their consumer practices. We are now familiar with the power of ethical consumer boycotts applied to specific regimes or companies, as in the recent case of Brent Spar. But the careful, discriminatory exercise of 'selective buying' (Nava, 1991, p.168), extended to a widening range of goods and services including ethical finance and investment, tourism, leisure activities and other spheres, has also grown rapidly over the last few years. As Nava (1991, p.171) argues, '(I)t may well be the case that late twentieth century Western consumerism contains within it far more revolutionary seeds than we have hitherto anticipated'.

Given that the moralization of consumption requires the informed and deliberate attempt to buy virtue, to combine lifestyle preferences with 'goodness' — an essentially symbolic quality — it seems valid to claim that some forms of signifying culture can be made to work for the environment and other desirable social goals rather than against them, as has normally been the case. However, this particular form of symbolic consumption has also been reinforced by long term socio-cultural changes taking place in Western societies. One is the rise of what Beck (1992) calls the 'risk society'. Untrammelled industrialization has generated human-made environmental hazards and so endemic insecurity on an unprecedented scale. But the social changes associated with late industrialization have simultaneously reduced citizen dependence on older class, family, community and national structures. These supposedly liberating forces have propelled citizens towards greater individualization or self-determination — albeit it at the cost of growing personal insecurity in social life — while enabling them to acquire lay expertise with regard to scientific and other matters assisted by the growing importance of education in a knowledge-based economy and the growth of information technology. Citizens are therefore motivated and equipped to create and demand new forms of participation while insisting on their right to question the aims of science, corporate capital and the intrinsic value of material progress as consumers or as participants in new social movements.

Secondly, some sociologists have recently claimed that alongside the widespread fear and awareness of environmental hazards has grown an increasing tendency for some postmodern citizens to seek much more direct control over their lives through the adoption of creative, self-conscious and carefully monitored life choices. In consequence, and whether as individuals or as members of active networks, reflexive citizens are becoming ever more active agents in shaping social structures. Writers stress different dimensions of reflexivity and the forces that fuel it. It may possess an underlying basis in cognitive learning, knowledge and the exercise of lay expertise (Giddens, 1991 and 1992); it may also involve a critical element of moral awareness (Beck, 1992); and reflexivity may contain an important element of expressive or aesthetic competence derived from participation in various forms of popular culture especially film or television (Lash and Urry, 1994). Here, it is possible that lifestyle preoccupations can help to inform as well as motivate citizen awareness of wider political issues.

Given the dominant materialist culture characteristic of postmodern society and the important and parallel nature of the changes outlined above it is hardly surprising that the twin spheres of consumerism and business have become important arenas for the expression of public concern over environmental and related ethical issues. Nor is it surprising that these have also become the political and cultural focus for experimentations with 'alternative' lifestyles such as the recent rise of community barter schemes or LETS (Local Exchange and Trading Systems), anti-consumption groups, ethical investment trusts, community re-cycling organizations, anti-road groups, and so on.

As part of this process, an expanding cohort of green and ethical business interests have increasingly emerged in response to the market opportunities created by the increasing moralization of certain consumption practises. In this growing sphere of green and ethical enterprise the market relationship locks both entrepreneurs and consumers into a mutually validated cultural embrace. At the same time, this sphere is marked by contradictions, particularly for the former, precisely because it involves a confrontation between the conflicting orientations of commercial pressure — the logic determined by considerations of price, competition and profit — and moral or political obligations fed by all-encompassing cultural change. How do green and ethical businesses, especially the more radical ones, cope with these contradictions?

The study; methodology employed and variations in the sample

This chapter is based on the findings derived from in-depth interviews with the leading figures in seventy four enterprises located mostly in Northern Britain and especially in the North West region. 38 were situated in the Manchester conurbation, 19 were located in West Yorkshire and the remainder were scattered across Derbyshire (6), Merseyside (4) and contiguous regions. A lack of resources prevented the study from including enterprises further afield. The interviews were conducted between May 1993 and June 1994. The enterprises selected for inclusion were ones that directly or indirectly served the market niches created by final consumers for a wide range of products that intrinsically seemed to offer the potential for embodying a greater or lesser element of greenness or ethicality. Many of these firms promoted their products precisely on this basis, claiming that they were responding to public concern. Thus, the sample included firms engaged in producing the following: re-cycled textiles, clothes, plastics, wood and paper products (20 firms); cruelty-free, non-animal based body products, cosmetics, soaps, etc. (4); environmentally-friendly, biodegradable chemicals and household cleaning agents (5); organic, vegetarian, wholefoods and beverages (24); the printing, publishing and retailing of radical literature (5); the provision of services such as ethical investment and loans, green management consultancy and accountancy (10); and retailing of a range of green and ethical products including educational materials, fair-trade, Third World craft products etc. (6). The sample included 15 worker's cooperatives, 5 community or social enterprises, 27 limited liability companies and 27 partnerships or sole proprietorships. Most firms had been established since 1980 and more than half were founded after 1987, that is, during the period when there has been a marked increase in concern with environmental and animal rights issues by the British public. 32 firms were engaged in manufacturing activity, 5 were wholesale suppliers and distributors, 18 were retailers and 19 firms were engaged in the services sector.

Not surprisingly, there were considerable variations in the structure and patterns of enterprise displayed by these firms. The key difference, however, was the extent to which a mainly commercial and profit-driven ethos prevailed. Approximately thirty enterprises were designated as 'mainstream'. Mostly these were medium or large in their scale of operations and might be affiliated to a group of companies. Their management structures were conventional; hierarchic, specialized and professional. Assets were privately owned and remuneration was highly unequal as between employees. Involvement in green or ethical business activity normally generated only a part of their sales turnover and was motivated first and foremost by profit considerations. Nevertheless, they were not exempt from many of the pressures and dilemmas that affect firms operating in this market niche and which are outlined below.

A second group of about thirty-three enterprises are designated as 'radical'. Much of the later discussion in this paper concentrates on this group. Their proprietors and members displayed most of the following orientations: a strong leaning towards democratic, equalitarian organization and work practices; a wide ranging and deep commitment to incorporating a moral and/or quasi political ethos into the heart of enterprise operations; and a preference for

229

alternative, relatively non-materialistic lifestyles in their private non-work relationships. Clearly, the determination to express this high incidence of personal moral or political commitment through business endeavour creates a powerful internal momentum for participating in wider cultural change, one that considerably reinforces the economic motivations for doing so. It also makes them especially susceptible to the kinds of external pressures to which all such green, ethical businesses are prone and which are discussed in the next section.(1)

The logic of green, ethical enterprise; marrying profit and principle

1. All these enterprises were compelled to respond to the inescapable logic of a capitalist economy; seeking to compete, survive, increase profits and cultivate particular market niches. In this sense they are no different from any other capitalist enterprise.
2. Nevertheless, whatever else these firms are engaged in selling — the provision of quality goods at reasonable prices capable of fulfilling certain utility functions, the means for satisfying consumers' social, private aesthetic or lifestyle aspirations — they are also engaged in providing products perceived by consumers as embodying some elements of moral or political credibility. Thus, they are involved in commodifying ethicality; in marketing the proofs of their own virtue or political commitment as well as those of their customers. This generates several important consequences.
3. One is that whether they like it or not these enterprises are driven towards accepting a much more interactive relationship with their immediate consumers as well as various citizen groups. The consumers who purchase such products, as we have seen, are engaged in moralizing their consumer practices. Such customers tend to be highly informed, reflexive, discerning and ethically caring. Many reject the relative passivity of 'normal' consumers where buyers exercise a certain postmodern 'free' choice in their personal selection of predetermined images from an array of market-researched goods but have little say in the way goods are actually produced, packaged and presented. Instead, such consumers are trying to develop a demanding and participatory role as agents in the various stages of the economic decision-making process, especially those of production and the disposal of waste — spheres from which

they were previously excluded.

4. The commodification of ethicality as a market strategy also requires entrepreneurs to adopt certain minimum criteria of green or ethical purity concerning what ingredients are permissible in production, the nature of the production process employed, the range of goods and services that are legitimate to market or the methods used for packaging and procedures for waste disposal. Such purity criteria may be adopted with varying degrees of strictness and may cover a narrow, wide or even complete range of products. Any compromises may need to be justified, particularly to discerning customers.

5. The business of selling products that embody certain ethical claims necessarily invites scrutiny and calls for proof. This has two consequences. Firstly, it increases the likelihood of much greater exposure not only to the demands of discerning and scrupulous immediate consumers, demanding accountability, but also to the political pressures exercised by a much wider range of external non-economic interest groups than is normal in more conventional business sectors. Secondly, it generates increased dependence on these same external forces. The power and ability to influence public opinion exercised by such groups is growing all the time; non-governmental organizations (NGOs) such as Greenpeace and Friends of the Earth, local voluntary or community groups engaged in campaigning on various environmental or other issues or in re-cycling activities; schools and colleges, the media, national consumer research organizations concerned with these issues, for example the Ethical Investment Research Service or the Women's Environmental Network, to name but a few. Not the least of such external pressures are those emanating from other companies operating in the immediate supply or market chain on which a given firm is directly dependent for contracts. Such companies are likely to require reassurance concerning the 'clean', environmentally or ethically valid nature of enterprise operations for fear of jeopardizing their own reputations with respect to consumers and pressure groups. Alternatively, they will not wish to risk contravening the growing volume of green laws and policies enacted in recent years as a result of their dealings with an unreliable company. Enterprises operating in this area may also require special resources that only sympathetic support agencies sharing similar aims are able or willing to supply: technical advice and information concerning the shifting debates and

research findings on environmental issues or changes in public opinion; training; or financial assistance from unconventional lending agencies such as the Industrial Common Ownership Movement or radical labour councils with social or political objectives that permit them to provide funding on favourable terms, and so on. These enterprises also need to feel confident about trusting the claims of their own suppliers that the inputs provided meet the required ethical standards demanded by their own clients further down the production chain or by final consumers. This, in turn, may rely critically on the generation of close personal friendships based on pleasurable and genuine mutual liking as well as on shared political or ethical commitments. Such relationships offer a potentially fertile ground for moral conversion and the reinforcement of already shared values. Some of these firms relied for some of their raw materials on the campaigning skills and goodwill of citizens, private charities, schools and church groups who collected re-cycled paper, clothes and other artifacts through kerb-side or workplace collection schemes. Sympathetic media coverage and free advertising had also helped a number of firms in their search for greater market impact. Moreover, some enterprises had relied partly on the trading sections of various NGOs, for example, Friends of the Earth, as key purchasers of a considerable part of their output.

Three important conclusions follow from this discussion. One is that these entrepreneurs have powerful economic reasons for participating directly in cultural change. Market expansion requires nothing less than the conversion of increasing numbers of consumers to the significance of the various green or ethical causes and here they can make a major contribution themselves. This explains, secondly, why many of these firms had adopted a clear campaigning profile in their own right, assuming some quasi political or educational role not normally associated with capitalist enterprises. Thirdly, the need to respond to reflexive consumers and a wide range of pressure groups is not only good for business it also further intensifies firm exposure to the agendas of groups whose interests and orientations are quite clearly moral and political rather than purely commercial.

Radical firms; green or ethical business as a moral obligation

Although the radical entrepreneurs were endeavouring to run a reasonably successful enterprise, and so they were accountable to market pressures, they were simultaneously dedicated to using their firms as vehicles for the attainment of wider non-economic goals. These were 'profit-plus' businesses or as one informant expressed it; "this is so much more than just a business". This moral and/or political intentionality had normally been present from the time of their foundation so that their histories were saturated with this ethos. Indeed, most of the radical proprietors had originally established their present business or had sought some kind of later involvement precisely so they could make a living without the necessity to compromise their private morality. They desired an occupation offering real scope for the exercise of personal autonomy, power and creativity.

This key characteristic of the radical enterprises generated important consequences. Firstly, they adhered very strictly to the criteria of purity appropriate to their particular sphere of business. Normally, the operationalization of such purity criteria extended to all or most areas of marketing, unlike the mainstream firms where such activity typically encompassed only a fairly recent and incremental addition to long-established practices. In the radical enterprises, any compromises had to be justified both to discerning customers and among enterprise members, where they might occasion disputes. At times, such rationalizations concerning the occasional resort to compromises were even offered to the interviewers. For example, one member of a wholefood cooperative, highly dependent for its clientele upon vegan and vegetarian students, argued that they occasionally stocked 'forbidden' goods such as white sugar and the odd loaf of sliced, wrapped bread in order to attract some local non-student residents whose own food preferences for ethically sound food products were rather limited. This was justified in terms of the precarious nature of the business given the prevailing poverty among most local residents, the need to charge low prices, and the resulting slim profit margins. She displayed obvious relief, however, in declaring that they had always resisted the ultimate 'sin' of stocking Nescafe and other Nestle's products. Such notions of clear moral lines that must never be crossed were ubiquitous in these radical enterprises.

Secondly, there was a marked tendency for radicality with respect to marketing activity to spread to other areas of business activity. One such area was the sphere of labour relations and everyday management practices. A lack of alternative job opportunities partly explained the presence of many radical members but this was normally far from being their only or main concern. They had also sought a working environment that offered an equalitarian, democratic and participatory atmosphere shared with like-minded individuals. Here, jobs were rotated, special skills were not given any particular recognition, divisive pay differentials were largely absent, there were opportunities for regular consultation, even in the case of volunteer probationers seeking a permanent job, and all could be held accountable for their decisions including the more long-serving members. All of these characteristics were especially evident in the workers' cooperatives (14) and the community/social cooperatives (5) included in the sample. In addition, non-sexist, racist or ageist practises with respect to recruitment, pay and promotion were adhered too firmly and as a matter of course in these radical firms.

Generalized radicality was also readily discernible in the commitment to implement a range of environmentally-friendly policies wherever practicable. This might take one or more of the following forms: participation in voluntary, community re-cycling schemes; using re-cycled stationery and other paper products in everyday communications; and engaging in various energy-saving exercises such as operating a door-to-door bicycle delivery service to the homes of final consumers or sharing transport and distribution arrangements with other enterprises. In some enterprises a commitment to wider radicality was also demonstrated through an involvement in community service: giving donations of food, labour or money to local causes or permitting such associations to borrow business equipment or premises free of charge; cooperating with local government policies designed to encourage the training and employment of people with various disabilities; or the tendency to attract and offer subsidized facilities and preferential market terms to a cluster of tiny satellite businesses.

A third consequence of radicality clearly evident in these enterprises involved their marked tendencies towards de-differentiation. Thus, and to a much greater extent than in the case of the mainstream firms included in the study, whose managers also have to contend with the pressures arising from their engulfment in the cultural stream of change, the radical entrepreneurs had assumed activities of a quasi-moral, educational, political and cultural nature. These are much more typical of an overt campaign linked to a social movement than a business.

Some theoretical underpinning for this phenomenon of de-differentiation can be found in the recent writings of sociologists. According to Crook (1992) and others, in late capitalist society the relentless process characteristic of an earlier stage of modernity — involving the emergence of highly specialized institutions, clearly demarcated by function and ethos — has continued such that structures have become further fragmented into numerous sub and sub-sub-systems. But the point has now been reached where social actors have found it both meaningful and possible to generate counter-tendencies towards de-differentiation. Here, individuals are discovering ways to creatively amalgamate previously separate practices, life experiences and meanings across political, economic and cultural institutions. Several converging aspects of the postmodern condition have apparently combined to make this both possible and desirable: the increasing opportunities for citizens to plan their own biographies; the progressive de-linking of individuals from community, class and family; the rise to dominance of cultural concerns associated with the vast proliferation of media images, the growth of the cultural industries and the corresponding influence of the so-called new cultural intermediaries in popular culture and so on; and the tendency for citizens to express their political concerns through participation in the new social movements as the relevance of formal institutional politics and earlier class-based ideologies presumably declines.

There were several ways in which those running these radical enterprises were actively engaged in constructing instances of multi-functional social practice. Firstly, they offered an all-encompassing cultural experience of alternativeness and community participation. Here, customers could enjoy the personal contact with sympathetic fellow consumers and business proprietors and the feeling of friendliness that is far-removed from the impersonality of large chain stores. Secondly, they provided the opportunity for personal networking into various quasi-political groups and their local representatives. Thirdly, involvement in these enterprises generated an affirmation of personal as well as business responsibility. Both kinds of evidence, of personal and business responsibility, may assume various forms: the back-up information supplied with the commodities on sale, including guarantees of purity, and which assumes a degree of acquired knowledge as well as ethical awareness on the part of customers; the simplicity of the packaging, resonant with images of naturalness and simplicity; and a milieu that stresses wholesomeness, informality and an absence of pretension. All of this evokes a sense of unity and common purpose between buyers and sellers where customers can feel that their own identity and ethical commitment is acknowledged, validated and valued. Fourthly, there is likely to be an abundant supply of information concerning radical events, issues and movements that require participation as well as adverts inviting customers to support housing cooperatives, local charities, alternative health therapies or radical cultural events.

In all these ways the radical entrepreneurs were engaged in fusing together a number of normally separate cross-institutional orientations and meanings that are not typically found so closely bound together or in such an intensive way in conventional businesses nor perhaps, in most institutions outside the family. At the same time they were acting in the capacity of cultural intermediaries; inventors and purveyors of meaning. And their capacity to do so required the active complicity of their customers.

The opportunities experienced by radical firms

The unique qualities and orientations typical of the radical enterprises provided certain opportunities or resources. These strengths basically stemmed from three factors: the kinds of people who were attracted by the experience of employment in such enterprises; the advantages of networking; and the peculiar characteristics and loyalties displayed by many of their consumers.

Employee commitment and skill

Despite their apparently informal business style, many of these enterprises adopted careful procedures for selecting and socializing some or most of their new recruits. At the same time, many potential participants were seeking employment niches that formed one complementary and overlapping dimension of a total and alternative lifestyle. These circumstances enabled the radical enterprises to enjoy two key advantages. One was the high degree of 'commitment' that employees and members — especially those working in the cooperatives — could normally be relied upon to display including a degree of support and creativity not justified or matched by a commensurate level of financial remuneration. For such employees this involved a trade-off between the relative insignificance of income and the greater or equal rewards of ethicality, a fulfilling work experience and the right to democratic participation. Secondly, most potential recruits, whether as proprietors, cooperative members or employees, tended to be young, relatively well-educated people, often with degrees (60%) or an equivalent qualification. Many had also previously worked in a wide range of occupations as secretaries, teachers, social workers, radio broadcasters, rock musicians, hotel workers and so on. Such experiences combined with Higher Education had equipped radical participants with a variety of concrete skills such as a familiarity with information technology, the ability to drive, some knowledge of commerce, advertising and other media techniques and the capacity to present ideas in a clear written format. They were not intimidated by the prospect of tackling new skills nor of assuming responsibility and exercising self direction. This rich diversity of talents and experiences had helped these enterprises to withstand tough market competition for a minimum financial outlay.

The advantages of embeddedness in a supportive network

Because they had chosen to rely as far as possible upon an array of suppliers, market outlets and support agencies whose organizers shared similar aims and orientations, the radical enterprises could normally count on sympathetic treatment and support. This was based on trust derived from a shared cultural ethos and ethical commitments reinforced by common economic interests. But trust between network participants was often further enhanced by close personal contacts engendered by frequent business interaction, joint participation in non-business activities and friendships. A common perception that 'straight' businesses were sometimes hostile towards radical ventures might also be present.

The advantages of network support are several. Reportedly, such enterprises were easy to communicate with, generally sympathetic to another's needs and problems and relaxed in their demeanour. Consequently most business dealings are relatively uncomplicated, informal, enjoyable and free of 'hassle' or acrimony. Secondly, these enterprises need to rely on the green or ethical credentials displayed by those on whom they depend for supplies or for high quality information. This requires the kind of trust, supported by mutual personal liking, described above, although shared economic interests are also important. It is not in any firm's interest to knowingly act in such a way that a client firm's own final consumers later become alienated. A third advantage of network membership and support — one that was frequently mentioned by our respondents — was the willingness to pay invoices promptly, in full and with few attempts to haggle over price. None of the radical enterprises included in this study reported that during the recent recession they had been forced near to bankruptcy by the non-payment of outstanding debt from network enterprises as has clearly occurred in the mainstream economy.

Consumer practices and loyalties

Relying on our respondents' own impressions of their customers it appears that these radical enterprises enjoy several important advantages with respect to retaining the loyalty of their main clientele. Firstly, they are much better placed to offer the cultural package that radical consumers demand than large, national and international firms whose managers must cater primarily for mass markets and respond to the demands of shareholders and the big institutional investors. Given the present structure of British society it is hard to imagine that they could seriously emulate the style of intimacy and quasi-political and community involvement, offer the same quantity and quality of knowledge or create the same campaigning milieu that the radical enterprises can generate so effortlessly, at least not without increasing their costs or risking the alienation of the majority of their clientele. Secondly, many of the respondents observed that their consumers were often antagonistic towards the supermarkets and big chains such as Boots or Hollands and Barrett. Allegedly, these customers regarded such companies as the 'great devils' guilty of a multiplicity of unethical and environmentally unfriendly activities including the recent tendency for supermarkets to set up huge hyper-stores at the edge of towns and cities. They were also perceived as fundamentally untrustworthy when they tried to increase their range of green or ethical products.

Thirdly, many respondents argued that they relied on key groups of informed, ethically aware and relatively wealthy consumers — mostly people in 'two career' families with professional occupations — for at least a critical minimum of their final market demand. Despite their own relative affluence, such consumers were apparently disdainful of what they regarded as the rampant materialism of postmodern society. They also felt the need to legitimize their privileged position. To these ends they were willing to pay premium prices for certain goods or services rather than buy much cheaper alternatives from large companies or stores even when there was considerable evidence that the latters' goods were equally green or ethical in content.

Each of these forms of market attractiveness bestow a competitive edge that allows radical enterprises to charge higher prices than their rivals without losing too much of their potential market. In fact, they may have little choice but to actively foster and promote a total cultural package. Many of their clientele expect nothing less and this is the primary condition for their continued patronage.

The constraints on radical enterprises

The radical enterprises faced certain difficulties. To some extent these were also shared by their mainstream counterparts but others were particular to the radicals' mode of operation. Perhaps the most severe threat to their long-term viability and growth prospects was not only the rather limited nature of market demand for green or ethical products in Britain at the present time, as experienced by all the firms operating in this sector, but also their need to share this narrow market base with much more powerful mainstream rivals. Although they enjoy certain advantages in their struggle to retain their client base, as we have seen, they also face certain competitive disadvantages. This dual constraint contains several dimensions.

One is that many of the 'natural' reservoirs of potential market support for these products exist among people living on relatively low incomes and who are relatively marginalized from the main economy whether by choice or necessity. The more affluent professionals provide only one source of demand. Students, nurses and other members of the 'caring professions' were often cited by the radical respondents, and others, as important clients yet many of these are not especially well-off. Students, for example, have suffered a substantial drop in their grant incomes in recent years and the need to resort to various loan commitments and this at a time of dwindling prospects of future job security. Then there are groups with health problems; diabetics, families where a child suffers from some kind of allergy or elderly people who believe that the additives present in conventional foods are responsible for some of their persistent maladies. Similarly, there are those who have deliberately rejected the careerist and materialistic preoccupations of the majority of citizens and which they identify as the chief causes of the environmental and social malaises of contemporary life. While all these groups may lean heavily towards ethical buying for reasons of health or personal preference, by definition, their economic circumstances may prevent them from doing so on a regular or wide-ranging basis.

Since price considerations were rather important to many of their customers the radical businesses were also faced with the dilemma of how to retain their clientele given that it was often difficult for them to compete on cost terms with their larger, mainstream rivals. The latter enjoyed lower overheads and the economies of scale. Supermarkets and other chains could negotiate very favourable price terms from suppliers on bulk orders and so undercut the small radical businesses. Indeed, large chains had far fewer scruples generally about stocking their 'own brand' versions of green or ethical products. The competitive superiority of mainstream retail chains and manufacturers was further reinforced by additional advantages: the ability to engage in expensive advertising campaigns to promote their ethical image; the availability of an established distribution system set up to deal with conventional lines; and the opportunities for large national manufacturers to counteract the narrowness of the British market by exporting to countries like Germany and Holland, where green, ethical consumerism is far more developed. The inability of the high street retailers to out-compete the large chains on price simultaneously threatens both the manufacturers and the wholesale merchant suppliers and distributors, who deal in green, ethical goods, since the former often represent their sole or most important market.

As we have seen, what the radical businesses could and did offer was a gamut of additional services that large firms cannot supply; an ambience of alternativeness and moral or political activism, the opportunity for customers to 'tune in' to a set of networking opportunities, and so on. Thus, their attempt to create a lively cultural milieu, though sincerely intentioned, must be viewed against this economic backdrop. A business rationale is at work here, alongside ethical commitment, one that strengthens their competitive edge while simultaneously generating the space in which to play the role of cultural intermediaries. But, this 'strategy', too, may generate certain disadvantages. While it attracts certain types of customer and engenders their loyalty, at the same time, the central message may not only fail to reach the majority of less informed and rather uncommitted citizens it may also repel them. A number of respondents observed that working class men, in particular, often perceive such radical firms and their products as faddish, cranky, even effeminate. They resent the atmosphere of 'political correctness' and are antagonistic to the associations such products supposedly have with alternative/new age or hippy lifestyles and middle class 'do-gooders'. A key problem for such radical enterprises, therefore, is how to extend their market reach to majority groups and achieve long term expansion but without simultaneously alienating their committed repeat customers. Here again, the large, more mainstream enterprises enjoy many clear advantages, especially their ability to use their more conventional business lines in order to 'carry' the more precarious minority sector involved in green/ethical marketing. The latter might be regarded as a form of loss-leader, providing a company with a high social profile in the short term whilst ensuring that they remain 'ahead of the game' until such time as the mass market for such products begins to expand.

Location also affects competition and market consolidation. Many radical retailers tended to cluster at convenient city centre locations adjacent to popular shopping areas, restaurants, hospitals, theatres and universities, areas from which so many of their typical clients were drawn. But this also had certain drawbacks. One is that in these times of bulk-purchasing, motorized shopping, out-of-town hyper-markets, capable of providing parking facilities as well as cheap goods, a city centre location is not always convenient. Even very loyal customers may find it much easier, as well as cheaper, to shop at the supermarkets especially when they are engaged in bulk purchasing for the weekly family budget. Secondly, even the most committed clients, and certainly the majority of more conventional consumers, seem likely to succumb, at times, to the postmodern attractions of central shopping malls and arcades as sites for what Shields (1992) calls 'the enactment of lifestyle' (p.16) and 'zones of permitted, legitimated pleasure' (p.8). The powerful temptations of glitzy exoticism, narcissistic escapism, sheer convenience and cost-saving vie with those provided by moral and political correctness, community feeling and a cultural empathy with alternativeness.

There were at least three additional constraints confronting the radical businesses. Firstly, to the extent that these enterprises actively prefer to operate within a network of like-minded and sympathetic suppliers and support agencies then, any difficulties experienced by some members inevitably creates insecurity for others. Interdependence generates de-multiplier effects in a contracting network. For example, some of these firms had relied at some time on the provision of grants, loans at a reasonable rate of interest and technical advice from various sympathetic local authorities. But such dependency carries certain dangers. Thus, the composition and loyalties of local politicians can change with shifts in voting patterns. Also, the supply of such assistance has generally contracted as local government has experienced a progressive tightening of its spending powers and priorities.

Secondly, whereas these radical enterprises enjoy certain strengths, their preferred style of organization also contains certain inherent dangers, as has been documented elsewhere in the case of worker's cooperatives (for example: Thornley, 1981 and Mellor et al, 1988). Thus, the relatively non-hierarchic, democratic and participatory nature of such businesses, reinforced by the attractions of personal autonomy, positively encourages internal debate and, perhaps, disagreement while inviting demands for consultation. Providing they are not too deep or prolonged, disagreements and even conflicts over policy may have productive consequences; stimulating new ideas and creative dialogues, releasing energy and reinforcing a sense of personal commitment. On the other hand, democratic participation can slow down decision-making and even paralyse business operations at times when, as during a recession, key decisions need to be made.

Another hazard is the risk of severe personality clashes between particular individuals who then force other members to take sides, so undermining the inter-personal goodwill upon which such organizations so clearly depend. These, in turn, may also be linked to fundamental differences of opinion concerning the goals of the enterprise, for example, the key question of how far principle should be compromised for the sake of market survival or expansion. In extreme cases such conflicts may lead to the disintegration of the entire enterprise. However, internal dissension is normally resolved in less destructive ways, such as splitting a business into two semi-autonomous units or the decision by certain members to leave and join another group.

Thirdly, and however reluctantly, most of these enterprises were driven to make certain compromises with their ethical principles in order to ensure business survival. These might take many forms: attempts to reduce weekly running costs by employing cheap or 'free' labour, such as volunteers-probationers, part-time casual workers or the use of 'self employed' contract labour, paid on a commission basis according to their sales; subsidizing minimum wage payments through the receipt of housing benefits and family income supplements; stocking a limited range of items of dubious ethicality, such as stock cubes, vitamin pills or margarine, in order to accommodate the occasional more conventional purchasers; incorporating certain colourings and perfumes in the manufacture of organic or cruelty-free cosmetics and body products; or placing a higher mark-up on some vegan goods than might be strictly justified by their cost, possible because of the difficulties vegans face in finding reputable and regular suppliers. Such compromises involve clear breaches with established principles that are not easy to resolve or justify; acquiescing in the state system, exploiting a few employees in ways not dissimilar to those used in mainstream businesses, straying, at times, outside the 'normal' network of like-minded radical outlets, supplying a proportion of their products to conventional firms which were not committed to ethical business practice, pandering to majority consumer preferences for 'pretty' goods, and so on.

It is difficult, perhaps impossible, to draw a clear distinction between acceptable levels of compromise, carried out in very limited areas and under strict surveillance, and those situations where so many criteria of ethicality are disregarded that radicality itself becomes questionable. More important from the standpoint of this discussion is the question of the risks attendant upon such activities, especially the possibility of alienating their core, committed customers and engendering internal divisions between members. These represent very real constraints.

This discussion concerning compromise brings into focus a final and very important constraint on these radical enterprises, namely, their largely self-imposed reluctance to pursue expansion beyond a certain point. This, in turn, raises central issues concerning the fundamentally contradictory position within the capitalist system in which these firms find themselves.

The contradictions of business growth; ethical peril or gain?

Radical enterprises are attempting to survive and prosper in a market economy whilst simultaneously trying to perform certain quasi-political, cultural and moral roles. Yet, implicitly if not explicitly, the latter presuppose a commitment to changing the very economic system on which they depend for their personal livelihoods and market opportunities. This raises the question of how two such potentially contradictory goals can be reconciled. A large part of the problem here revolves around the issue of business expansion. There were several reasons why, despite their underlying desire to pursue market growth, in the final analysis the majority of radical entrepreneurs held back from doing so beyond a certain point.

Firstly, the most likely prospect for widening market appeal probably requires the attempt to achieve a break-through into mass marketing. This, in turn, and depending on the particular position a given firm occupies in the production chain, may involve one or more of the following: winning contracts with supermarkets and so moving towards the manufacture of 'own brand' products using the client's name; stocking a wider range of products of lower or more dubious ethical content but which are either cheaper or that comprise the kinds of purchases regularly made by poorer and/or less sophisticated and scrupulous consumers; becoming more lax over the implementation of strict purity criteria; de-emphasizing their present alternative or quasi-political image, and so on. But all of these possibilities incur certain dangers. Thus, several of the radical manufacturers who were engaged in producing organic or cruelty-free cosmetics and similar body products or environmentally friendly domestic cleaning goods claimed that any attempt to win contracts

244

with supermarkets and other chains invariably led to a progressive tightening of control by the latter over their suppliers. As a condition for agreeing to market their products at all such chains would require goods to be re-packaged under their 'own brand' name which involved an immediate loss of identity. Once a supplier became dependent upon such large outlets, the latter were also likely to demand a lowering of the ethical standards used in production in order to ensure cheapness. Finally, with greater integration into the larger company's activities so bargaining power over price negotiations would diminish leading to the imposition of cost-cutting demands and reduced profit margins. Meanwhile, previous outlets might be lost as the main buyer absorbed an ever greater proportion of resources and capacity. In this scenario, it was argued, both firm autonomy and ethicality were seriously at risk.

A second reason for fearing expansion was that extending the sphere of operations might require the introduction of more impersonal, hierarchic, technically specialized forms of organization characteristic of more orthodox firms. Such moves were perceived both as ethically undesirable and as likely to increase exposure to external pressures from unsympathetic financial organizations and technical agencies who might be the only available sources of new capital for investment. Thirdly, the kinds of changes that might be necessary to facilitate business expansion — more compromises with purity criteria, a reduced emphasis on presenting a radical, quasi-political *milieu*, a progressive loss of firm autonomy, and so on — might well provoke internal disagreements and divisions, perhaps even the disintegration of the enterprise as a viable entity in its own right.

Lastly, even if diluting standards in the attempt to reach more conventional customers proved acceptable to members of the enterprise as a path to expansion there remains the risk of alienating their original and most ethically committed core clientele whose willingness to pay premium prices may have previously helped to ensure survival. Of course, a successful transition to supplying a larger market may reduce overheads and unit costs and so bring down prices. This might compensate committed customers for any diminution in the expression of radicality. However, once these former attributes are reduced or even lost such customers might equally feel that there is no longer sufficient reason why they should not purchase their green or ethical goods directly from the chains and

245

supermarkets, especially if the latters' products are offered at even lower prices. Also the willingness of affluent consumers to pay premium prices as evidence of their own moral responsibility, and disdain for destructive commercialism may lose its former rationale.

One solution to this dilemma is to decide that the political and ethical campaign objective is more worthwhile than giving precedence to the economic goal of business growth. That many of the radical firms chose to prioritize the campaign, so creating self-imposed restraints on economic expansion, did not therefore appear to them as tantamount to business 'failure' though outsiders who judged solely by the criteria of profit might consider such a venture to be a rather unenterprising one. Nevertheless, this 'solution' creates its own contradictions. Thus, if carried too far, resistance to the 'normal' capitalist goal of expansion and an unwillingness to accept commercial compromises may threaten long run business survival as well as individual employment. In a capitalist economy, businesses that do not expand tend to fail sooner or later. In these circumstances choosing to prioritize the campaign may actually become self-defeating if the risk of economic failure removes or cripples the chosen vehicle for conducting the campaign in the first place. In a very real sense, the ability to influence the wider public and shape cultural change only thrives on the back of the resources, venue and market reach generated by the business as an economic means to a campaigning end.

Equally, the decision to avoid the opportunities for reaching a wider public through various forms of mass marketing or by seeking joint ventures that could increase size and access to more investment capital, for fear of engaging in deeper compromises, closes the door to a far more urgent problem. Thus, in environmental terms, achieving a genuinely safe economy requires the conversion of the currently less scrupulous and relatively unaware citizen majority to something approaching the same level of greenness displayed by the more radical consumer minorities. In short, any serious attempt to achieve a viable form of sustainable development in future years depends critically on the ability to channel much of the potential power of symbolic consumption in the direction of greener lifestyles but as practised by the entire population and not merely by small minorities, clinging to enclaves of enlightened greenness. Anything less may constitute failure. The same argument may be relevant to issues of social justice. Meanwhile in the absence of such an approach the citizen majority are left directly exposed to the full glare of powerful, manipulative and entirely commercial forces. Perhaps, therefore, these radical enterprises should consider playing not merely a symbolic and educational role — reinforcing the commitments of the already converted at the leading edge of minority cultural change — as at present, valuable though this is, but a key one at centre stage where major influences for change are shaped and negotiated.

Notes

1. A third group of eleven firms were mainly involved in using their businesses as vehicles for expressing a highly individual or family concern with health matters, such as worries about allergies, or the desire to exercise a very personal artistic or craft fascination with particular types of materials or skills. That such activities had generated certain environmental or wider ethical advantages was therefore largely coincidental and unintentional. Accordingly, the discussion omits this group.

References

Baudrillard, J. (1988), *Selected Writings*, edited by Poster, M. Polity, Cambridge.

Bourdieu, P. (1984), *Distinction; a Social Critique of the Judgement of Taste*, Routledge, London.

Crook, S. et al (1992), *Postmodernization; Change in Advanced Societies*, Sage, London.

Featherstone, M. (1987), 'Lifestyle and consumer culture', *Theory, Culture and Society* 4,1, pp.55-70.

Giddens, A. (1990), *The Consequences of Modernity*, Polity, Cambridge.

Giddens, A. (1991), *Modernity and Self Identity*, Polity, Cambridge.

Lash,S. and Urry, J. (1994), *Economies of Signs and Spaces*, Sage, London.

Mellor, M. et al (1988), *Worker Cooperatives in Theory and Practice*, Open University Press, Milton Keynes.

Nava, M. 'Consumerism reconsidered; buying and power', *Cultural Studies*, 5,2, pp.157-173.

Shields, R. (ed.) (1992), *Lifestyle Shopping*, Routledge, London.

Thornley, J. (1981), *Workers' Cooperatives; Jobs and Dreams*, Heinemann, London.

9 Shouting in the street: Popular culture, values and the new ethnography

Andy Lovatt and Jonathan Purkis

We can pool information about experiences, but never the experiences themselves (Aldous Huxley, *The Doors of Perception*, 1954).

The resistance of the popular occurs on terrains altogether different from that of culture in the strict sense of the word ... and it takes the most unexpected forms, to the point of remaining more or less invisible to the cultivated eye (Pierre Bourdieu, *In Other Words*, 1990).

Introduction

'These days they don't make academics like they used to do, do they?' And for some of us this is cause for celebration rather than nostalgia or the wringing of hands. The academic — like God, history, or society — is dead, long live the academic!

Such remarks would seem trite and needlessly provocative if it wasn't for the fact that there is more than a whiff of truth to them. The fact of the matter is that academia — like the leopard — is changing its spots. Increasingly in an underfunded education sector new relationships have begun to emerge, bridging the gap between the academy and cultural producers, the media and business. Just as there is a whole strata of 'cultural intermediaries' (Bourdieu, 1984) operating between business and the arts, so there now exists the (usually reluctant) intellectual equivalent (Featherstone, 1991). As cultural, social and urban policy is increasingly dictated by an amalgam of experts from each of these areas, so the academic is required to play a number of different roles and occupy a number of positions related to the work which s/he does.

This is not a new revelation obviously. There has always been something of a relationship between academia, politics, business and the media. Yet as a result of economic restructuring during the 1980s, massive expansion of the media and media driven knowledge systems and an increasing turn to (popular) culture in the regeneration programmes of many city centres, we are now witnessing both a changing role for the academic researcher and the conditions of ownership of 'expert' knowledge within the field of popular culture. This is clearly a controversial assertion, but if one considers some of the implications of this in terms of the nuts and bolts of researching popular culture in a rapidly changing world system — who does it? how is it carried out? who is it for? — the answers to these questions may well be more complicated than they previously appeared to be.

This chapter focuses on the ethnographic research role within the sociology of popular culture; an interest fuelled by the observation that so much contemporary work in this area is being carried out by younger and younger academics, many of whom are already immersed in their chosen culture prior to intellectual engagement with it (Redhead 1993; Marcus 1992). In such circumstances, the role of the ethnographic researcher becomes problematic, both in terms of their 'tactics' and their identity — for example, are they a fan, an interpreter, a researcher, an essayist, or all four? We want to suggest that by examining how research is done, and exploring its mode of operation in the field of popular culture, we can see the emergence of a new type of sociological researcher; one who may be called upon to adopt many different 'tactics' and identities during the course of their various research activities (Clifford 1986; Hobbs 1988).[1]

We feel that this view is vindicated by the changing circumstances within which the concept of 'culture' comes to be understood. In recent years there has been a conscious commitment in sociology to engage with popular cultural forms previously hidden from history or subject to a process of academic objectification (Schirato, 1991). Work by Chambers (1990), McRobbie (1994) and others suggests that there has been a 'turn to the popular', and integral to this switch has been the frustratingly complex debate surrounding postmodernism. Whilst it is not our intention here to revisit this extensive literature and comment on the relative merits of each of the various versions of postmodernism, we do welcome its controversial reputation in sociology, and see it as an opportunity rather than a threat. There has been a tendency for this debate to be read as the symptom of the disruptive ingression of popular culture into a previously privileged intellectual domain. In a sense then, this forms the second line of our inquiry: to assess the value of the theoretical material which informs the study of popular culture. In doing so, we take the view that understanding popular culture requires a theoretical flexibility — putting empathy before explanation; thus avoiding the temptation to lapse into objectifying meta-theories of culture, be they the old (e.g. Marxism) or the new (e.g. Baudrillard). We would agree with Chambers that the world is no longer 'tied to traditional discourses, institutions and voices for information about its meaning' (1990, p.217), and proffer that new areas of study demand understanding on their own terms. Furthermore, the fact that new areas of study may emerge from groups previously marginalized by power relations, suggests that the theory and practice of popular cultural research can be done in such a way as to put some (political) principles (back) into postmodernism (if they were ever absent).

In this respect then we find ourselves turning to a reading of postmodernism that occupies a similar orbit to the 'low modernism' proffered by Marshall Berman (1984). Here Berman's 'low modernism' provides a cultural and political critique of the failed and failing meta-narratives of 'high modernity'. Accordingly, we have used this as a touchstone to explore some of the rocky extremities of the postmodern terrain. Berman's is a modernism characterized by movement, flux, change and unpredictability; characteristics which are conventionally associated with the postmodern but which, according to Berman, contain a substantial thrust of the modern (see also Lash and Friedman, [eds.] 1992). The work of Berman as we shall see is akin to that of Walter Benjamin, and offers a figural vision of the *flaneur*, of the popular, of the streets. Berman's low modernism wants to work towards an ethics but an ethics without blueprints, to develop 'principled positions' (see Squires, [ed.] 1993) which emerge from detailed exposure to the everyday worlds of the popular order and a consequential erosion of objectifying distance between the researcher and the researched.

It is this exposure that leads us to outline the essence of a new ethnography for popular culture. However, to reach this point we will first contemplate the sociologists place in a changing world, particularly how the study of culture has moved from the margins to the centre of academic interest, and at the same time effectively undermined its pedagogical role. Secondly we wish to examine the theory and practice of doing ethnography, specifically the need to avoid the pitfalls of 'realist' ethnography (Marcus 1986), and to recognize that the role of the 'new' ethnographer carries certain responsibilities which liberate yet complicate the researcher's task.

Intellectuals and the politics of the distribution of knowledge

We begin with the rudimentary observation that despite a partiality for experimentation with methodological and epistemological structures throughout its history, sociology is unquestionably a modernist discipline. It was part and parcel of Enlightenment rationalism and instrumental in the development of knowledge based state systems in Western democracies at the end of the nineteenth century. Subsequently the project of sociology has, until fairly recently, been one of producing scientific research in order to contribute to some sort of societal progress. Whether it has succeeded in achieving this is not our concern. The most significant factors for us are: that sociological research into culture does not befit the reflexive characteristics which modern institutions are supposedly embracing (Giddens, 1991); that instead of engaging with the uncertainties of contemporary cultural developments sociology chooses to deploy the certainties of particular modernist sensibilities and in so doing deposits its intellectual baggage upon the culture it seeks to understand.

Although the intellectual fear of mass culture can be traced back to the coming of industrialization, the die was cast by early sociologists of popular culture like the Frankfurt School. Their work was set in the context of the expanding capitalist leisure industry, with the emphasis on the stupefying effects which the consumption of 'popular culture' (the culture industry) had on people's ability to transform the world. The Frankfurt School, and in particular the work of Adorno, illustrates the legacy of an economic reductionist view of culture that leaves little space for treating culture as flexible in its own right (Gendron 1986). Deterministic assessments of the effects of 'mass culture' have also passed into everything from semiology and structuralism to both feminism and postmodernism. Much of this we would argue stems from a certain distance — in terms of social and class — between the academic and the 'object of study' (sic). This is an obvious but crucial point, as the academic has tended to occupy an extremely privileged position in society, and all too frequently is reflecting the aims and ambitions of a particular group. In the case of modernism, it was largely a project of a particular social and cultural class — namely bourgeois white European men — and the search for 'truth' in science, literature politics or history, was done on their terms and for their interests.

In the late twentieth century the challenge presented to sociology is to engage with the move away from the traditional cultural and intellectual projects of the white European male. For, if we are to believe the claims of authors such as Andreas Huyssen (1986) and Patrice Petro (1989), that the whole invention of modernism in the nineteenth century was driven by a deliberate attempt to distance serious male culture from the growth of a 'feminized' culture of the popular,[2] then there are good reasons for a feminist (along with other excluded) voices to want to reclaim some of the theoretical ground. What is clear to us, is that in the post-colonial world in which we live, the processes of globalization of culture and thought, further underlines the limitations and authority of the European Modernist vision (see Bauman, 1987; Owens, 1985). There are two factors which stand out here.

Firstly, the ivory towers no longer hold special status regarding the collection and dissemination and legitimation of knowledge, especially that of popular cultures. Secondly that the growth of lifestyle-oriented economics, and the rapid circulation of ideas and identities from the city to the Global Village, leads us to believe that studying these phenomenon is not only academically imperative, but perhaps more importantly, that it is done in a way which reflects the sensibilities of the age. In the first instance we will illustrate our point with reference to the media and in the second turn to Walter Benjamin for inspiration.

(i) We would agree with Bauman (1987; 1988) for instance, that the changing relationship between the state and the academy in recent decades — resulting in a decline in the importance of large scientifically driven state sponsored research — has led to a 'status crisis' within academia. This and the 'opening up' of culture through 'mass' consumption has ensured that intellectual debate has become both freer and more democratic. There is a sense now that alongside the 'new intellectuals' (Bourdieu, op cit) — TV managers, cultural producers, publishers and so forth — the academic is no longer elevated as a special case. In part this is a result of the rise of the multi-institutional research project, funded by city councils, leisure industries, development and tourist sectors of the market and local state, but also the growth of popular intellectual programmes in the media. There is, according to Featherstone (1992, p.45) 'a new breed of celebrity intellectual' afoot 'who have little distaste for, indeed who embrace, the popular'.

This populism often brings with it a different — more media orientated — research agenda with the 'new intellectuals' being afforded access to people and places where the academic of a previous age would never be.(3) Whilst in some cases there is little doubt that 'TV does it better', this will not always be so. Perhaps more important then is the wider access to research findings which the telecommunications age brings with it — as academic claims are picked up and discussed in a variety of cultural mediums, such as BBC 2's *The Late Show* , Radio 4's *Start the Week*, the *NME*, *The Face* and so forth. Subjects for discussion and investigation are boundless and can vary from the latest Baudrillard book, debates about the impact of television violence, or the significance of the latest 'do-it-yourself' cultural phenomena.(4) Once again this is not to detract from the academy's critical role in the development of theoretical and empirical work within and for academic consumption but an attempt to highlight the opportunities for fruitful collaboration between the academy and other cultural intermediaries with a shared interest.

The sociological response to the media and to popular culture (often treated as one and the same thing) seems to be at best ambiguous and at worst damning. As is noted by McRobbie (1994, p.185) there is a tendency to relegate culture to 'the field of the arts and literary criticism or else package(e) it up with (the) political economy of mass communications'. This reflects a double pedagogical problem: that of interdisciplinary research and of the fragmented identity which many academics researching popular culture cannot help but embrace.

Although sociology has long been a parasitic discipline (Urry, 1981) and draws upon all sorts of philosophical influences for inspiration, a central need for empirical validation from a standpoint of scientific correctness still exists (Strianti, 1994). This hangover from the days when most sociology was quantitative also applies to the flexibilities of the modern research role, whereby an academic researching into popular culture might spend some of a week in night-clubs or football matches, take time out to appear on or even present media programmes and still sit on academic committees and give lecturers. Such fractured lifestyles do not yet stand easy with many academics although the diverse requirements of the aforementioned multi-institutional research projects tend to suggest that the sociology of popular culture is starting to venture out of the security of the ivory tower.

We are aware of the importance of not confusing these developments with the legacy of Thatcherism, which throughout the eighties disenfranchized the academic more on the issue of funding specific projects rather than aiming to undermine their authority as such. Consequently we feel much more comfortable with the tradition of left libertarianism of writers such as Illich (1973) and Gorz (1981) who offer a critique of the modern institution — educational, medical, or administrative — in terms of its impersonality, unaccountability, and meritocracy. Thus we welcome the fact that new relationships are beginning to be forged with groups outside the academy, and also take inspiration from the fact that even within academia itself there has begun a slow but a healthy dismantling of the boundaries between disciplines, helped in particular by developments in the sociology of scientific knowledge.(5) These studies free qualitative sociologists of popular culture from the ideological questions of whether the research is scientific or not, and the blurring of disciplines has led to interesting relationships between the sociology of culture and art or literature (Chaplin, 1994; Fyfe and Law, 1988; McRobbie, 1994) in terms of both representation and subject matter (Marcus, 1992). Similarly, there are indications that in academic practice there are signs of openness also befitting the information age, particularly where sharing knowledge is concerned. These days we are used to the idea of working papers — unfinished reports for wider circulation and discussion, whereas in the 1970s this was rare indeed (Clark, 1990). With the expansion of access to information technology, particularly the Internet, the time and space of the academic is on the move, and the mystique of the 'expert' swept away on a wave of possible new openness.(6)

(ii) To talk then of carrying out research into popular culture and to talk of modernist sociology in the same breath would seem incongruous, thus we feel that it is necessary to make the rather obvious distinction between high modernism and low modernism. If the former is as indicative of sociology historically — certain, self-assured, scientific, distanced from the research that is done, and producing knowledge for select groups in society — then low modernism is rooted in the culture of the popular: of the streets. It is uncertain, contingent, ephemeral, subjective and for de Certeau (1986) frequently subversive of the interests of dominant cultures.

Here we take inspiration from the work of Walter Benjamin, a low modernist in the lion's den of elitism: the Frankfurt School. Benjamin introduced an ambivalence and agnosticism to his writing on culture and the city (Docker, 1995) — playfully evoking the disparate and often contradictory voices of the popular that echoes the spirit of other authors of low modernism such as Baudelaire and Dickens. The nineteenth century cities described by Baudelaire and those discussed by Benjamin were the sites of the artistic and intellectual counter cultures whose members sought to capture and evoke the essence of the age (Featherstone, 1992). Bohemians and intellectuals acted as (cultural) intermediaries in stimulating, formulating and disseminating the sensibilities of the age to wider audiences and publics (Seigal, 1986). Once more they pursued their task using the various media available to them in order to articulate the range of new sensations encountered. Thus the sense of closeness, immersion and participation evident in Benjamin's work strikes a chord with those of us engaged in contemporary cultural research in the city. We would concur with McRobbie that:

> ... Benjamin ... recognised with some urgency, the need to extend the role of the intellectual in order to engage with the people and to do this through transforming the existing mass media while simultaneously making use of their technological advances (1994, p.96).

The growth in leisure-based economics, and new technologies such as the Internet with their democratizing possibilities provide both a framework for recognizing that the 'logic of late capitalism' (Jameson, 1985) is driven by cultural imperatives, and that it's analysis exceeds the parameters of the modernist sociological preoccupation with white male European bourgeois society. The question one is left with is this: if research into popular culture in particular and within sociology in general now operates within a different set of parameters, then how should it be conducted and how should it be consumed? If we take a lesson from the Situationist critique of society and culture (Debord, 1987; Plant, 1992), the popularizing of academic discourse is not necessarily anything special in itself if it is part of the same general power nexus. The postmodern celebration of the popular and the lowbrow means very little if it is done as though such phenomena were interesting only as a lifestyle and not linked into a capitalist power matrix. Academic driven knowledge remains part of the spectacular rather than lived cultures; as de Certeau has demonstrated 'Knowledge remains linked to the power that authorises it' (op cit p.121). We feel that evocation of the essence of these lived cultures can be done through the re-discovery of the language and practice of the authors of low modernism, and it is to the specifics of its practice that we now turn.

"That's not what I said!": doing ethnographies with yer mates

We wish to approach our concept of the 'new ethnography' firstly in terms of its practice and then in relation to representation. In the first instance we wish to take some fairly progressive ideas concerning the practice of ethnography to task, and secondly to suggest that the 'voices' of such research must stand on their own terms and not succumb to meta-theoretical manipulation. It should be noted that although the term 'ethnography' has its roots in the anthropological rather than sociological tradition, we consider the manner in which it informs both traditions to be of particular relevance to our argument.

Doing the ethnographic business?

Historically speaking the classic anthropological ethnography was suffused with a sense of the exotic and mysterious, to such an extent, notes Brewer (1994), that readers often had little option but to rely on what was said in the text without recourse to other sources of information. He argues convincingly that this was also the case with regard to the Chicago School, in the 1920s and 30s, who studied snooker players, jazz musicians and gamblers with a similar fascination. Today the 'the margins (of society) are so well mapped and encountered' (ibid. p234) that it is difficult to say anything without somebody wanting to take issue with it. We wish to develop this point later, but here will relate it to various weaknesses within the sociology of popular culture in Britain, specifically the work of the ground-breaking Birmingham Centre for Contemporary Cultural Studies (CCCS). Focusing on the production of meaning in 'deviant' youth cultures and their relationship to the 'parent culture', the work of Hall and Jefferson (1976 [eds.]), Willis (1978), Hebdige (1979) and others has been of seminal influence on the sociology of culture. However, CCCS is also typical, on three counts, of engaging in the kind of ethnographic theory and practice which we would like to see less of within the sociology of popular culture.

Firstly and most importantly CCCS can be seen to be following firmly in the tradition of a high modernist sociology. Just as with the 'old' material, the subject and the object of research were separated out quite clearly, and there was never any sense of the researchers being part of a culture — surely a crucial point.(7) Secondly, as Muggleton (1994, p.4) notes, there is a heavy structuralist — read determinist — dimension to the texts, and it is apparent that some authors — notably Willis (op cit) — are keen to use the research to support their own particular world view (in Willis' case Marxism) rather than letting the voices speak for themselves (Marcus 1986, p.173-88). Thirdly, there is the issue of academic sensationalism to be addressed. Careers can and are made on 'daring research', particularly those focusing on so called 'deviant' cultures. It is important that in the race to publish and satisfy the demands of the educational establishment (both funding bodies and institutions) that these professional motivations should never be held above the needs and desires of those being studied — an extension of the first point perhaps.

So, when we come to 'do' ethnographies it is important that these shortcomings are addressed and in turn provide the basis for new ethnographic principles. Even though the problems of doing ethnographies and being participator and academic at the same time have been well documented — most impressively in Burawoy et al (1992) — there are certain problems which require reassessment. One is the assumption that the ethnographer can rely upon the stable foundational notions of class, community, gender, subculture, tradition and structure in order to reference a particular identity which emerges as a compromise of resistance to and/or incorporation of the larger whole (Marcus, 1992). Subsequently there are few authors who problematize these 'framing assumptions' (ibid) and rise to the challenge of recognizing uncertain and persistently ephemeral conditions let alone place them at the very centre of their work. In part this suggests a 'freeze-dried' methodology, and to illustrate its limitations we will take one fairly contemporary example — John Van Maanen's *Tales from the Field* (1988) — and develop this critique.

Our reason for choosing this text is that it advocates a convenient separation of fieldwork from office work; suggesting that 'ethnography as a written product ... has a degree of independence (how culture is portrayed) from the fieldwork on which it is based (how culture is known)' (1988, p.4). There are several assumptions at work here: (a) that the process of doing research fits into a clean ideal type situation where detachment from the field is possible; (b) that ethnography occurs in easily controllable spatial and temporal situations; (c) that the theorizing by the academic is somehow privileged above and beyond what those being studied think about the significance of their activities. Each of these points need clarification.

(a) The complexities of doing research in a post-industrial society, where there is an increasing de-differentiation of work and leisure roles, makes Van Maanen's assertions a little simplistic. This challenge is well documented by Dick Hobbs in his classic ethnography of the London docklands, *Doing the Business* (1988). Here he expresses the dilemma of writing up field notes obtained with disarming honesty. Often he was uncertain whether to 'write them up or throw them up'. Like Hobbs' relationships with both criminals and the police in the public houses of the East End, almost every researcher engaging in popular cultural fieldwork quickly finds themselves in a series of complex and shifting situations which requires an almost constant interchangeability of roles.

(b) The processes of globalization and 'space time compression' (Harvey, 1989) mean that it is no easy task to simply step outside the research role as though one were simply leaving an island in the Pacific or a working class community in another city from one's own. Obligations established during the research period, mean that distancing oneself from the subjectivities of lived experiences is often simply not possible. It might also be ethically questionable, particularly if the 'research' involves responsibilities such as caring for people, staffing 'helplines' or having a crucial administrative role

(Marcus, 1992). In addition research situations can produce a multitude of complicated challenges to the ethnographers ethics, loyalties, even friendships and we would again follow Marcus in arguing that this web of preexisting historic or contemporary connections — even autobiographical motives behind a particular project — must not be relegated to the footnotes but be foregrounded; woven like a thread through the text and made central to the work produced. In short we feel that the 'I' needs to be constantly identifiable as the author moves with their subjects from one research position to another.

(c) Furthermore, although it may seem tantamount to academic sacrilege, we have to accept that it is perfectly possible for the research 'subjects' to be reflexive to the extent that they can locate themselves in theoretical, historical and political terms. As Mascia-Lees et al (1989, p.9) note on the postmodernist trend in anthropology, the situation is such between researcher and researched that 'the native informant may read and contest the ethnographers characterisations — indeed, may well have heard of Jacques Derrida and have a copy of the latest *Banana Republic* catalogue'. This is almost certainly the case with much of the ethnographic research into popular culture which has emerged from Britain during the last 30 years and certainly true of many contemporary efforts.(8) These situations further reveal the fragility of the pedagogical role of the academic and how even in a highly reflexive and often intellectually equal situation, there exists formal hierarchies in the production and dissemination of knowledge.

Minding your own ethnographic business?

Much of the aforementioned critique of Van Maanen is in keeping with some of the recent debates within anthropology concerning the 'new ethnography' (see Marcus and Clifford, 1986). Since the history of colonialism sits uneasily on the shoulders of ethnographic research within anthropology, in the post-war period there has been something of an attempt to distance the new tradition from these associations. Instead, there is a desire to understand cultures on their own terms; thus the fundamental goal of the new ethnography is for Mascia-Lees et al 'to apprehend and inscribe 'others' in such a way as not to deny or diffuse their claims to subjecthood' (op cit p.2). The issue of offering a providing space for 'subjects' has therefore become important to many areas of the academic cannon as well as anthropology and sociology.(9) Although still very much in its infancy, a new politics has emerged in these and related fields, one which recognizes that too often academic research has been the site for the exercising of a middle class curiosity upon 'the Other' — whether 'natives', the working class, deviant groups, or something else — for the purposes of improving knowledge and social policy (the benefits of which to the subjects is highly debatable). In this respect it is important for the 'subjects' (sic) to recognize themselves and that the representations remain open-ended enough to provide for amendments or 'notes in the margin', in much the same way as in the development of mediaeval texts. For Marcus this means re-shaping the translation of concepts at the core of realist ethnography:

> Perhaps moments of exegesis, of definitions in context would be replaced by the exposure to moments of dialogue and their use in the ethnographers revision of familiar concepts that define the analytic limits of his or her work, and of anthropological discourse more generally. Such a move would open the realm of discussion of ethnographies to organic intellectuals (to use Gramsci's term) and readerships amongst one's own subjects (ibid, p.320).

It is vital then, that these representations do not get lost in the subtleties and enigmas of the 'new ways of structuring', which Mascia-Lees et al (1989, p.10) argue is a tendency in the new ethnographies (see also Woolgar, 1988).

Furthermore, if we are to get away from the realist ethnography — 'based in mimesis' (Tyler, 1986, p.130) and choose like Marcus (1986, p190) to 'evok(e) the world without representing it' then we must avoid the temptation to use the 'voices' of our 'subjects' to justify particular positions that we as privileged polemicists might want to adopt. Willis' book *Learning to Labour* (1978) — though old — is a lesson in how not to do this: indicating that the ethnographic technique is merely a means of collecting data he overtly overlays his ideological principles and his critical world view onto the ethnographic environment. Such a technique is really no better than the imperialisms of the classical anthropological researchers.

There is an additional point here which follows along the same political lines — that of academic competition. In the process of representation ethnographies must not become the football. For example, the tendency towards more experimental and phenomenological 'tales' has caused concern in some circles (see Porter, 1993) with the call to reintroduce structure — via 'critical realism' (i.e. Marxism) — back into the ethnographic equation. Regardless of the politics of these perspectives, the crucial point is that in terms of representation of research it is the data which should come first not, academic empire building. This serves to reify the voices still further if they become casualties of what Stanley and Wise (1990, p.46) dub the 'academic three-step', whereby the merits of a particular theory are not judged on their own terms but in terms of the academic's own 'better' standpoint. Any attempt to introduce ethnographic data into the academic snake pit will merely ensure that it is 'the subjects' who get stung.

Conclusions and beginnings ...

Our intention finally is to lay down a number of trails which we hope those engaging in new ethnographic research will consider — in terms of practice, theory and representation. We are aware of the fact that these are, in many respects, inextricably interlinked.

Future practice

In view of the problems of representation already outlined and the increasing amount of good research being done by young academics into popular culture, it is critical that prospective researchers are familiar with the territory which they are to study. In the postmodern age there are few sociologists of the exotic, and it is rare for one to enter 'the field' innocent of what we may find. The ethnographer needs the ability to understand the signs, signals and nuances of a culture which may be implicit to the everyday world of a particular culture yet which are not articulated explicitly to the researcher. They require the ability to make explicit 'the systems of operational combination' (de Certeau, 1986) which compose a culture; to understand both the individual and group stories along with the background noise of the practices of everyday life.

Similarly, if we aim to evoke the essence of a particular culture or set of cultural practices then we will need a degree of emotional investment in it which is, at present, anathema to the persistently scientific methods favoured by sociology. Empathy cannot be manufactured in the text nor can it be secured by the distanced dispassionate observer, it comes from involvement with and an immersion in the field. The other side of the same coin is recognizing that in the process of doing ethnographies, the culture will effect the researcher just as much as they will effect it (Harrison & Lyon, 1993, p.105). The construction of separate worlds between the ethnographer and the subject has long been used as some sort of critical juxtaposition and the coevalness of the ethnographer with the Other has for the most part been denied (Fabian, 1983). Moreover we would assert that this so-called problem of 'contamination' (Burawoy, 1991, p.2) is rapidly becoming one of a different research age; where there were clearly identifiable research 'subjects' with whom the ethnographer had a relatively distanced and controllable relationship. As we have said above, the situation whereby an ethnographer can be active alongside city planners, business people, the person in the street or in a position of 'cultural policy' decision making, challenges the academic 'purity' of non-intervention.

There is a case then for seeing ourselves as privileged — and accountable — delegates from the culture (our culture) which is being studied. In the process something of an awareness of the equation of means with ends needs to be demonstrated. In this respect three questions stand out: 'who constitutes popular culture?'; 'from where are they speaking?' and 'for what purpose?' (Schirato, 1994). Since the aforementioned new relationships between academia and the rest of society are most evident in the field of popular culture, it is important that the 'intellectual intermediaries' here set an example for sociology in general.

Future theory

A crucial ingredient in the move toward theorizing the new ethnographic practice is positioning 'popular culture' in such a way that it has both a basis in empirical research — unlike the Frankfurt School and some of their postmodernist equivalents — and is at least engaged with or consumed by its authors (the subjects) on a reasonably regular basis. Far from following either the collapse into relativism or the retreat into absolutism we suggest that it is possible

263

to celebrate in postmodernism what others (Berman, 1992; Walzer, 1987; de Certeau, 1988) have seen in modernism: an opportunity to clarify values, to embrace heterogeneity, pluralism and to mix the pessimism and optimism, the possibility and danger of everyday life. Thus in turning to 'low modernism' we are able to convey and evoke what was 'Other' to high modernism but has never really been ascribed with the same degree of intellectual seriousness. Here we can learn from Benjamin's figural vision of 'the *flaneur*' as a model for a new kind of intellectual observer; one at ease in the crowd and fascinated, not alarmed by the constant flow of commodities and constantly changing signs and images of the arcade, of the street, of the city. It suggests a modernism which is open ended and contingent, characterized by the uncertainty normally associated with the postmodern where 'a thousand little stories' compose rhizomic ephemeral cultures of the contemporary urban *milieux* (Deleuze & Guatarri, 1981). We would concur with Walzer when he suggests that 'we would do better to study the internal rules, maxims, contentions, and ideals, rather than detach ourselves from it in search of a universal and transcendent standpoint' (1987, p.ix). Such a standpoint does not lead to the abandonment of values or principles but stresses the values of the lived experience where, as Laclau puts it, 'if the word of God can no longer be heard, we can start giving our own voices a new dignity' (1989, p.14).

The implications of this may be unpleasant for some, particularly because it puts the history of the sociology of culture on trial for being political through a policy of theoretical exclusion. However, by conducting research as outlined above, and adopting a 'low modernist' position — which is equally theory, artform and text — spaces can begin to emerge in the knowledge monopoly, as 'real life' becomes fused with research. Our own experience at Manchester Institute for Popular Culture has sometimes felt akin to jumping backwards and forwards through epistemological hoops, as other departments and institutions have struggled with the interdisciplinary nature and content of our research. This is their problem not ours.

Future representations

Readers can be forgiven for thinking that thus far we have assumed that if new ethnographic practices and theories are followed then some coherent representation will automatically follow. This however is not the case. As has been only too clearly observed by Latour (1988) it is when the new ethnographers get to work that the problems of representation become even more pronounced, as theorists believe that either through different writing styles or jargon there is always some final level of meta-reflexivity which can be reached. Here, even in the most iconoclastic of genres — the sociology of scientific knowledge and the 'new ethnographies' — we see the spectre of ideology rising from the ashes of ideology.

In this respect we warm to the notion of de Certeau's that each time we attempt to call up the popular, or more specifically popular practice by scientific representation there is a death. This death applies equally to trying to read texts authentically as it does to writing them. As noted earlier, Tyler (1986, p.137) claims that to try and depict reality is merely to engage in mimesis, and that every attempt will inevitably produce situations where crucial factors will be missed with the end result a representation which borders on the verge of fantasy. This of course is not a problem if it is recognized that in trying to represent the unrepresentable (i.e. living popular cultures) one is really drifting into the art of story telling. Marcus argues convincingly for the development of this craft — for story telling through the form of 'the modern essay' which by definition undermines realist accounts 'by seeking to evok(e) the world without representing it'(1986, p.190). For him the modern essay:

> ... opposes conventional systematic analysis, absolves the writer from having to develop the broader implications of his thought (while nonetheless indicating that there are such implications) or having to tie loose ends together. The essayist can mystify the world, leave his subjects actions open ended as to their global implications, from a rhetorical posture of profound half-understanding half-bewilderment with the world in which the ethnographic subject and the ethnographer live (ibid. p191).

Stories also play an important role in the work of de Certeau. As Schirato notes:

> ... he refers to the 'transgressive stories' of Foucault and Bourdieu, where the law, the system, and theories are re-told and at the same time undone by the interpolation of certain moments

in the story — what he calls 'coups' — when 'thinking otherwise' becomes possible (1991).

For de Certeau story telling and story writing is not a substitute for reality — merely a move in a game, yet a move which can contest hegemonic meanings and 'create space out of place'. So rather than aiming to present holistic views of systems, communities or events the story telling of the modern essay 'legitimates fragmentation, rough edges and the self-conscious aim of achieving an effect that disturbs the reader' (Marcus 1986, p.191). The interpretive task becomes shared as the stories of the subjects weave around themselves and those of the ethnographer. With the ethnographer foregrounded yet another story emerges, and we need look no further than the Gospels of the Bible to reveal how representation can work in this fashion; there is a break with reality but the fragments and evocations of the events allow us the impression of an experience (see Tyler, 1986).

In this respect the treatment of popular culture by sociology could learn more from art than science, and perhaps receive more respect and a degree of legitimacy from those who it is claiming to represent. We also must face the fact that the conventional sociological text itself has a 'sell by' date on it and that other modes of representation should be explored. To follow Redhead (1993) we feel that it is vital to recognize that so called 'pulp' or 'trash' novels about popular, and particularly, youth culture may well capture and inform us more about what it means to be involved with them than yet another academic exposition. The telecommunications revolution in the form of interactive information distribution only serves to underline this point.

We are living in an increasingly DIY culture where the means of entertainment to the means of employment, the means of exchange to forms of representation are being attempted with varying degrees of success outside of formal institutions. If sociology is not to become another redundant craft and the ethnographic researcher just another outmoded artisan it is important that we think creatively about that craft and that we are allowed to take the risks necessary to produce meaningful research. The rediscovery of the values and principles of low modernism along with the experimentation implicit in it, may allow both the form and context of ethnographic writing to create a space for the marginalized practices of popular culture to emerge and contest versions of both the 'high' and the 'post' — to provide space for thinking otherwise.

Note and acknowledgement

The story of this chapter is an ethnography in itself, and at times it has felt as though we have been trying to take on the entire history of the sociology of culture. This has not been something we have been afraid of more that it has set us wondering if anybody else is on the same planet! Fellow iconoclastic terrestrials include Justin O'Connor, Steve Redhead, David Muggleton, Bernice Martin and Richard Smith and we thank them for their encouragement and helpful remarks on this project.

Notes

1 Here we deliberately utilize de Certau's use of the word 'tactic' (the makeshift creativity and disruptions of the popular) as opposed to the disciplinary 'strategies' of the establishment of which sociology has become embedded.

2 Characterized by Adorno's and Horkheimers derisory reference to 'girls in the audience' in *The Culture Industry*.

3 Here we recall recent programmes such as the Cook Report for ITV on drug gangs in the inner city (July 1994) and Panorama's (BBC) exposure of protection and extortion on several of Britain's most notorious housing estates (January 1995).

4 Numerous documentaries during 1994/5 on rave culture, New Age travellers, anti-roads direct action groups to name a few illustrate this point — all executed with sober accuracy and depth.

5 Woolgar (1988) in particular draws attention to the fact that scientific knowledge these days is no longer regarded as a special case in the field of knowledge — suffering from the same social constructions as the humanities. See also Bijker, Pinch and Hughes ([eds.] 1987).

6 William Mitchell from MIT recently 'placed' his forthcoming book *Digital Cities* on the Internet for 'comments in the margins'

which could then be incorporated into the 'hard' copy.

7   For a rigorous critique of CCCS and especially Paul Willis' *Learning to Labour* see George Marcus in Clifford and Marcus (eds.) *Writing Culture* 1986 pp.175-188.

8   For instance, Purkis, whilst participating in a radio feature as an academic 'expert' on the anti-roads movement in November 1993, was only too aware that he hadn't said anything more profound than the people he was supposed to have been assessing (the Donga Tribe of Twyford Down fame).

9   See Knights (1995) for the problems of representation in *Business Studies and Economics* and Hollway (1989) for organizational and behavioural psychology.

References

Adorno T. and Horkheimer M. (1991), *The Culture Industry*, Routledge, London.

Baudrillard, J. (1983), *Simulations*, Semiotext, New York.

Bauman, Z. (1987), *Legislators and Interpreters*, Polity Press, Cambridge.

Bauman, Z. (1988), 'Is There a Postmodern Sociology?', in *Theory, Culture & Society*, Vol.5.

Benjamin, W. *One Way Street*, New Left Books, London

Berman, M. (1988), *All That Is Solid Melts Into Air: The Experience Of Modernity*, Verso, London.

Berman, M. (1992), 'Why modernism still matters', in Lash, S. and Friedman, J. (eds.) *Modernity and Identity*, Sage, London.

Bijker, W. E., Pinch, T. and Hughes, T. (eds.) (1987), *The Social Construction of Technological Systems*, MIT Press, Cambridge, MA. Bourdieu, P. (1990), *In Other Words: Essays Towards a Reflexive Sociology*, Polity, Cambridge.

Bourdieu, P. (1984), *Distinction*, Macmillan, London.

Brewer, J. (1994), 'The Ethnographic Critique of Ethnography', in *Sociology*, Vol.28, No.1, February.

Burawoy, M. et al (1991), *Ethnography Unbound*, University of California, Berkeley.

Chambers, I. (1990), *Popular Culture: The Metropolitan Experience*, Routledge, London.

Chaplin, E. (1994), *Sociology and Visual Representation*, Routledge, London.

Clark, J. (1991), *New Times and Old Enemies*, Harper Collins, London.

Debord, G. (1987), *The Society of the Spectacle*, Rebel Press, AIM.

de Certeau, M. (1986), *Heterologies*, Manchester University Press, Manchester.

de Certeau, M. (1988), *The Practice Of Everyday Life*, California University Press, California.

Deleuze and Guatarri, (1980), *A Thousand Plateaus: Capitalism and Schizophrenia*, University of Minneapolis Press, Minnesota.

Docker, J. (1995), *Postmodernism and Popular Culture*, Cambridge University Press, Cambridge.

Fabian, J. (1983), *Time and the Other; How Anthropology Makes Its Object*, Columbia University Press, New York.

Featherstone, M. (1991), *Consumer Culture and Postmodernism*, Sage, London.

Fyfe, G. and Law, J. (1988), *Picturing Power: Visual Depiction and Social Relations*, Routledge, London.

Gendron, B. (1986), 'Theodore Adorno Meets the Cadillacs', in Modleski, T. (ed.), *Studies in Entertainment*, Indiana University Press, Bloomington.

Giddens,, A. (1991),*Modernity and Self-Identity*, Polity, Cambridge.

Gorz, A. (1981), *Ecology as Politics*, South End Press, Boston.

Grossberg, L. (1992), *We gotta get out of this place*, Routledge, London.

Hall, S. and Jefferson, T. (eds.) (1976), *Resistance through Rituals*, Hutchinson, London.

Harrison, B. and Lyon, E. S. (1993), 'A Note on Ethical Issues in the Use of Autobiography in Sociological Research', *Sociology*, Vol.27, No.1, February.

Harvey, D. (1989), *The Condition of Postmodernity*, Basil Blackwell, Oxford.

Hebdige, D. (1979), *Subculture: the meaning of style*, Methuen, London.

Hobbs, D. (1988), *Doing the Business*, Clarendon, Oxford.

Hollway, W. (1994), 'Fitting Work; Psychological Assessment in Organisations', in J. Henriques et al, *Changing the Subject*, Methuen, London.

Huxley, A. (1954), *The Doors of Perception*, Chatto & Windus, London.

Huyssen, A. (1986), 'Mass Culture as Woman: Modernism's Other', in Modleski, T. (ed.) *Studies in Entertainment*, Indiana University Press, Bloomington.

Illich, I. (1973), *Tools for Conviviality*, Harper and Row, New York.

Jameson, F. (1985), 'Postmodernism and Consumer Society' in Foster, H. (ed.) *Postmodern Culture*, Pluto, London.

Knights, D. (1995), *Organisation Theory In the Age of Deconstruction: Dualism, Gender and Postmodernism Revisited*. Paper given to Action, Structure & Organisation Conference, May, 1995, Paris.

Lash, S. and Friedman J. (eds.) (1992), *Modernity & Identity*, Blackwell, Oxford.

Latour, B. (1988), 'The Politics of Explanation: an Alternative', in Woolgar, S. (ed.) *Knowledge and Reflexivity*, Sage, London.

Marcus, G. (1986), 'Contemporary Problems in the Modern World

System', in Clifford, J. and Marcus, G. (eds.), *Writing Culture*, University of California, Berkeley.

Marcus, G. (1992), 'Past, present and emergent identities: requirements for ethnographies of late twentieth century modernity worldwide', in S. Lash & J. Friedman (eds.), *Modernity & Identity*, Blackwell, Oxford.

Mascia-Lees, F. et al (1989), 'The Postmodernist Turn in Anthropology: Cautions From A Feminist Perspective' in *Signs*, Vol.15, No.11.

McRobbie, A. (1994), *Postmodernism and Popular Culture*, Routledge, London.

Muggleton, D. (1993), *The Relationship Between Theory and Ethnography in Neo-Marxist Studies of Youth Cultures*. Unpublished paper, Department of Sociology, University of Lancaster.

Owens, C. (1985), 'The Discourse of Others: Feminists and Postmodernism' in Foster, H. (ed.), *Postmodern Culture*, Pluto, London.

Plant, S. (1992), *The Most Radical Gesture*, Routledge, London.

Porter, S. (1993), 'Critical Realist Ethnography', in *Sociology*, Vol.27, No.4, November.

Redhead, S. (1993), 'Disappearing Youth?', in *Theory, Culture & Society*, Vol.10.

Schirato, T. (1991), 'My Space or Yours? de Certeau, Frow & the Meanings of Popular Culture', in *Cultural Studies*, Vol. 7, No.2, May 1993.

Seigal, J. (1986), *Bohemian Paris*, Viking, New York.

Stanley, L. and Wise, S. (1990), 'Method, methodology and epistemology in feminist research processes', in Stanley, L., *Feminist*

Praxis, Routledge, London.

Strianti, D. (1994), *An Introduction to the Theories Of Popular Culture*, Routledge, London.

Squires, J. (ed.) (1993), *Principled Positions*, Lawrence and Wishart, London.

Tyler, S. (1986), 'Post-Modern Ethnography: From Document of the Occult to Occult Document', in Clifford, J. and Marcus, G. (eds.), *Writing Culture*, University of California, Berkeley.

Urry, J. (1981), 'Sociology as a Parasite' in Abrams, P. (ed.), *Practice and Progress*, Allen and Unwin, London.

Van Maan, J. (1988), *Tales of the Field: On Writing Ethnography*, University of Chicago Press, Chicago.

Walzer, M. (1987), *Interpretation and Social Criticism*, Harvard University Press, Cambridge, Mass.

Willis, P. (1978), *Learning to Labour*, Saxon House, Farnborough.

Woolgar, S. (1988), 'Reflexivity is the Ethnographer of the Text', in Woolgar, S. (ed.) *Knowledge and Reflexivity*, Sage, London.

RAVE OFF

POLITICS AND DEVIANCE IN CONTEMPORARY YOUTH CULTURE

Edited by STEVE REDHEAD

POPULAR CULTURAL STUDIES: 1

"...recommended as student reading." Youth and Policy

"...stimulating and provocative opening contribution to the Popular Cultural Studies series. Courses on youth culture will look a little incomplete if they do not now include them as set reading ...central texts for any up-to-date specialist course." Leisure Studies Association Newsletter

Steve Redhead and a team of authors associated with the Manchester Institute for Popular Culture at Manchester Metropolitan University have written a unique account of deviant youth culture at the end of the century, concentrating on the much-hyped 'rave' scene and its connections to recreational drug use - for instance Ecstasy - contemporary pop and dance music, youth tourism, football hooliganism and the 'enterprise culture'.

The book attempts to provide answers to such questions as: What is 'rave culture'? What had 'Madchester' got to do with it? Has the rave (formerly acid house) scene merely parodied an earlier moment in pop history (60s psychedelia, 70s punk or Northern Soul)? Is illegal 'party drug' use a passing fad or here to stay? What political and legal implications are there of this new 'hedonism in hard times'? Has 90s youth culture embraced or rejected the values of the market, individualism and enterprise?

1993   208 pages   Hbk   1 85628 463 8   £29.50
         Pbk   1 85628 465 4   £12.95

Price subject to change without notification

arena

THE LADS IN ACTION

SOCIAL PROCESS IN AN URBAN YOUTH SUBCULTURE

DAVID MOORE

POPULAR CULTURAL STUDIES: 3

"This is a much needed, adventurous work..." Professor David Parkin, University of London

The Lads in Action, based on long-term participant observation with Australian skinheads, portrays the social processes which underlie and constitute the skinhead subculture.

The book begins with a critique of existing studies of youth. Moore then presents a phenomenological analysis of the meaning of skinhead expressive activity for the skinheads themselves, heavily influenced by anthropology of social process. After dispensing with the static concept of 'gang' in favour of a more processural framework, he deals in turn with the meaning of visual and performative style for skinheads, interaction between skinheads and the members of other youth subcultures, the significance of drinking, and the public and private representations skinheads make about the young women with whom they form relationships. He also outlines the part played by 'memories', the stories of past exploits which skinheads tell to one another, in the creation of the skinhead's categorical and personal identity. These issues are examined in the light of extensive ethnographic material.

David Moore is a Visiting Research Fellow in the Addiction Studies Unit, School of Psychology, Curtin University of Technology, Perth.

1994   192 pages   Hbk   1 85742 203 1   £29.50
Pbk   1 85742 204 X   £12.95

Price subject to change without notification

THE MARGINS OF THE CITY

GAY MEN'S URBAN LIVES

Edited by **STEPHEN WHITTLE**

POPULAR CULTURAL STUDIES: 6

Within cities, gay life has always been marginalised. Despite the fact that their significant places are often centrally placed geographically within cities, gay communities are not centrally placed in the political, social and cultural lives of cities. These international accounts draw on first hand ethnographic research and reflect the responses of gay men in particular to the changes that have taken place during the last 25 years in urban settings. They look at the physical and spatial development of gay places, at the same time as viewing the social placing of the communities that use those places.

The cross-disciplinary studies within this book look at the tensions that arise between gay communities and their cities, the political and economic implications to city planners of the "pink pound" and the legal and social implications for gay men as they attempt to reconcile being both the outsiders and insiders of city life.

Stephen Whittle is Lecturer in Law at Manchester Metropolitan University.

1994   184 pages   Hbk   1 85742 201 5   £29.95
Pbk   1 85742 202 3   £12.95

Price subject to change without notification

THE GULF WAR DID NOT HAPPEN

POLITICS, CULTURE, AND WARFARE POST-VIETNAM

Edited by **JEFFREY WALSH**

POPULAR CULTURAL STUDIES: 7

This interdisciplinary collection of essays breaks new ground in studying the complex relationships between the historical Gulf war of 1990–91, and those myths, narratives and extended images commonly drawn upon to explain it. Such a distinctive mode of enquiry reveals the ideological symmetry between the political debate and popular culture, or between foreign policy and artistic production. A linking theme running through the volume is the shadow of Vietnam, how the Gulf war was perhaps the culminating event in what has come to be known as "the Vietnam syndrome".

As well as focusing upon the central role of mass media the contributors address issues and events that are not usually treated in the same political and historical context, for example, popular music, comic books, war memorials, anti-war expression, literature, and the effects of war upon language. These essays will be of great interest for students of history, politics, war studies, American studies, cultural studies, oriental and Middle Eastern studies, the social sciences, media studies, literature and art history.

Jeffrey Walsh is Principal Lecturer in English at Manchester Metropolitan University.

1995   224 pages   Hbk   1 85742 292 9   £35.00
Pbk   1 85742 286 4   £12.95

Price subject to change without notification

arena